## Geologic Time Scale

| | Period | Era | Eon |
|---|---|---|---|
| Present — | Quaternary | | Cenozoic |
| 1.6 — | Neogene | Tertiary | |
| 24 — | Paleogene | | |
| 66 — | Cretaceous | Mesozoic | Phanerozoic |
| 144 — | Jurassic | | |
| 208 — | Triassic | | |
| 245 — | Permian | Paleozoic | |
| 286 — | Pennsylvanian | | |
| 320 — | Mississippian | | |
| 360 — | Devonian | | |
| 408 — | Silurian | | |
| 438 — | Ordovician | | |
| 505 — | Cambrian | | |
| 545 — | Precambrian | Proterozoic | |
| 2500 — | | Archean | |

Millions of years before present

# *Hiking* THE
# GRAND CANYON'S GEOLOGY

**LON ABBOTT & TERRI COOK**

THE MOUNTAINEERS BOOKS

Published by
The Mountaineers Books
1001 SW Klickitat Way, Suite 201
Seattle, WA 98134

*The Mountaineers Books is the nonprofit publishing arm of the Mountaineers Club, an organization founded in 1906 and dedicated to the exploration, preservation, and enjoyment of outdoor and wilderness areas.*

First edition, 2004

Published simultaneously in Great Britain by Cordee, 3a DeMontfort Street, Leicester, England, LE1 7HD

Manufactured in the United States of America

Acquisitions Editor: Cassandra Conyers
Project Editor: Christine Ummel Hosler
Editor: Paula Thurman
Series Cover and Book Design: The Mountaineers Books
Layout: Peggy Egerdahl
Mapmaker and Illustrator: Moore Creative Designs
All photographs by the authors unless otherwise noted.

Cover photograph: *Morning light on cliffs near Fossil Canyon—Colorado River Mile 125, Grand Canyon National Park, Arizona.* Photo © Ralph Lee Hopkins, Wilderland Images. Frontispiece: *Hiker silhouetted against the Redwall Limestone, South Kaibab Trail.*

*Library of Congress Cataloging-in-Publication Data*

Abbott, Lon, 1963-
  Hiking the Grand Canyon's geology / Lon Abbott and Terri Cook.— 1st ed.
    p. cm.
Includes bibliographical references and index.
  ISBN 0-89886-895-5 (paperbound)
  1. Hiking—Arizona—Grand Canyon National Park—Guidebooks. 2. Geology—Arizona—Grand Canyon National Park—Guidebooks. 3. Grand Canyon National Park (Ariz.)—Guidebooks. I. Cook, Terri, 1969- II. Title.
  GV199.42.A7A22 2004
                                    2003016710

# Dedication

For our parents, whose love and support
helped us create our own tracks.

*Tracks left by an ancient inhabitant of Hermit Creek.*

# Acknowledgments

We are indebted to many people who helped this project come to fruition. Many thanks to Linda Jalbert of the National Park Service for her review of the "Preparing to Hike" chapters, and to Steve Sullivan and all the rangers in Grand Canyon National Park for their help, suggestions, and hard work. The book's illustrations were greatly enhanced by Dona Abbott's contributions, as were the photographs by Bill Ervin's seasoned critiques. This project would not have been possible without The Mountaineers Books and our supportive editors, Cassandra Conyers, Christine Hosler, and Paula Thurman, as well as Tom Fleischner, who suggested it to us. Finally, many thanks to Logan, who patiently logged many miles riding on Mom and Dad's backs (as long as we kept singing).

# Contents

*Grand Canyon hikes*

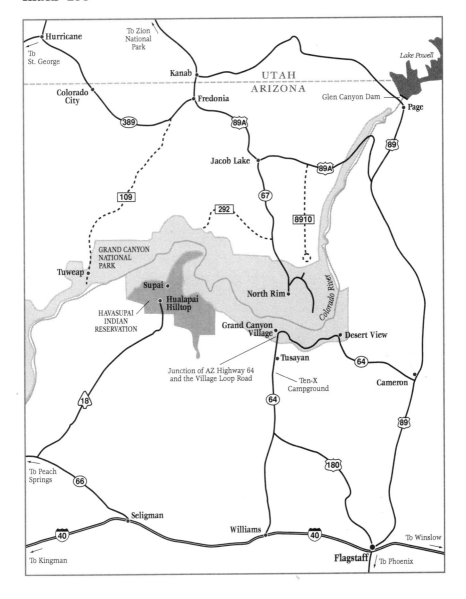

# Preface: A Journey through Time

The Grand Canyon is the world's most celebrated geologic showpiece, a place where the rocks span 2 billion years of earth history. Each step down transports you an astounding 60,000 years back in time. Numerous guidebooks are available to help hikers navigate the extensive network of trails, and many fine geology and natural history guides help visitors interpret their amazing surroundings. The goal of this book is unique: to combine all the geology *and* all the hiking information you need to transform your Canyon hike into a journey through time.

We have endeavored to make this book useful for everyone interested in the Grand Canyon's geologic history, whether you are an experienced desert hiker or prefer a brief stroll along the rim. We have included a broad spectrum of hikes, from rugged, multiday backpacks to gentle, half-day rim walks. This book contains all the popular Corridor trails, plus several remote routes that will appeal to veteran backpackers. In addition, we have included Global Positioning System (GPS) coordinates as navigation aids to points of interest, ensuring that you will be able to find an unsigned trail junction as well as a 545-million-year-old island along the path.

Part 1 gives a brief account of the Grand Canyon's fascinating stories in stone so you can place what you observe along the trail in the overall context of its geologic evolution. Part 2 includes all the information you will need to plan, permit, and safely enjoy your hike. Trails from the South Rim are described in Part 3 and hikes from the North Rim in Part 4. Each hike has its own geologic theme, focusing on the aspects of the Canyon's evolution that are particularly well illustrated along its length.

When selecting a hike, we recommend that you skim the trails' information blocks and the "About the Landscape" sections in order to find the difficulty level and the geologic theme most suitable for your interests. Then read Part 2 to properly plan for your adventure.

Appendixes A through C briefly summarize some key geologic concepts for those with limited exposure to geology's technical terms. Key reference materials, both technical and nontechnical, are noted in the trails' information

*The Colorado River meets Nankoweap Creek in beautiful Marble Canyon.*

*Chuar Butte looms above the Colorado River at the end of the Tanner Trail.*

blocks and refer to the list in Appendix D. Map numbers in the information blocks refer to the topographic maps listed in Appendix E.

Be sure to inquire about trail conditions and questionable water supplies before starting your trip, and please follow all Park Service regulations to minimize your impact on this wonderful landscape. Whether you descend a frozen stream of lava to the Canyon's most thunderous rapid, journey to the center of an ancient supercontinent, or step across a major geologic fault near the Bright Angel Lodge, we hope that this book will increase your enjoyment and awareness of this incredible place.

*Sunset at Toroweap Overlook.*

*Part 1*

# STORIES IN STONE
## THE GEOLOGIC EVOLUTION OF THE GRAND CANYON

Etched on the Grand Canyon's steep walls are the stories of sweeping changes the region has endured through the enormity of geologic time. The horizontal layers of the upper Canyon tell vivid tales of tropical seas come and gone, immense mudflats stretching from horizon to horizon, vast deserts filled with sand dunes a thousand feet high, and the histories of the plants and animals that have made this place their home. The narrow confines of the Inner Gorge whisper of volcanic violence, mountain ranges raised by a clash of tectonic plates, and the slow, inexorable forces of erosion that laid the mountain cathedrals low.

As you hike, you can trace the Grand Canyon's awe-inspiring evolution, piecing together the saga of the long and tortuous transformation to its present grandeur. The next four chapters narrate this epic, providing an overview that will help you place the geologic features you observe along the trail in their broader context as you hike the Canyon's incredible journeys through time. If you are unfamiliar with the concepts of plate tectonics, geologic time, or rock classification, or simply need a refresher, please read Appendixes A through C at the back of this book first.

*A hiker surveys the vista along the Tanner Trail.*

# Chapter 1
# THE PRECAMBRIAN

The Precambrian Eon covers vast sweeps of time, from the formation of the earth 4600 million years ago to the beginning of the Paleozoic Era 545 million years ago (Appendix B). During this time, chains of volcanoes, early continents and oceans, bacteria, and the forces of plate tectonics (Appendix C) interacted to form the Grand Canyon's oldest rocks.

## THE GEOLOGIC TIME SCALE

During the eighteenth and nineteenth centuries, geologists used the succession of fossils in *sedimentary* rocks (rocks formed by the consolidation of loose sediment) to construct the Geologic Time Scale (see first page of this book). They broke geologic time into two eons: Rocks belonging to the older eon (the Precambrian) contained no visible fossils; those of the younger eon, the Phanerozoic, contained many fossils. The Phanerozoic was then subdivided into three eras, based on the general resemblance of the fossils to modern organisms. The oldest sedimentary layers contained fossils that are dramatically different from modern ones. These rocks were assigned to the Paleozoic Era, meaning the era of "ancient" life. The middle layers contained slightly more recognizable organisms and were assigned to the Mesozoic Era, the era of "middle" life. Finally, the highest and therefore youngest layers contained the most modern organisms and were assigned to the Cenozoic Era, that of "recent" life. Each era was then subdivided into periods. Through the use of this time scale, a geologist from England could conduct a study of sedimentary rocks in Australia or America and know when, in a relative sense, the rocks were deposited. However, this same geologist was completely powerless to say precisely when, in years, that deposition occurred. With the twentieth century discovery of radiometric dating (a method by which radioactive elements are measured to determine age), geologists could make comparisons between radiometric dates and sedimentary fossils, and then assign numerical ages to the beginning and end of each period in the Geologic Time Scale (Appendix B, Figure 44).

# FORMATION OF THE EARTH

The Grand Canyon's story begins a mind-boggling 4600 million years ago with the formation of our earth. Along with our sun and the rest of the solar system, the earth coalesced out of a swirling cloud of interstellar gas resulting from the supernova explosion of a nearby giant star. We are, quite literally, stardust.

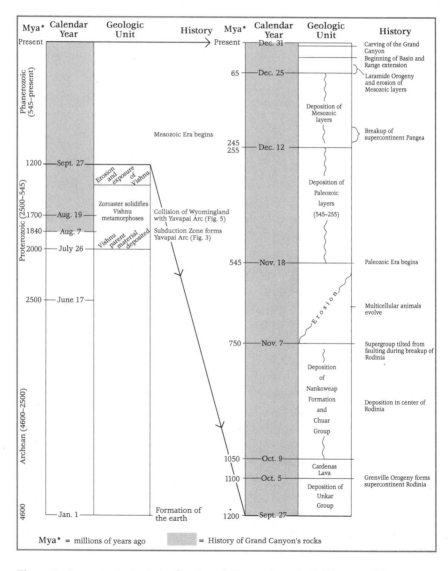

Figure 1. Important events in the Grand Canyon's geologic history with a comparison of the time involved to a calendar year.

The early planet was so hot and turbulent that no rock record exists of its first days. However, recent discoveries show that by 4400 million years ago, rocks and oceans had formed on the earth's surface. Numbers such as 4400 million are difficult for any human being to comprehend, especially in reference to time. As an aid to grasping such vast spans, geologists often compare the age of the earth to a smaller, more comprehensible slice of time, such as a year (Figures 1, 2). If the earth coalesced at the stroke of midnight on New Year's Day, then these first rocks formed on January 16.

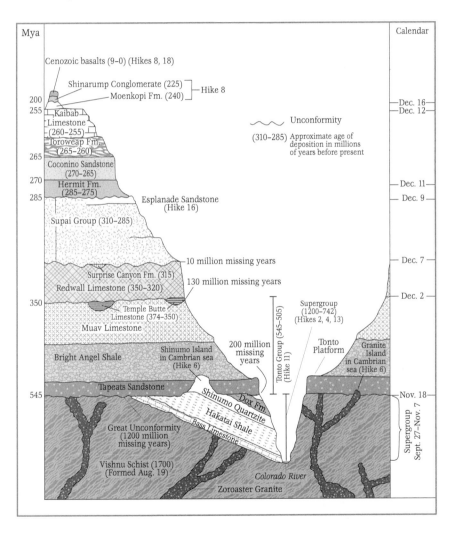

*Figure 2. Rock layers of the Grand Canyon.*

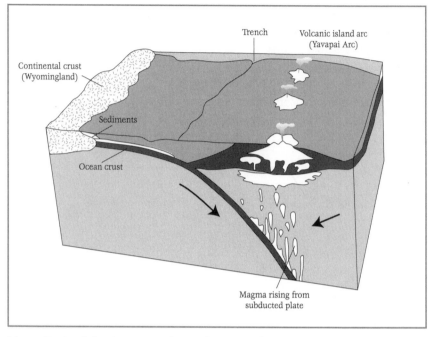

*Figure 3. A subduction zone. The modern Grand Canyon region was part of the Yavapai volcanic arc 1750 million years ago.*

By this time it is likely that a version of *plate tectonics* (whereby giant rock slabs, moving and interacting with one another, create the earth's major landforms) was operating, but because the early earth was considerably hotter, the pace and scope of those tectonic interactions were probably different from today's. Most of the planet's face, including the Grand Canyon area, was covered by a primordial form of dense *oceanic crust* (the variety of the earth's topmost layer that floors the ocean basins) destined for obliteration in a *subduction zone* (an area where oceanic crust is destroyed when one plate dives beneath another and melts, creating a chain of volcanoes—Figure 3). Because no rock record from this early phase remains, we can say little about what the area looked like so long ago.

## THE YAVAPAI ARC

Rocks from about 1840 million years ago, more than halfway through the earth's history (August 7 on our compressed scale), tell the earliest known chapters in the story of the Grand Canyon. By this time, plate tectonics was functioning as it does now, and the modern Grand Canyon region was a subduction zone, crowned by a volcanic island chain in the midst of a vast ocean.

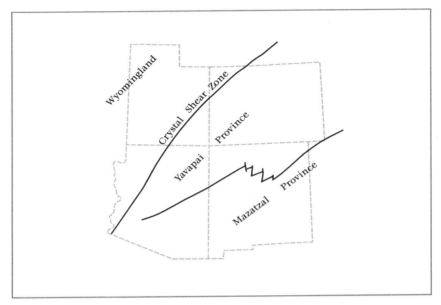

*Figure 4. The regional extent of the Yavapai and Mazatzal volcanic arcs (provinces). The Crystal Shear Zone runs through Crystal Rapid, a short distance downstream of Phantom Ranch.*

Far to the northwest of the Grand Canyon region (in this story we will use modern geographic reference marks, but as we discuss in Appendix C, the movements of the continents through time mean that what is north today was not necessarily north in the past) lay the shores of a small continent that later became the nucleus of North America. This continent stretched from modern southern California through Wyoming and into central Canada. The Wyoming-through-southern California portion of that continent, which many geologists call Wyomingland, plays a significant role in our story. Attached to Wyomingland was a slab of oceanic crust that was gradually subducting to the southeast, in the process forming a chain of volcanic islands (Figure 3). Known collectively as the Yavapai Arc, the islands stretched like a string of pearls across a thousand miles of ocean, resembling Alaska's Aleutian Islands. They covered a swath of terrain from modern Sonora, Mexico, through Arizona and Colorado to Nebraska (Figure 4), including the Grand Canyon area.

Over the next 150 million years, subduction brought Wyomingland ever closer to the Yavapai Arc. Along the arc, generations of volcanoes evolved and died. Lava and ash flows from the birth of one volcano mixed with layers of sand and mud created by the erosion of its ancestors. Over time, a pile of interbedded lava, ash, sand, and mud accumulated to a depth of 40,000 feet.

## COLLISION OF THE YAVAPAI ARC WITH WYOMINGLAND

Wyomingland finally reached the Yavapai subduction zone 1700 million years ago, around August 19 on our calendar. Because Wyomingland's continental crust was too buoyant to dive below the Yavapai Arc, a massive collision between continent and arc occurred (Figure 5). At that time the Grand Canyon would have borne a physical resemblance to New Guinea, where a similar collision between a volcanic arc and the Australian continent is occurring.

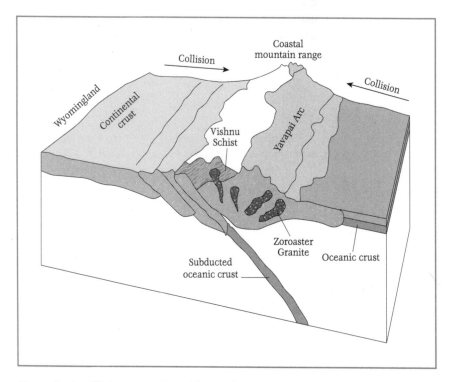

*Figure 5. A collision zone. The Vishnu Schist was metamorphosed in such a collision 1700 million years ago.*

The Yavapai Arc was forced up and over the edge of Wyomingland, welding it to the continent and forming a dramatic coastal mountain range. The heat and pressure of the collision *metamorphosed* the pile of lava, ash, sandstone, and mudstone into the rock unit we know today as the Vishnu Schist (Color Plate 9, Figure 5). The magma chambers feeding the Yavapai volcanoes solidified to become the Grand Canyon's Zoroaster Granite. Together these two rock units form the soaring walls of the Canyon's Inner Gorge (Photo 1).

## A ROCK BY ANY OTHER NAME

The Zoroaster Granite (Color Plate 9) was named by two geologists working in the Canyon during the 1930s. Because the group of rocks they identified contains other plutonic rock types in addition to granite, recent geologists have coined a more cumbersome (but technically correct) name for them: the Zoroaster Plutonic Complex. Most geologists find that name too unwieldy for everyday use; they still call these rocks the Zoroaster Granite, and we will do the same.

The Vishnu Schist also suffers an identity crisis brought about by a tongue-twisting official name. The Vishnu consists of *schist* and *gneiss* (two varieties of metamorphic rocks, which have been transformed by heat and pressure) and other rock types that were all metamorphosed about 1700 million years ago. One of the Canyon's early geologists, Levi Noble, termed the rocks "Vishnu Schist" back in 1914. Later geologists renamed it the Granite Gorge Metamorphic Suite and subdivided it into the Brahma Schist, Rama Schist, and Vishnu Schist. The three are similar enough that most geologists (except a few specialists) call these rocks the Vishnu Schist, and we will too.

## THE MAZATZAL ARC

Once the Yavapai Arc was securely welded to the continent, the old subduction zone was destroyed and the Grand Canyon lay at the edge of the continent. But a second subduction zone lay southeast of the Grand Canyon region, along with its chain of volcanoes, the Mazatzal Arc (Figure 4). In turn, about 1600 million years ago (August 26), this arc also collided with Wyomingland, plastering the arc onto the continent and thus shifting the continental edge far to the south of the modern Grand Canyon. A spasm of melting 1400 million years ago (September 10) added more volume to the Zoroaster Granite, but the cause of this event remains mysterious.

## EROSION OF A MOUNTAIN RANGE

A relatively quiet period in the region's history began 1400 million years ago. The mountains raised during the Yavapai collision slowly eroded away. As more material was removed from the mountain tops, the deeply buried Vishnu Schist and Zoroaster Granite were slowly unearthed. By 1200 million years ago (September 27) they lay exposed on the earth's surface. Ultimately, the mountains were completely leveled by erosion, and the Grand Canyon region consisted of a nearly flat plain lying at sea level.

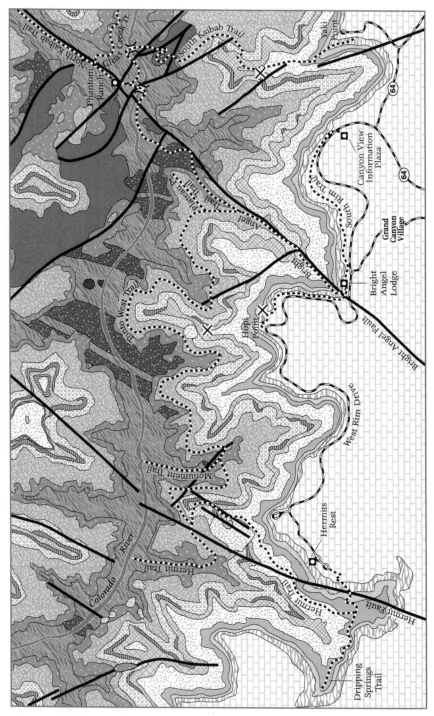

*Figure 6. Geologic map of the central Grand Canyon.*

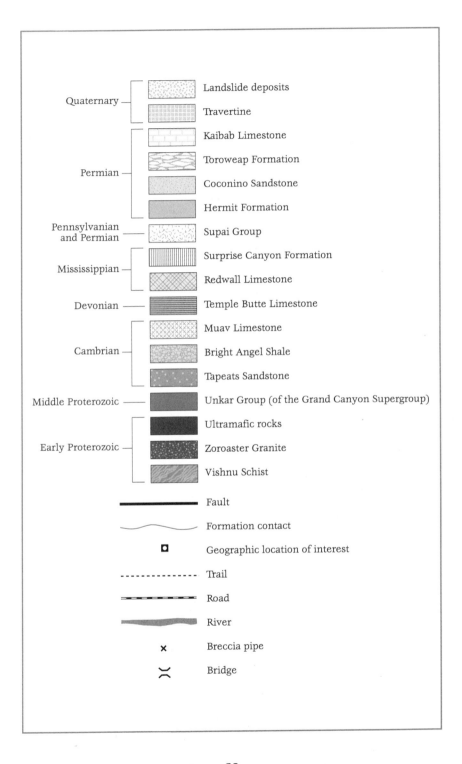

| | | |
|---|---|---|
| Quaternary | | Landslide deposits |
| | | Travertine |
| Permian | | Kaibab Limestone |
| | | Toroweap Formation |
| | | Coconino Sandstone |
| | | Hermit Formation |
| Pennsylvanian and Permian | | Supai Group |
| Mississippian | | Surprise Canyon Formation |
| | | Redwall Limestone |
| Devonian | | Temple Butte Limestone |
| Cambrian | | Muav Limestone |
| | | Bright Angel Shale |
| | | Tapeats Sandstone |
| Middle Proterozoic | | Unkar Group (of the Grand Canyon Supergroup) |
| Early Proterozoic | | Ultramafic rocks |
| | | Zoroaster Granite |
| | | Vishnu Schist |

Fault

Formation contact

□ Geographic location of interest

Trail

Road

River

✕ Breccia pipe

Bridge

## FLUCTUATING SEAS:
## DEPOSITION OF THE SUPERGROUP

At this time the sea encroached upon the region from the west, depositing the first layer in a series of rocks called the Grand Canyon Supergroup (Photo 1, Figure 20). This first warm, shallow ocean was the Bass Sea, and the sediment

*Photo 1. Horizontal layers of the Grand Canyon Supergroup overlie dark cliffs of Vishnu Schist along the South Kaibab Trail.*

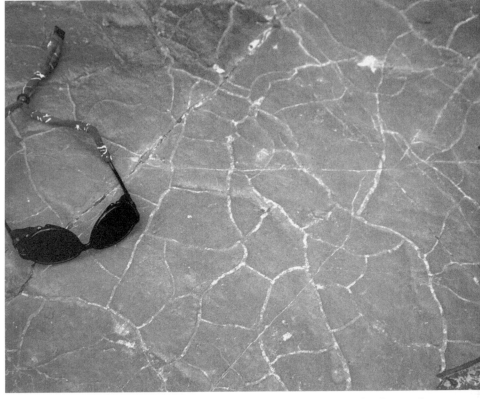

*Photo 2. Mudcracks crisscross a slab of Hakatai Shale deposited on the shores of a retreating sea.*

that accumulated in it and along its shore eventually formed the Bass Limestone. Although life originated on earth over 3500 million years ago, 2300 million years later, when the Bass Sea existed, it still consisted of simple, single-celled bacteria. These bacteria formed huge, slimy mats on the shallow seafloor, the remnants of which are preserved today as *stromatolite fossils* (Photos 79, 82) in the Bass Limestone and other rocks along several of the Canyon's trails (Hikes 2, 4, 15, 16).

Sea level fluctuates constantly, and before long (geologically speaking!) the Bass Sea began to retreat, draining away from the Grand Canyon region. The muddy sediment deposited on the shores of this retreating sea formed the Hakatai Shale (Photos 2, 3). Geologists suspect this coastline was arid because of the presence of salt crystal casts and mudcracks found throughout the formation (Photo 2). These features tell of repeated periods of drying on these huge mudflats. In addition, the Hakatai's vivid orange and red colors are the result of iron oxidation in dry conditions.

## THE SEA IS NEVER STILL

Because most of the Canyon's sedimentary rocks were deposited at or near sea level, geologists are keenly interested in past sea-level fluctuations. Along a gently sloping shore, a mere 10-foot rise in sea level can drown hundreds of square miles of previously exposed land, completely changing the sediment types deposited in those areas.

Sea level is almost never fixed for very long; it is continually rising and falling. These fluctuations can have either local or global causes. For example, a local rise in sea level can occur when the coastline drops down along a *normal fault,* which is a break in rock where one side slid down. Or the establishment of a new river in an area can create a growing delta, resulting in a fall in local sea level.

Other processes can change sea level globally. The two main triggers for such worldwide changes are (1) major glacial episodes and (2) periods of faster or slower *extension,* or spreading, that occurs at ridges in the middle of the ocean. When the earth enters a glacial interval, water evaporated from the oceans falls on the continents as snow, which is then locked up in glacial ice, preventing its quick return to the ocean. This transfer of water from the oceans to the ice caps produces a global drop in sea level. When the glaciers melt, the water is returned to the ocean, once again raising sea level. Because changes in the earth's orbit (known as *Milankovitch cycles*) tend to repeatedly warm and cool the globe on time scales of hundreds of thousands of years, these glacially driven sea-level fluctuations tend to be large (as much as 500 feet) and relatively rapid (100,000 to 1,000,000 years).

Changes in the rate of *seafloor spreading* (the growth of ocean basins through the eruption of basaltic volcanic rocks where two plates pull away from each other) can also alter sea level by changing the amount of space available in the ocean basins. If seafloor spreading speeds up, more basalt is erupted at the *mid-ocean ridge* (the volcanic ridge formed where two plates pull apart). The newly erupted basalt occupies space that before had been filled with water, thereby displacing it from the deep ocean basins onto low-lying continental areas. Picture filling your bathtub to the brim and then climbing in. Your body displaces water from the tub onto the floor, which had previously been dry.

In the ocean, the reverse effect also occurs when extension slows down, reducing the amount of basalt erupted at mid-ocean ridges. The basalt that already exists cools and contracts as it ages, deepening the ocean basins and causing global sea levels to drop as much as 100 to 200 feet. Global changes in the amount or speed of seafloor spreading occur slowly, resulting in gradual sea-level fluctuations lasting 20 to 30 million years.

Sea level is thus constantly on the move, profoundly influencing other forces that shape the landscape, from the depositing of sediments to the cutting of the Grand Canyon.

*Photo 3. In the center and lower-right corner of this photo, tilted layers of Hakatai Shale and Shinumo Quartzite underlie horizontal Paleozoic rock layers along the New Hance Trail.*

*Photo 4. At Tanner Rapids, movement along the Butte Fault has placed a dark cliff of Cardenas Lava between softer, less resistant Dox Formation. The lighter, resistant layer above the lava is the Nankoweap Formation.*

Overlying the Hakatai Shale are the bold, pink cliffs of the Shinumo Quartzite (Photo 3). A subtle *unconformity,* or gap in geologic time, separating these rock units was probably caused by the movement of reverse faults (Figure 50) running northeast to southwest across the region. Today the most prominent of these is the Bright Angel Fault (Figure 9), and you can see evidence of its motion along the Clear Creek Trail (Hike 6). The Bright Angel and North Kaibab Trails (Hikes 5, 15) both follow the Bright Angel Fault.

The Shinumo is composed of sand deposited on beaches and in river deltas. This material was later metamorphosed into a hard quartzite, making the Shinumo one of the Canyon's hardest, most resistant, layers. The overlying Dox Formation, with its interbedded sandstones and mudstones (Photo 4), records additional, small changes in sea level, showing that a shoreline setting was present in the Grand Canyon area until 1100 million years ago.

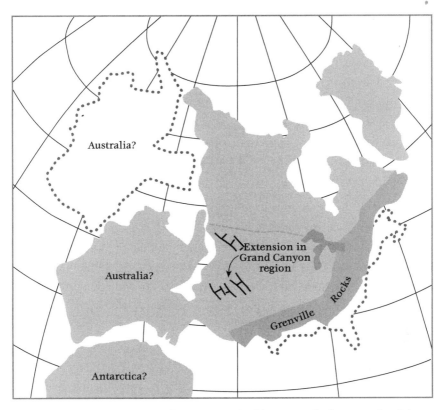

*Figure 7.  Extent of the Grenville mountain-building episode that completed the assembly of the supercontinent Rodinia. Simultaneous extension in the Grand Canyon region led to eruption of the Cardenas Lava. Note that Antarctica and Australia lay to the west of the Grand Canyon at that time. Modified from Key Reference 10 (see Appendix D).*

## RUMBLINGS OF CHANGE: THE CARDENAS LAVA AND THE FORMATION OF A SUPERCONTINENT

Just as the final grains of the Dox Formation were deposited, signs of major regional changes appeared; the Cardenas Lava (Photo 4) began to ooze across the landscape. Such outpourings of basalt typically occur in areas of crustal extension or *rifting* (where plates thin and pull apart). Minor extension was happening in the Grand Canyon area, probably as a byproduct of a massive continent-to-continent collision that was uplifting mountains along what is now North America's East and Gulf Coasts (Figure 7). Known as the Grenville Orogeny, this collision 1100 million years ago (October 5) was the final event in the formation of a supercontinent known as Rodinia. A modern example of this same process is found in Tibet, where basalt is being erupted at a small rift zone located behind the Himalaya Mountains, themselves the product of a continent-to-continent collision similar to the Grenville Orogeny.

## THE INTERIOR OF RODINIA

After the Grenville Orogeny, essentially all of the planet's continental crust was bound together to form Rodinia, and the Grand Canyon area lay locked in the center of that huge continent. Most geologists believe that the real estate that lay immediately west of North America consisted of a combination of Australia and eastern Antarctica (Figure 7). They are of different opinions, however, as to whether it was the Australian portion or the Antarctic portion that butted up against the Grand Canyon region.

Two rock units deposited then provide evidence of what the Grand Canyon region was like. The Nankoweap Formation (Photo 4) and the Chuar Group (Photo 5) were deposited between about 1050 and 750 million years

*Photo 5. Thinly bedded layers of Chuar Group (right side) were deposited in the center of a supercontinent. Nankoweap Trail.*

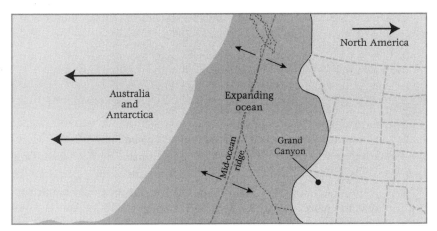

*Figure 8. The supercontinent Rodinia split apart very near today's Grand Canyon.*

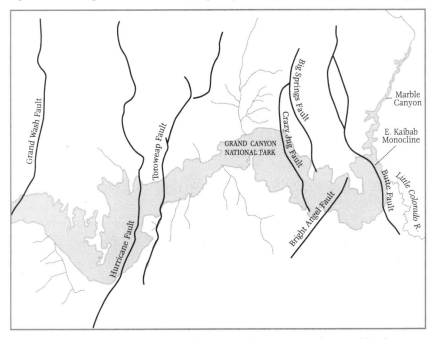

*Figure 9. Major faults in the Grand Canyon. The Butte Fault is visible along Hikes 1 and 13, and the Toroweap Fault is seen from Hike 18. The Grand Wash cliffs rise above the Grand Wash Fault.*

ago (between about October 9 and November 7 on our calendar). The characteristics of these two rock units, which can be seen along the Tanner and Nankoweap Trails (Hikes 1, 13), indicate that the land surface was low and that, despite being in the center of the supercontinent, the region was flooded by seawater. A modern example is Canada's Hudson Bay, which floods a low-lying portion of central North America.

## BREAKUP OF RODINIA AND TILTING OF THE SUPERGROUP

Rodinia began to break up about 750 million years ago, as Australia and Antarctica pulled away from western North America and the Grand Canyon (Figure 8). A group of normal faults split the Grand Canyon region in a northwest-southeast direction, offsetting adjacent blocks of crust almost 2 vertical miles (Figures 9, 10). Movement along these faults tilted the rocks of the Grand Canyon Supergroup (Photo 3). The faults and the tilted rock layers are visible on several Canyon trails, particularly the South Kaibab (Hike 4).

Landslides tumbled off cliffs formed by this fault movement. The rubble that accumulated at the base of the cliffs hardened over time into a *breccia* (a type of sedimentary rock consisting of big, jagged particles). This breccia makes up the Sixtymile Formation, the uppermost layer in the Grand Canyon Supergroup (Figure 20, 21). Most of the large blocks in the Sixtymile breccia consist of Chuar Group sedimentary rocks that were only partially hardened when they fell onto the rubble pile, demonstrating that the fault moved (and therefore Rodinia broke apart) immediately after the time when the youngest Chuar Group sediments were deposited, about 750 million years ago. The largest rubble blocks are 130 feet long and 26 feet wide, telling us that they had a short but very violent trip to their resting place.

## MOUNTAIN EROSION AND PRESERVATION OF THE SUPERGROUP

The rifting of Rodinia left the Grand Canyon region looking much like modern Nevada, with a series of uplifted mountain ranges separated by downdropped basins. As Australia and Antarctica disappeared into the sunset, the newly formed ancestral Pacific Ocean grew larger (Figure 49), and the tectonic violence that had shaken the Grand Canyon region ceased once again. The patient forces of erosion began to remove the Nevada-like mountains, and by the dawn of the Paleozoic Era 545 million years ago, the landscape was once again nearly flat, with the exception of a few hills of Shinumo Quartzite and Zoroaster Granite, which you can still see along several trails (Hikes 2, 6, 11, 16).

Where the rift-related normal faults had uplifted the crust, the Grand Canyon Supergroup was exposed to such vigorous erosion that it was completely removed, reexposing the Vishnu Schist and Zoroaster Granite. In contrast, in the downdropped areas, the Supergroup was preserved and formed the land surface (Figure 10). This was the situation 545 million years ago (November

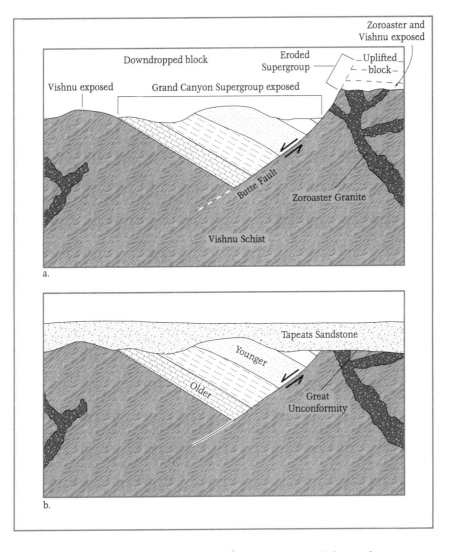

*Figure 10. a. Where the Grand Canyon Supergroup dropped down along extensional faults, it was protected from erosion in a geologic "grave" or graben. Where the Supergroup was uplifted, erosion completely removed it, leaving the older Vishnu Schist and Zoroaster Granite at the surface. b. Much later, Tapeats Sandstone blanketed the nearly flat surface, creating the Great Unconformity.*

18), when the Canyon's first Paleozoic rock layer, the Tapeats Sandstone, began to blanket the Precambrian rocks. This rock boundary forms the Canyon's world-famous Great Unconformity.

*Photo 6. The 1200 million-year time gap of the Great Unconformity lies between the horizontal Tapeats and the massive Zoroaster and Vishnu on the left.*

## THE GREAT UNCONFORMITY

The boundary between the Tapeats Sandstone and the older Precambrian rock units represents a massive gap in time. In areas that dropped down during the rifting of Rodinia, the Tapeats overlies one of the units of the Supergroup (Figure 10b). The contrast between the gently tilted Supergroup rocks and the overlying horizontal Tapeats identifies this as an *angular unconformity* and causes the Tapeats to overlie progressively older Supergroup rocks the farther west one travels in the Canyon (Figure 10). The amount of time missing from the record varies from about 200 million years at the Nankoweap Trail (Hike 13), where the Chuar Group underlies the Tapeats, to about 600 million years in places where the Unkar Group (Figure 20) is found below the Tapeats. The really great unconformity, though, is found where the uplift along the normal faults completely removed the Supergroup (Photo 6). In these areas, the 1700-million-year-old Vishnu and Zoroaster rocks directly underlie the 545-million-year-old Tapeats, so the paper-thin boundary between these rocks represents almost 1200 million years of missing time. This means that at these locations, no record exists for one-quarter of the earth's history! Fortunately, the preservation of the Supergroup in the downdropped blocks has allowed geologists to reconstruct what happened during much of this missing time.

Key references for Chapter 1 are 1 through 11. See Appendix D.

*Chapter 2*

# THE PALEOZOIC

*Photo 7.  Sunrise on O'Neill Butte's beautiful Paleozoic layers. South Kaibab Trail.*

The Paleozoic Era marks a particularly tranquil time in the Grand Canyon's history. After the breakup of Rodinia, for hundreds of millions of years the region lay along a passive continental margin far from tectonic activity (Appendix C). During this time all the sediments forming the Canyon's famous horizontal layers were deposited (Photo 7). The rocks' distinctive alternations between cliffs and slopes, as well as their radiant colors, were controlled by fluctuations in sea level and climate throughout the era. The walls of the Canyon expose outstanding examples of Paleozoic sedimentary rocks, providing geologists with one of the world's best natural laboratories for reconstructing ancient geographies and climates (Hike 5).

*Photo 8. Bold cliffs of horizontally bedded Tapeats Sandstone guard the Tonto Trail.*

## THE TONTO GROUP: ENCROACHMENT OF THE SEA

Not long after the dawn of the Paleozoic Era, around 545 million years ago (November 18), fingers of the ancestral Pacific Ocean began to lap across the Grand Canyon region. Extensive erosion had occurred during the millions of years represented by the Great Unconformity, leaving behind large amounts of quartz sand to form beaches and offshore sand shoals. These quartz sands eventually formed the Tapeats Sandstone (Photo 8), the Canyon's oldest Paleozoic layer. While sands accumulated along this ancient shoreline, small mud particles that could be carried farther from shore were deposited to the west, where the water was deeper, forming the Bright Angel Shale (Photo 9). Even farther west, beyond the reach of terrestrial sediments, *calcite* accumulated in still deeper water, forming the Muav Limestone (Photo 10). Some of this calcite was crystallized directly from seawater; the rest consisted of shell fragments secreted by the newly evolved organisms. Together, these three layers comprise the Tonto Group.

*Photo 9. The Bright Angel contains soft, green shales with a few thin, cliff-forming sandstone layers. Hermit Trail.*

Photo 10. *Outcrops of thinly bedded Muav Limestone hug Nankoweap Creek and form the tower in the distance.*

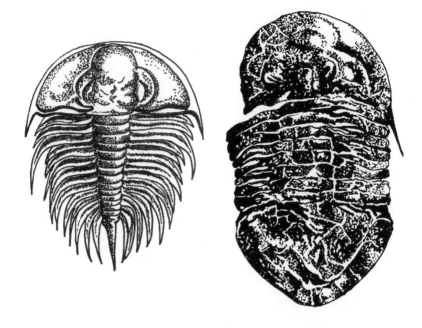

*Figure 11. Cambrian-age trilobite fossils (© 2004 by Dona Abbott).*

## EXPLOSION IN LIFE

Multicellular animals first evolved 650 million years ago (about November 10), after a mind-boggling 3000 million years of single-cellular life on the planet. However, it was not until the Cambrian Period (545 to 505 million years ago) that their population really diversified, offering the advantage of vastly greater complexity. By this time, these multicellular organisms had developed the ability to burrow through sediments for food and had learned to secrete hard shells for their protection. The advent of hard shells led to a dramatic increase in fossilization of organisms, so Cambrian rock layers throughout the world are loaded with visible fossils, something rarely seen in older rocks. The Canyon's Cambrian rocks contain many fossils, especially trilobites (Figure 11), but far more abundant are the remains of their tracks and burrows. Known to geologists as *trace fossils*, because they preserve evidence of the organism's activity rather than pieces of the organism itself, these tracks and burrows cover the faces of the Tonto Group along trails throughout the Canyon. A particularly impressive display lies along the Deer Creek Trail (Hike 17, Photo 86).

As the ancestral Pacific crept eastward, the locations where sand, mud, and calcite were deposited shifted with it, in the process stacking muds of the Bright Angel Shale on top of Tapeats sand, and Muav Limestone on top of the shale (Figure 12). Such a rise in sea level is known by geologists as a *transgression*, and the stacking of the Cambrian Tapeats, Bright Angel, and Muav layers visible in the Canyon's walls today is considered one of the world's best records of such an event.

## 130 MILLION MISSING YEARS

Although the Grand Canyon's layers comprise one of the world's best records of events during the Paleozoic Era, even this record is incomplete. The biggest

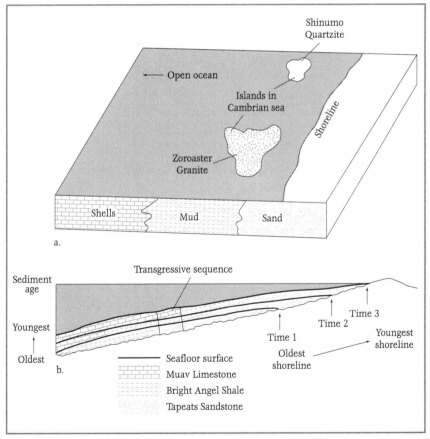

*Figure 12. A transgression (rising) of sea level formed the Tonto Group. a. Sand was deposited near shore, with mud and shell fragments deposited farther offshore. b. As the sea level rose, first mud (Bright Angel Shale) and then shell fragments (Muav Limestone) were deposited over the nearshore sands (Tapeats Sandstone). Modified from Key Reference 1 (see Appendix D).*

*Photo 11. A lens of elusive Temple Butte Limestone (middle) fills an ancient tidal channel between horizontal layers of Muav Limestone (below) and Redwall Limestone (above). Marble Canyon.*

gap occurs directly above the Tonto Group. In much of the eastern Grand Canyon, the layer lying directly above the Muav Limestone is Redwall Limestone (Figure 2) dating from the Mississippian Period. In the western Canyon, the Temple Butte Limestone, deposited during the middle Devonian Period, rests on the Muav (Figure 46). Nowhere in the Canyon are rocks visible that tell the story of the Ordovician, Silurian, and early Devonian Periods, meaning that we are in the dark about what occurred here for a period of 130 million years, between about 505 and 374 million years ago (November 21 and December 2). Based on evidence found in Ordovician and Silurian rocks exposed in adjacent states, geologists think that sediment probably continued to accumulate in a shallow ocean-to-shoreline setting during most of this time. A drop in sea level during the late Silurian or early Devonian probably exposed these soft sediments to erosion before they had a chance to consolidate, thus removing all traces of them.

## THE TEMPLE BUTTE LIMESTONE:
## ANCIENT TIDAL FLATS

We pick up the story's thread again in the Devonian Period with the formation of the Temple Butte Limestone (Photo 11). It was deposited when an arm of the ancestral Pacific again stretched eastward into Arizona. The western

Grand Canyon region was covered by the sea and received a thick, even blanket of sediment, but deposits were spotty in the eastern Canyon area, which was the shoreline. Therefore, western trails (Hikes 12 and 17) cross a continuous layer of Temple Butte, but this rock unit is missing entirely along many eastern trails. Along the North and South Kaibab Trails, small lenses of Temple Butte Limestone fill tidal channels that in their day drained extensive mudflats stretching to the horizon. The Grand Canyon area 374 million years ago (December 2) bore a strong physical resemblance to the arid, tidal mudflats that line today's Persian Gulf.

## THE REDWALL LIMESTONE: A VAST SEA

Another drop in sea level eroded the upper portion of the Temple Butte Limestone, removing it entirely from some areas. But the sea is ever restless, and it returned with a vengeance about 350 million years ago (December 4) during the Mississippian Period, when it deposited one of the Canyon's most dramatic layers, the Redwall Limestone (Photo 12). During this period the ocean came and went several times, but at its zenith it covered virtually all of western North

*Photo 12. The breathtaking Redwall Limestone towers above the Hermit Trail.*

America. By this time the complex marine life that had evolved in the Cambrian Period exploded into a fantastic diversity, and fossils of creatures such as brachiopods, corals, bivalves, crinoids, bryozoans, and gastropods are abundant in the Redwall (Hike 9).

## THE SURPRISE CANYON FORMATION: ANCIENT ESTUARIES

By 320 million years ago (December 7) the Redwall Sea receded westward, leaving the newly deposited limestone high and dry. Rivers began to carve channels up to 400 feet deep in the top of the exposed rock. In the meantime, the climate had become humid again, causing the limestone to rapidly dissolve, leading to the formation of caves and sinkholes. Such pockmarks are characteristic of *karst* topography; the sinkholes found throughout Florida are examples of this. When the sea inevitably returned about 315 million years ago (December 8), these sinkholes were filled with the sediment of a new formation, the Surprise Canyon (Figure 13).

Deposited in a series of river estuaries, the Surprise Canyon Formation is one of the Grand Canyon's most elusive rock units. Nowhere does it form a continuous layer; it is only exposed in Redwall sinkholes and in channels scoured out by ancient tides. Although most of these lie far from established trails, you can glimpse the Surprise Canyon Formation along Hikes 2 and 3.

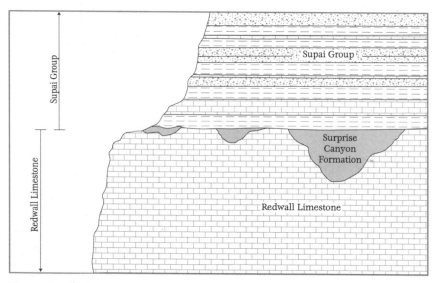

*Figure 13. The Surprise Canyon Formation is found only in isolated channels and caves carved into the top of the Redwall Limestone. Modified from Key Reference 12.*

*Photo 13. The Supai Group's distinctive cliffs and slopes (at left) formed from rapid changes in sea level caused by glaciers half a world away.*

Where it does occur, the formation provides a rich trove of fossils, both terrestrial and marine, and geologists regard it as one of the best examples ever found of an ancient estuary.

## THE SUPAI GROUP:
## GONDWANALAND AND GLACIATIONS

As the Pennsylvanian Period dawned, deposition of the Supai Group's distinctive red sediments began (Photo 13). This continued, with a few breaks, until early Permian time, so the Supai covers the story between about 310 and 285 million years ago (December 8 to 9). At that time, North America straddled the tropics, but it was profoundly affected by the advance of glacial ice sheets in the Southern Hemisphere. Many of the Supai Group's distinctive characteristics are the result of these southern glaciers.

## MILANKOVITCH CYCLES AND THE SUPAI GROUP

During the Pennsylvanian Period, South America, Africa, Australia, India, and Antarctica were combined in the supercontinent Gondwanaland. This huge continent had parked itself squarely over the South Pole, triggering one of the earth's largest ice ages.

Because of variations in the earth's orbit known as Milankovitch cycles, the amount of solar radiation received by the planet fluctuates in cycles lasting about 100,000 years. During ice ages like those in the Pennsylvanian Period and the much more recent (and famous) Pleistocene Epoch, reduced sunlight would plunge the earth into a glacial period, dropping sea level as water was locked up in ice. Then, as the sun intensified, the glaciers would melt, and sea level would rise.

During the Pennsylvanian, rapid and dramatic global changes in sea level caused by the waxing and waning of the southern glaciers affected the coastline and sediment deposition patterns in the Canyon region. The Canyon lay close to the shoreline of the ancestral Pacific Ocean, so a slight rise in sea level caused by glacial melt would flood the area and deposit marine muds and a few limestones. Then the following fall in sea level as the glaciers waxed again would expose the area as a gentle coastal plain. The Canyon climate at this time was arid, so sand dunes would march across this plain (Figure 14), forming sandstone. This pattern repeated itself for cycle after cycle until Gondwanaland moved off the pole and brought the glacial period to an end. The Supai's distinctive series of cliffs and slopes (Photo 13) were deposited during this time. The cliffs are composed of the coastal-dune sandstones, and the slopes consist of the marine mudstones.

## THE HERMIT FORMATION:
## SEDIMENTS FROM THE ANCESTRAL ROCKIES

As the Southern Hemisphere glaciers melted later in Permian time (December 9), the Grand Canyon region was flooded by river sediments washed down from the ancestral Rocky Mountains, which had risen in Colorado and New Mexico during a massive continent-continent collision. By the time the rivers draining these mountains reached the Grand Canyon, they were sluggish, meandering streams wandering across a vast plain, much like the modern Mississippi lazing its way across the low-lying portions of Mississippi and Louisiana. The muddy sediments deposited by these rivers formed the Hermit Formation (Photo 14).

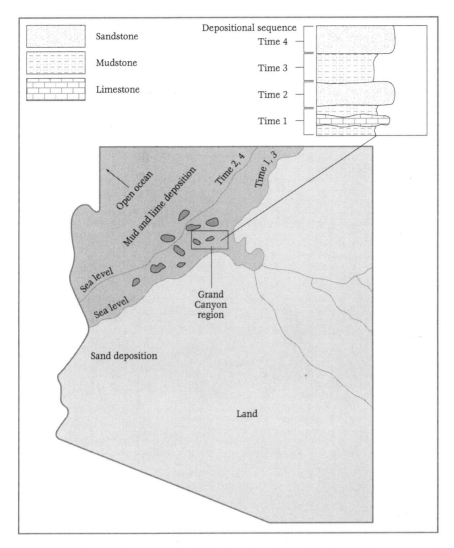

*Figure 14. Fluctuations in sea level during deposition of the Supai Group caused the Grand Canyon region to be alternately submerged by a shallow sea, where mud and lime were deposited, and then exposed as land, where sand was deposited. This sequence creates the Supai's distinctive cliff-slope-cliff appearance.*

## THE SUPERCONTINENT PANGEA

As Gondwanaland moved off the South Pole, it took up a collision course with North America. By early Permian times its African portion was grinding into the eastern seaboard of the United States and uplifting a Himalayan-scale mountain range: the Appalachians. Simultaneously, the South American portion of Gondwanaland was wreaking havoc on the Gulf Coast, uplifting mountains from Arkansas to the panhandle of Texas. The ancestral Rockies were created by this collision. By the Triassic Period the fireworks were over and these mountain ranges were being eroded away, but this massive collision put the finishing touches on the assembly of a new supercontinent, Pangea (Figure 15).

*Photo 14. The bold and beautiful Coconino Sandstone formed in a Saharan dunescape. The rubble-covered slope below it is composed of Hermit Formation, and the vegetated slopes above (at far right) are the Toroweap Formation.*

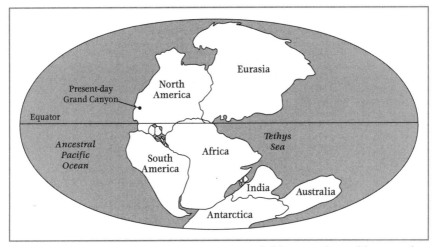

*Figure 15. The supercontinent Pangea, surrounded by a single world ocean, the ancestral Pacific.*

## THE COCONINO SANDSTONE:
## A SAHARAN LANDSCAPE

The rivers that supplied the Hermit Formation flowed across the Canyon from about 285 to 275 million years ago, but then they stopped, and a period of erosion set in. The climate was changing again, getting ever drier, and huge cracks, some as deep as 20 feet, formed in the surface of the drying Hermit muds (as seen on Hikes 5 and 10). By 270 million years ago (December 11), the region became a desert, the size of which rivaled the modern Sahara. Sand dunes up to 1000 feet tall covered the landscape from the Grand Canyon to Montana. These dunes are now preserved as the sheer cliffs of Coconino Sandstone (Photo 14, Figure 27).

## THE TOROWEAP AND KAIBAB FORMATIONS:
## ONE LAST SEA

Sand dunes marched across the Canyon for 5 million years, but by 265 million years ago the sea was also on the move, and it encroached on the area yet again. The climate was still extremely arid, so huge quantities of seawater evaporated in the intertidal area, forming salt, gypsum, and other *evaporite minerals*. As you can see along many trails (Hikes 4, 9), these evaporites are a distinctive component of the Toroweap Formation (Photo 30). In the western Canyon the proportion of evaporites in the Toroweap decreases and the amount of limestone increases, pointing the way to the open ocean (Hike 16).

The sea continued its eastward expansion, with a few pauses, and by 260 million years ago it stretched beyond the modern Grand Canyon into eastern

*Photo 15. Cliff of Kaibab Limestone seen along the South Rim Trail.*

Arizona. The Canyon was covered by a shallow sea inhabited by brachiopods, sponges, bivalves, corals, crinoids, gastropods, bryozoans, and other marine organisms (Figure 29). The Canyon's capping layer, the Kaibab Limestone (Photo 15), was deposited in this sea (Hikes 7, 14).

By 255 million years ago (December 12), the magnificent Paleozoic rock grouping of the Grand Canyon was complete, but that is far from the end of its story. On December 12 the limestone that comprises the modern Canyon rim lay at sea level, not at its current elevation of 7000 to 9000 feet. And the Canyon itself was not yet carved!

Key references for Chapter 2 are 1 and 12. See Appendix D.

*Chapter 3*

# THE MESOZOIC

Although the Kaibab Limestone forms the modern rim of the Canyon, it was not the last sedimentary rock deposited there. Nearby Cedar Mountain and Red Butte (Hike 8) preserve remnants of two additional layers deposited across the region during the Triassic Period that were later eroded. The lower layer is the brick-red Moenkopi Formation (Photo 49), whose mudstones and sandstones were deposited by lazy, meandering rivers about 240 million years ago in a setting similar to the earlier Hermit Formation. Above the Moenkopi lies the 225 million-year-old Shinarump Conglomerate, whose distinctive pebbles and cobbles were deposited by more powerful, swiftly flowing streams. Something was happening to lift up the land south of the Canyon, the direction of the streams' headwaters.

## THE BREAKUP OF PANGEA

That "something" was another major reorganization of the earth's face, the largest since the breakup of Rodinia back on November 3. Pangea, like Rodinia before it, was destined to break apart, and it began to do so in the Triassic Period. Rodinia broke up right in the Canyon's backyard, causing faulting and erosion throughout the region. In contrast, Pangea came apart far to the east, so the Canyon was not directly affected this time. However, an event of this magnitude has indirect effects across the globe, and the Grand Canyon certainly did not escape completely.

Given that Pangea was the one-world continent, there was also only one world ocean, the ancestral Pacific. As Pangea began to break up, Europe and Africa drifted away from North and South America, and the modern Atlantic Ocean was born (Figure 49). As the Atlantic grew, it did so at the expense of the Pacific. *Subduction zones* (areas where one plate dives beneath another) formed around the shrinking Pacific (Figure 3), creating today's infamous "Ring of Fire." One of these subduction zones formed near Phoenix, Arizona, uplifting mountains that were drained by the swift-flowing rivers that deposited the Shinarump Conglomerate.

## DEPOSITION OF ADDITIONAL MESOZOIC SEDIMENT

Throughout the Paleozoic, western North America was tectonically quiet, but with the breakup of Pangea it became a dynamic place complete with volcanoes, earthquakes, and the birth and demise of mountain range after mountain range. The Grand Canyon region and the rest of the Colorado Plateau occupied a particularly strong block of crust, so while this tectonic tempest raged all around, they remained tranquil by comparison. Because of the Plateau's relative inactivity, it remained near sea level. Therefore, many of the sediments eroded from the surrounding volcanoes and mountain ranges ended up accumulating there. In the Grand Canyon area, over 4000 feet of Mesozoic sediment piled on top of the Kaibab Limestone, burying the Paleozoic sediments deep enough to cement them into rock. Later events eventually removed all traces of these Mesozoic rocks from the Canyon, except for the small scraps of Moenkopi and Shinarump at Red Butte and Cedar Mountain. These missing sediments still exist today in the canyon country of southern Utah, and some of the layers stand sentinel over Marble Canyon, forming the Vermillion Cliffs that loom over Lees Ferry, the launching point for all Grand Canyon river trips.

## REMOVAL OF MESOZOIC SEDIMENT

What event could have stripped 4000 feet of sediment from the region? The answer lies in the continued breakup of Pangea and an important mountain-building episode, the Laramide Orogeny, which uplifted the Kaibab Plateau.

### LARAMIDE MOUNTAIN BUILDING

As North America continued to move westward to make room for the growing Atlantic Ocean, Pacific Ocean crust was subducted beneath the western edge of the continent. This formed a chain of volcanoes extending from British Columbia to California's Sierra Nevada, then down through southern Arizona and into Mexico.

About 65 million years ago (December 25), the angle at which this oceanic plate was subducting under North America shallowed, causing it to rub against the base of the continental plate much farther east than it did before (Figure 16). One likely cause for this shallowing was an abrupt acceleration in North America's westward movement; the continent raced over the oceanic plate faster than it could dive out of the way. Friction generated by the rubbing of the two plates created compressional forces that heaved up the modern southern Rocky Mountains and Colorado Plateau, an episode known to geologists as the Laramide Orogeny.

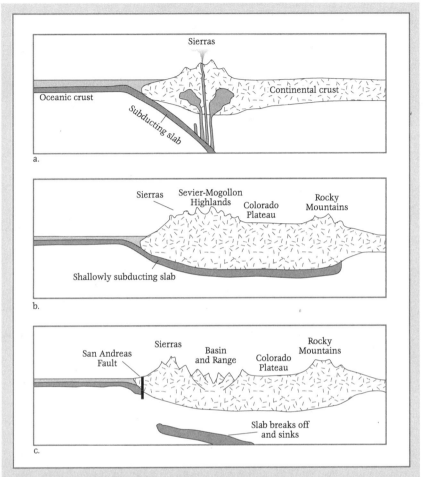

*Figure 16. Evolution of the Colorado Plateau. a. Subduction off the western edge of North America formed a chain of volcanoes whose core now forms California's Sierra mountains. b. The shallowing of the subduction angle under North America caused two mountain-building episodes, uplifting the Colorado Plateau, the Rocky Mountains, and the Sevier-Mogollon Highlands. c. After subduction ceased, the Sevier Highlands collapsed, forming today's Basin and Range province. Modified from Key Reference 1.*

Immediately prior to the Laramide Orogeny the Colorado Plateau, including the Grand Canyon area, consisted of coastal swamps where the coal now mined throughout the Four Corners region was formed. When the orogeny was complete, the region stood as the high plateau we see today.

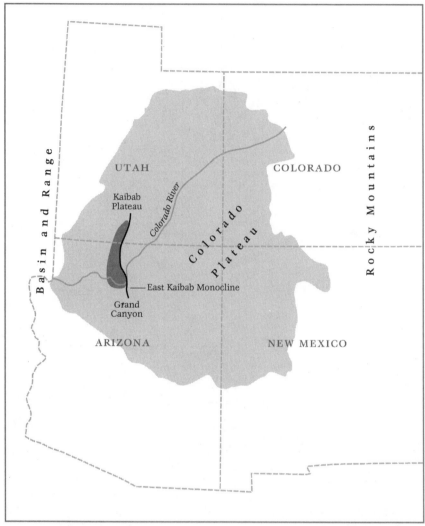

*Figure 17. The Colorado Plateau lies between the Rocky Mountain and Basin and Range provinces. The Kaibab Plateau is a smaller plateau-on-a-plateau formed by uplift of the East Kaibab Monocline by reactivation of the Butte Fault.*

During the Laramide Orogeny, most of the Colorado Plateau's rocks were uplifted nearly horizontally, as if they were riding an elevator. But in places ancient faults that had lain dormant since the breakup of Rodinia 700 million years earlier lurked below the thick sedimentary rocks, just waiting for something to disturb their slumber. The Laramide Orogeny renewed movement along many of these faults, which caused layers of rock to bend in steplike folds, creating the dramatically folded *monoclines* seen on the Colorado Plateau (Figure 50). The Grandview Monocline (Photo 28), visible along the Grandview Trail (Hike 3), is a striking example of one.

But by far the most important monocline in the Grand Canyon was formed by the renewed movement of Marble Canyon's mighty Butte Fault, visible along the Tanner and Nankoweap Trails (Hikes 1, 13). Its Mesozoic movement created an especially large and long fold, the East Kaibab Monocline (Photo 68, Figure 21). The uplifted western side of this monocline forms the Kaibab Plateau (Figure 17), a broad dome that rides piggyback on top of the more extensive Colorado Plateau.

As the Mesozoic Era drew to a close, the Laramide Orogeny was still actively raising the Colorado Plateau, its monoclines, and the Rocky Mountains. The uplift of the Kaibab Plateau soon exposed its rocks to intense, high-elevation storms, greatly accelerating their erosion rate relative to nearby areas. This erosion eventually stripped the Grand Canyon of the 4000 feet of colorful Mesozoic rocks that still exist elsewhere on the Colorado Plateau.

Key references for Chapter 3 are 1 and 13. See Appendix D.

*Chapter 4*

# THE CENOZOIC

Although very few of the Grand Canyon's spectacular rocks formed during the Cenozoic Era, this is the time when the Canyon was finally carved by the Colorado River, creating the famous abyss that exposes nearly 2000 million years of the earth's history.

## END OF LARAMIDE MOUNTAIN BUILDING

When the Laramide mountain building finally subsided around 45 million years ago (December 27), the American Southwest consisted of two large mountain ranges encircling the high Colorado Plateau (Figure 16b), physically resembling modern Tibet or Bolivia. The western mountain range, known as the Sevier and the Mogollon Highlands, used to run through Nevada and central Arizona. The eastern range, which still exists today, was the southern Rocky Mountains. Though the Colorado Plateau stood at a considerable height, it was low relative to its flanking mountains. Most of the runoff from these mountains therefore flowed onto the plateau and formed a series of lakes, much like Lake Titicaca on Bolivia's modern Altiplano plateau.

## ESTABLISHMENT OF THE MODERN DRAINAGE SYSTEM

The Colorado River headwaters probably formed around this time, carrying water from the Rockies to a lake in eastern Utah. But the portion of the Colorado that today flows southwest through the Grand Canyon did not exist. Instead, a series of rivers that drained the Mogollon Highlands flowed northeast across the area. As odd as it seems given Arizona's present geography, rivers with sources near Phoenix (present elevation 1500 feet) flowed downhill past Flagstaff (now at 7000 feet) and the Grand Canyon to a lake that stood in today's Bryce Canyon National Park. In fact, Bryce's signature spires are composed of sediments deposited in that very lake.

The southern Colorado Plateau's northeasterly flowing river system persisted until at least 18 million years ago (December 30), when tectonic events west of the Grand Canyon region began to lay the groundwork for the modern drainage system. The exact time at which the eastern Grand Canyon was carved remains a mystery because crucial rock evidence has been eroded away. However, the picture is clearer for the western Grand Canyon. Among

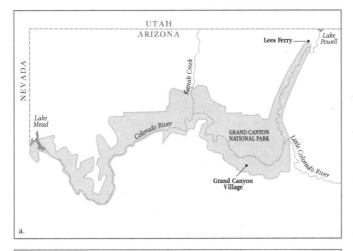

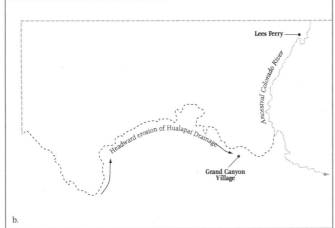

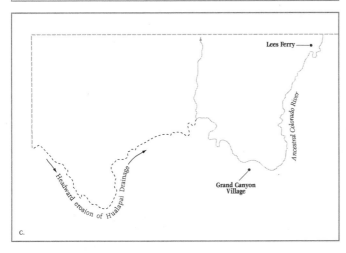

*Figure 18. Possible scenarios for the carving of the modern Grand Canyon.*
*a. Today's through-flowing drainage was established about 5 million years ago.*
*b. Prior to 5 million years ago, the Ancestral Colorado River may have flowed along the modern Little Colorado River before being captured by the Hualapai Drainage.*
*c. Alternatively, the Ancestral Colorado River may have flowed up Kanab Creek before being captured by the Hualapai Drainage.*

other clues, the Muddy Creek Formation, a rock unit that stretches across the Canyon's western mouth, contains clear evidence that the Colorado River did not flow here 6 to 8 million years ago, when it was deposited.

In contrast, 4- to 5-million-year-old rocks lining the valley of the lower Colorado River contain distinctive fossils that could only have come from rock formations on the Colorado Plateau. This demonstrates that the Colorado River must have flowed all the way through the Grand Canyon by that time.

Based on this evidence, geologists conclude that the Colorado River established its course through the entire Grand Canyon approximately 5 million years ago (about 2:30 P.M. on New Year's Eve; Figure 18a). But other evidence suggests that the upper Colorado River, the portion in Colorado and Utah, was established millions of years earlier. If the river didn't flow out through the western Grand Canyon, then where did it go? Geologists don't yet have a definitive answer to this question.

Among the many hypotheses regarding where the Colorado flowed, two have gained the most attention. The first suggests that the river flowed through Marble Canyon just as it does today, but rather than bending west to flow through the Grand Canyon, it instead headed south and flowed "up" the course of today's Little Colorado River (Figure 18b). "Up" here refers to modern geography; the river, of course, flowed downhill. It is hard for us short-lived humans to envision a landscape that is altered so profoundly that a river could completely reverse its course, but given sufficient time, the forces of erosion can work such feats of magic. From the Little Colorado the river likely flowed into New Mexico, where it connected with the Rio Grande and proceeded to the Gulf of Mexico.

The second hypothesis has the river flowing through the eastern and central portions of the Grand Canyon and then exiting up Kanab Creek, a major tributary that arrives from Utah at river mile 143 (Figure 18c). Some gravel deposits in Kanab Creek lend support to this idea, but where the river went once it reached Utah remains a mystery. Geologists would dearly love to have a more definitive answer to this crucial question regarding the Canyon's history, but thus far the Canyon's rocks have not revealed this cliff-hanging chapter of their story!

## THE LOWER COLORADO RIVER: THE PIRATE STREAM

Although the rocks have not revealed the location of the Colorado River 10 to 15 million years ago, geologists know that it was not in the western Grand Canyon. Clearly the Colorado River does flow there today, so how was its present course established?

About 30 million years ago (December 28), the subduction zone located off the west coast of North America since the Triassic Period died when it collided

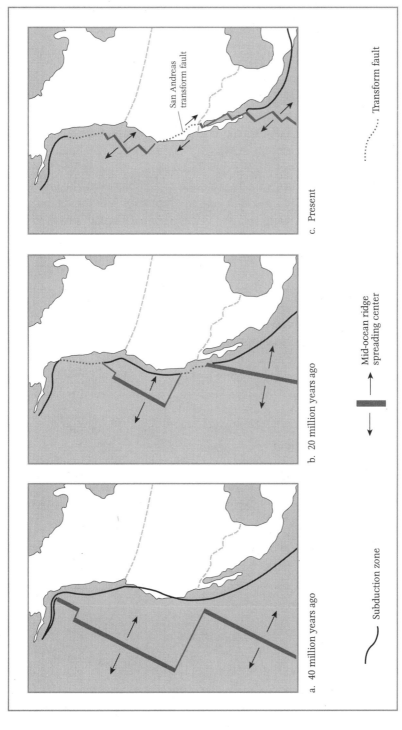

a. 40 million years ago

b. 20 million years ago

c. Present

San Andreas
transform fault

Subduction zone

Mid-ocean ridge
spreading center

.......... Transform fault

Figure 19. The arrival of a spreading center 30 million years ago eliminated the subduction zone offshore of southern California and gave birth to the modern San Andreas Fault.

with a *mid-ocean ridge* (where two plates pull away from each other) (Figure 19). This event gave birth to California's San Andreas Fault and ultimately caused the demise of the Mogollon and Sevier Highlands, the great mountain range bordering the western edge of the Colorado Plateau. Like any high area, the Southwest's mountains and plateaus were unstable, with gravity constantly trying to pull them down. Compression from the subduction zone had countered this tug of gravity and helped to hold the highlands up. When the compression was removed, gravity won out, and the highlands began to collapse along normal faults, brought low by their own weight. The Mogollon and Sevier Highlands suffered the greatest collapse, forming the Basin and Range topography that dominates Nevada, western Utah, and southern Arizona today (Figure 16c).

The formation of the Basin and Range had a profound influence on the Colorado Plateau. The plateau's western flank, which before had ended at the toes of a mountain range, now stopped along a dramatic escarpment plunging down into the Basin and Range. The Grand Wash Cliffs, which mark the western end of the Grand Canyon and the Colorado Plateau, form that escarpment today (Figure 9). Steep creeks began to drain that escarpment.

Steep streams erode their bedrock with great efficiency and through that process lengthen themselves by carving ever headward. One particular stream, known to geologists as the Hualapai Drainage, flowed from the Lake Mead area to its end in the newly formed Gulf of California. It rapidly carved its way headward, into the heart of the Colorado Plateau, forming the western portion of the Grand Canyon as it went. Eventually, it breached the last ridge separating it from the upper Colorado, and the full force of the river began coursing down this path to the sea (Figure 18). Geologists, ever fond of colorful language, refer to this process as *stream piracy* (Figure 22). The swift and nimble pirate Hualapai outmaneuvered his more lumbering foe and carried his spoils, the Colorado River, with him to the Gulf of California.

## POSTSCRIPT: FIRE, ICE, HUMANS, AND THE FATE OF THE GRAND CANYON

As of 5 million years ago, or 2:30 P.M. on New Year's Eve, we are nearing the end of our tale. The rocks of the Grand Canyon have been formed, the Canyon itself has been cut, but a few details are yet to be told. The first is the formation of the mountains that you can spy south of the Canyon rim (Hikes 7, 8, 14). As the Mogollon Highlands were collapsing, the landscape south of Grand Canyon Village was a vast, flat plateau. But deep below the earth's surface, magma was moving, and 9 million years ago it erupted in the first of many volcanic outbursts. Between 9 million and 1000 years ago, over 800 different volcanoes formed on the plain between the Canyon and Flagstaff. The vast majority of these are dark, basaltic *cinder cones* that stand a few hundred feet high. However, a handful of them erupted light-colored andesite or dacite (Figure 42) and grew larger in stature. The monarch of the volcanic field is San Francisco Mountain (Photo 48), an andesitic volcano born 2 million years ago. In the prime of its reign half a million years ago, San Francisco Mountain stood upwards of 16,000 feet high. At some point between 250,000 and 400,000 years ago, the mountain's northeast flank collapsed, shaving 3000–4000 feet off its elevation and turning its single cone into the current horseshoe-shaped ring of peaks. Despite this loss, the mountain still dominates the southern skyline from both the North and South Rim visitor areas.

The group of normal faults (Figure 50) that formed the Basin and Range has been creeping slowly eastward for the last 10 million years, stretching the crust and allowing magma to worm its way into cracks. The magma has erupted from many basalt volcanoes on the Canyon's North Rim. Within the last 1 million years, some of these volcanoes have either erupted within the confines of the Grand Canyon or

Photo 16. A conical cinder cone sits between the two cliff bands in this view from the Lava Falls Route.

spilled glowing lava down its flanking cliffs (Photo 16), hardening into lava plugs that dammed the river and turned the Canyon into an enormous reservoir. The Lava Falls Route (Hike 18) takes you down the steep lava cascades left by one of these eruptions.

These Basin and Range faults (including the Hurricane and Toroweap Faults on Figure 9) are still active and continue to drop the western Grand Canyon down in a series of stairsteps. In just a few million years these faults will turn the Grand Canyon area into an extension of the Basin and Range, and the region will look more like the area around Las Vegas than it will the present Canyon.

The final chapter of the Grand Canyon story is filled not only with fire but also with ice. As lava was pouring over the rim into the western Grand Canyon, the world plunged into its first major ice age since the Pennsylvanian Period. As is typical of ice ages, the Pleistocene ice age (1.8 million to 10,000 years ago) consisted of a series of glacial advances and retreats. As glaciers occupying the high mountain cirques in Colorado and Wyoming melted, they sent raging torrents down the Colorado, scouring the riverbed and carving the Grand Canyon deeper. Geologists believe that the Canyon may have deepened by 1000 feet during the last 1 million years (since 10:07 P.M. on New Year's Eve). No glaciers ever occupied the Canyon itself, but the significant cooling that occurred during these times caused the vegetation zones to migrate to lower elevations. Spruce trees flourished along the South Rim, and ponderosas marched down to today's sparsely vegetated Tonto Platform.

By the time humans arrived at the Canyon about 13,000 years ago (7 seconds before midnight on New Year's Eve), it had assumed its present form. However, the Grand Canyon remains a geologically dynamic place, and repeat visitors sometimes notice small changes such as debris from a flash flood covering a favorite campsite or a fresh scar marking where part of a cliff collapsed. These small changes don't seem to alter the Canyon in important ways, but their cumulative effect is awesome. The Canyon as we know it will likely disappear just a few short hours into the New Year, and before the end of the new month of January, the region could look like the plains of Kansas, the peaks of the Himalaya, or the tropical islands of the Bahamas.

Key references for Chapter 4 are 1 and 14–21. See Appendix D.

*Hiking the Hermit Trail.*

# Part 2
# PREPARING TO HIKE
# THE GRAND CANYON'S GEOLOGY

*Photo 17. Hikers emerging onto Cedar Ridge, South Kaibab Trail.*

Whether you choose to stroll along the rim or to explore the Canyon's Inner Gorge, this section includes all the information necessary to plan an enjoyable and safe trip. Remember that trails, access roads, and water sources can change over time. Check with Grand Canyon National Park's Backcountry Office (see "Permitting Your Trip" in Chapter 5) for current information before you embark, and remember that no guidebook is a substitute for adequate planning, conditioning, and good judgment.

*Chapter 5*

# PLANNING AND PERMITTING YOUR TRIP

If you plan to do overnight hiking in the Grand Canyon, you should obtain your permit before arriving because many camps are booked months in advance. As you plan, know your limits in order to devise a sensible and enjoyable itinerary. Without proper planning and preparation, what from your armchair appears to be an easy hike could instead become a dangerous undertaking. Please read this chapter carefully and contact Grand Canyon National Park's Backcountry Office at (928) 638-7875 if you have any questions.

## HIKING IN THE GRAND CANYON

Grand Canyon National Park hosts a vast system of trails, offering a splendid diversity of terrain, views, and geologic wonders. Short, nearly flat trails on both rims offer stunning panoramas for novice hikers or visitors with limited time. Strenuous rim-to-river trails offer experienced backpackers a range in difficulty levels to challenge their skills. Destinations below the rim but above the river offer more moderate excursions suitable for day hikers and backpackers who choose not to hike the long distances to the river.

## TRAILS

The condition of trails in the Grand Canyon varies widely, from well-groomed paths to rock-strewn routes requiring advanced navigation skills. The Park Service divides the backcountry into several types of use areas based on their level of management.

**Corridor** areas receive the most use and contain regularly maintained trails with generally smooth treads. These trails are regularly patrolled by rangers, and there is a high probability of coming into contact with other hikers. Corridor trails have permanent structures including toilets, ranger stations, purified water sources, and emergency phones. The Backcountry Office recommends that backpackers use Corridor trails during their first trip into the Canyon.

**Threshold** zones contain secondary trails that are not maintained but are generally easy to follow, although the tread can be rough. Trail junctions are signed, and there are nonpermanent toilet facilities. Along threshold trails there is a chance of frequent contact with other hikers.

**Primitive** zone trails are the most remote. They are seldom patrolled, and you will have infrequent (or no) contact with other hikers. Such trails do not have toilets, and water sources are usually few and far between. Detailed maps and advanced navigation skills are essential because the path is often faint, and junctions are not marked except by the occasional cairn. Only very experienced and self-reliant Canyon hikers should attempt primitive zone trails.

**Wilderness** zones are very low-density use areas without established routes and are therefore not covered in this book.

## MAPS

Under the information block for each trail, maps covering that hike are numbered and refer to the Map List found in Appendix E. The popular Trails Illustrated and Earthwalk Press Grand Canyon maps are available at many map dealers, the Canyon Village Marketplace and Canyon View Information Plaza, or from the Grand Canyon Association by telephone at (800) 858-2808, by fax at (928) 638-2484, or online at *www.grandcanyon.org*. The new Sky Terrain Grand Canyon National Park Trails map has an easy-to-read scale of 1:40,000 and is available at the Marketplace and online. These maps all have the park's use-area codes and boundaries marked, making them very useful for trip planning. The U.S. Geological Survey topographic maps (7.5-minute quadrangles) provide good landscape detail but do not list the backcountry use areas and do not always have the trails marked.

Although we provide a geologic map of the Corridor area (Figure 6), you may also want to bring the main geologic map, the Geologic Map of the Eastern Part of the Grand Canyon National Park, Arizona. It covers all but Hikes 8 and 18 in this book and is available at the Canyon View Information Plaza.

## CLIMATE

The best seasons for hiking in the Grand Canyon are spring and fall. During June, July, and August, when the Inner Gorge temperature exceeds 100°F almost every day, the extreme heat and lack of shade can pose serious dangers to unprepared hikers. In addition, the midsummer monsoons often bring violent thunderstorms with lightning and locally heavy rains, increasing the potential for flash flooding. During the winter, hikers must be prepared for extreme cold, snowstorms, and persistent snow and ice. Winter hikers often need instep crampons to negotiate the Canyon's steep, icy paths. During the spring, there are frequent storms, but the temperatures are more moderate. The most stable weather usually occurs in the fall, which, along with moderate temperatures, makes it an ideal time to hike the Grand Canyon's geology.

## BACKCOUNTRY REGULATIONS

It is your responsibility to be aware of and to follow all the backcountry regulations prescribed by the Park Service. These rules have been implemented to protect the fragile desert ecosystem that you are here to enjoy. The rules are posted at most trailheads, listed in the park's Backcountry Trip Planner (available from the Backcountry Office), and included on the Trails Illustrated, Earthwalk Press, and Sky Terrain maps.

## OVERNIGHT HIKING

Permits are required for all overnight use in the backcountry, including overnight use of rim sites not located in developed campgrounds. Permits are not required to sleep in the dormitories at Phantom Ranch, but you must have reservations (see "Lodging—North and South Rims" under "General Information"). The Grand Canyon backcountry is divided into use areas, each of which has a visitor quota. Camping in the Corridor and in Tapeats, Hermit, Monument, and Horseshoe Mesa use areas is restricted to designated campgrounds and/or campsites. From March 1 through November 14, you are limited to 2 nights' stay per site, per hike. From November 15 through the end of February, the allowance is 4 nights per campground per hike. In all other use areas, you are permitted to camp "at large" (i.e., at nondesignated sites). However, your campsites should be carefully selected to avoid hazards such as flash floods and to minimize your impact (Chapter 6). You may stay up to 7 nights per hike in each of these use areas.

## DAY HIKING

Permits are not required for day hiking, allowing for more spontaneity in your itinerary. Day hiking is a great way to get a "feel" for the Canyon and to study its amazing geologic history without having to carry a heavy backpack (Photo 17). At the end of this section, we have listed recommended day hikes, and ideal day-hike destinations are listed in the information block of each trail. Regardless of your choice, remember that day hiking in the Grand Canyon can be extremely challenging, particularly during the hot summer months. *Do not attempt to hike from the rim to the river and back in one day.* When you hike, be sure to bring a flashlight and plenty of water, food, and warm clothes.

## PLANNING YOUR TRIP

Before applying for your backcountry permit or hitting the trail for a day hike, you should carefully plan your itinerary to ensure a fun and safe trip. If you haven't yet decided which hike you'd like to tackle, we recommend that you skim the individual "About the Landscape" and hike information blocks to select which geologic themes and which trails hold the most appeal. The Bright Angel Trail is the best rim-to-river hike for first-time Grand Canyon backpackers. Buy the map(s) you will need, check out the National Park website at *www.nps.gov/grca,* and be sure to obtain the Backcountry Trip Planner from the Backcountry Office, either in person, by calling (928) 638-7875, or by writing: Backcountry Reservations Office, Grand Canyon National Park, P.O. Box 129, Grand Canyon, AZ 86023-0129. As you mull over the options, be sure to consider the following factors.

## DIFFICULTY RATINGS

When planning your itinerary, it is essential that you consider not only the mileage but also the amount of vertical elevation to be hiked. Some other factors you should take into account include the distance between water sources (and whether you need to haul water), the season, potential routefinding difficulties, and, of course, the amount of time you can devote. Every member of your group must be physically and mentally prepared for the challenges that lie ahead. To help you plan realistic trips, we have adopted a classification system rating the overall difficulty of each trail as follows:

**Easy:** A short, generally flat or gently inclined hike that can be completed in half a day or less.

**Moderately difficult:** A steep hike of short to intermediate length on a generally smooth tread.

**Difficult:** A very steep and/or long hike on a smooth to somewhat rocky tread. May require occasional routefinding skills.

**Very difficult:** An extremely steep and/or very long hike on an extremely rocky or nonexistent tread. Routefinding skills and water hauls are frequently required.

The "rule of thumb" used by many Grand Canyon hikers is that it will take twice as long to hike out as it does to hike down. However, this can vary greatly. Leave adequate time to hike out, and don't forget to leave your itinerary with someone you can trust to initiate a search. To report an overdue hiker, call (928) 638-7888 and dial 2.

## WATER SOURCES

One of the most important considerations in planning your trip is where you can count on finding water (Photo 18). Although it has played a critical role in shaping the Grand Canyon, there is precious little surface water to be found! And at 8 pounds per gallon, it does not take much to really load down your pack.

Except for the piped drinking water provided along some Corridor trails, all other sources in the backcountry should be purified before drinking. Filters are available at Canyon Village Marketplace on the South Rim and at many outdoor stores. You can also use iodine tablets or boil your water.

*Photo 18. Miners Spring, one of the Grand Canyon's welcome sources of perennial water. Grandview Trail.*

Many hikers choose to cache water on the descent to lighten their loads for the hike out. Be sure to store the water in heavy-duty containers and take careful notice of where you stash the bottles. Two to three quarts is generally adequate unless you will be camping en route. If you don't need your cache, dump the water and pack out all containers.

The Backcountry Office tracks seasonal water sources based on backpackers' reports. If you are counting on any water source other than the perennial ones listed for each hike, it is absolutely essential to check with the Backcountry Office before starting your trip.

## WHAT TO TAKE

Deciding what to take with you is a critical step in planning your trip. Take only what you will really need; every extra pound on your back will slow you down considerably and greatly increase the amount of water and food you need to consume. During the summer, consider leaving behind your stove and fuel. A bivvy sack can substitute for a tent, especially during the fall, when the temperatures are more moderate and rain and snow are less likely to fall.

A bandana can serve as a towel, a bandage, and a brimless hat. Carefully consider each item you put in your pack; you will appreciate it every step of your journey through time.

## THE TEN ESSENTIALS: A SYSTEMS APPROACH

The Mountaineers recommend that you plan ahead and equip yourself with systems to cover the following ten needs in case of an emergency.

1. **Navigation** (map and compass). See the map list at the end of the book for the appropriate maps to take on each hike. Also bring your compass and be sure you know how to use it.
2. **Sun protection** (sunglasses and sunscreen). Your sunglasses should block UV radiation.
3. **Insulation** (extra clothing). Remember to plan for inclement weather.
4. **Illumination** (headlamp or flashlight). Bring extra batteries and bulbs.
5. **First-aid supplies**. Hikers should be versed in basic first aid and, if possible, be certified in cardiopulmonary resuscitation (CPR).
6. **Fire** (firestarter and matches/lighter). As open fires are not allowed in the national park, use these only in an emergency.
7. **Repair kit and tools** (including knife). A pocketknife comes in handy for cooking, first aid, and a host of other uses.
8. **Nutrition** (extra food). If you bring enough food to tide you over during an emergency, you should have food left over at the end of an uneventful trip.
9. **Hydration** (extra water). A water purifier or iodine treatment is critical for ensuring a potable water supply.
10. **Emergency shelter**.

## AVOIDING THE CROWDS

Many people visit the Grand Canyon seeking replenishing solitude. The current permit system strictly controls the number of overnight visitors allowed in the Canyon, with the majority of these staying in the Corridor area. If you have previous Grand Canyon backpacking experience, consider hiking one of the more remote (and difficult) trails, such as Tanner (Hike 1), New Hance (Hike 2), Nankoweap (Hike 13), Thunder River (Hike 16), or Lava Falls (Hike 18). Plan trips in use areas where you camp at nondesignated sites so you can avoid other groups. Consider hiking from the North Rim, which receives only 10 percent of the park's annual visitors. Plan your trip during the spring, winter, or fall to avoid the summer crowds and the intense heat. Avoid holiday weekends and school vacations, particularly Spring Break. And when you do camp near other backpackers, be considerate; avoid excessive noise and lights.

## RECOMMENDED DAY TRIPS
**Easy:** Hike 7—South Rim Trail
Hike 11—Tonto Trail, Indian Garden to Plateau Point
Hike 14—Uncle Jim Trail
**Moderately difficult:** Hike 4—South Kaibab Trail to Cedar Ridge
Hike 5—Bright Angel Trail to 3-Mile Resthouse
Hike 8—Red Butte Trail
Hike 9—Hermit Trail to Santa Maria Spring
Hike 10—Dripping Springs Trail
Hike 15—North Kaibab Trail to Supai Tunnel
Hike 15—Phantom Ranch to Ribbon Falls
Hike 16—Bill Hall Trail to the Esplanade
**Difficult:** Hike 1—Tanner Trail to the top of the Redwall
Hike 3—Grandview Trail to Horseshoe Mesa
Hike 5—Bright Angel Trail to Indian Garden
Hike 15—North Kaibab Trail to Roaring Springs

## RECOMMENDED DAY TRIPS FOR
## RIVER RUNNERS
**Moderately difficult:** Hike 2—Hance Rapid to Bass Limestone
    stromatolites
Hike 9—Hermit Rapid to Hermit Camp
Hike 11—Granite Rapid to the Monument (Monument Creek)
Hike 13—Nankoweap Trail to Butte Fault
Hike 15—Phantom Ranch to Ribbon Falls
Hike 17—Deer Creek Trail to Deer Spring
**Very difficult:** Hike 12—Havasu Canyon Trail to Mooney Falls
Hikes 16 and 17—Tapeats Creek to Thunder River to Deer Creek

# PERMITTING YOUR TRIP

To enhance each visitor's experience and to avoid overusing precious resources, the Park Service has implemented and strictly enforces a backcountry permit system. Permits are issued by the Backcountry Office on a first-come, first-served basis. Because the demand for backcountry permits far exceeds the established use-area quotas, you should request your permit well in advance, *as early as the first of the month, four months before your intended start date.*

## BACKCOUNTRY OFFICES

The Backcountry Office at the South Rim is located at the Backcountry Information Center (near Maswik Lodge). It is open every day of the week, year-round, from 8 A.M. to noon and 1 to 5 P.M. When the North Rim facilities are open, generally from mid-May through mid-October, the North Rim Backcountry Office is located at the ranger station, 1.4 miles north of the Grand Canyon Lodge. Limited backcountry permits may also be obtained at Pipe Spring National Monument near Kanab, Utah, and at the Bureau of Land Management office in St. George, Utah.

## HOW TO APPLY

Once you have planned your itinerary, you must complete the permit application. This is available in the Backcountry Trip Planner as well as online at *www.nps.gov/grca*. Be sure to include the campground, campsite, or use-area code where you would like to stay each night. The codes are listed in the information block for each trail and are available in the planner, on the website, and on the Trails Illustrated, Earthwalk Press, and Sky Terrain maps. Also indicate alternative trips and dates if you are flexible; this will greatly increase your chances of receiving a permit. In 2003, the backcountry fees were $10 per permit, plus $5 per person per night. Infants and children are considered additional members of your party. Repeat visitors can purchase a frequent hiker annual permit for $25, which waives the $10 permit fee for one year.

After you have completed the application, there are three ways to apply for the backcountry permit. First, you can bring your completed request form in person to one of the Backcountry Offices. Second, you can fax your request to (928) 638-2125. Third, you can mail your request to Backcountry Reservations Office, Grand Canyon National Park, P.O. Box 129, Grand Canyon, AZ 86023-0129. At this time, you cannot apply for a permit by telephone or e-mail.

Written requests are processed on a first-come-first-served basis. All written requests are responded to by U.S. mail, so don't expect an e-mail or fax confirmation. You should allow at least 3 weeks for processing. If your itinerary is permitted and you requested it at least one month in advance, the permit will be mailed to the trip leader. If you haven't received your permit, you must pick it up at the Backcountry Office either the day before or the day of your intended start.

## LAST-MINUTE PERMITS

If you arrive at the Grand Canyon without a permit, you may still be able to get one. However, last-minute permits are very difficult to obtain, particularly during the summer and over holiday weekends. You must go in person to the

Backcountry Office and be prepared to wait. You should bring several itineraries, ranked according to your preference, in case your first choice(s) are unavailable. In the case that none of your itineraries are available, you should carefully consider the available options (which are often very difficult and/or remote trails) before you commit.

Once the quota for each campground or use area is exceeded, you may add your name to a waiting list. This option is only available to walk-in visitors, and you must be at the Backcountry Office at 8 A.M. each day to keep your spot. You may keep your name on the list for as many days as you need to obtain your permit.

Occasionally, you may be able to obtain last-minute permits at the remote Lees Ferry, Meadview, and Tuweap ranger stations for a limited number of use areas. You must have a valid credit card and should be aware that the rangers are not always present at these locations.

## ADDITIONAL INFORMATION

If you need additional information, please review the park's Backcountry Trip Planner, log on to *www.nps.gov/grca,* or contact the Backcountry Office at (928) 638-7875, Monday through Friday from 1 to 5 P.M. Mountain Standard Time, except for federal holidays. You may also go directly to the Backcountry Office.

## GENERAL INFORMATION
### LODGING—NORTH AND SOUTH RIMS

All lodging within the park, including Phantom Ranch, is run by the same company. To make reservations, call (888) 297-2757, fax (303) 297-3175, or write Xanterra Parks and Resorts, 14001 East Iliff, Aurora, CO 80014.

Outside the park at the South Rim, there are a number of communities where you can find a room, including Tusayan, 7 miles south of the park; Williams, 60 miles south; and Flagstaff, a larger community 80 miles away.

The North Rim is more isolated, with fewer options. Lodging is available seasonally at the Kaibab Lodge, 18 miles north of the park (928) 638-2389, as well as at the Jacob Lake Inn, 45 miles away (928) 643-7232.

## CAMPING

There are three designated campgrounds available at the South Rim. Two of these, Mather Campground and Trailer Village, are located in Grand Canyon Village. Sites at Mather are available on a first-come-first-served basis from December 1 through March 31. The rest of the year, reservations can be made at (800) 365-2267 or *reservations.nps.gov.* Trailer Village has hookups; call (303) 297-2757 for reservations. Desert View Campground is located 25 miles east of Grand Canyon Village and is available on a first-come-first-served basis. It is open seasonally, usually starting in mid-May.

Outside the park, 2 miles south of Tusayan, the Ten-X Forest Service Campground is open seasonally. Seven miles south of Tusayan, "Camper Village" (928) 638-2443 has hookups and coin-operated showers.

At the North Rim there is one Park Service campground located 1 mile from the rim. You can make reservations up to five months in advance at (800) 365-2267. Outside the park, you may camp seasonally in National Forest campgrounds or at the Kaibab Camper Village; call (928) 643-7804 (summer) or (928) 526-0924 (winter). Dispersed camping in the National Forest may also be allowed; check with the North Kaibab Ranger District at (928) 643-7395.

## SHOWERS AND LAUNDRY FACILITIES

There is nothing like a hot shower after hiking in the backcountry! At the South Rim, showers and laundry facilities are located near Mather Campground and operate from 6 A.M. to 11 P.M. At the North Rim, the facilities are located next to the General Store.

## PHANTOM RANCH

For lodging and meals (other than cafeteria-style snacks) at Phantom Ranch, you must have reservations, which can be made by calling (888) 297-2757. These services are often booked a year in advance.

## HAVASUPAI RESERVATIONS

Hike 12, the Havasu Canyon Trail, is located on private land administered by the Havasupai Indian Tribe. You must make advance reservations for camping at (928) 448-2121 or (928) 448-2141, or lodging at (928) 448-2111 or (928) 448-2201. Each visitor is also charged an entrance fee ($20 in 2003). You must pay 50 percent of your total costs in advance. Both the campground and the lodge accept credit cards. Helicopter flights into the canyon are also available; call (928) 282-1651.

## RIM-TO-RIM SHUTTLE SERVICES

For those contemplating a hike between rims (between Hike 15 and Hikes 4 or 5), transportation is provided seasonally by Trans Canyon Shuttle (928) 638-2820. Daily shuttles depart the North Rim at 7 A.M., arriving at the South Rim at noon. South Rim departures leave at 1:30 P.M. and arrive at the North Rim at 6:30 P.M.

## MULE RIDES

Mule rides leave year-round from the South Rim and must be booked in advance at (888) 297-2757. From the North Rim, trips are available from mid-May through mid-October through Canyon Trail Rides at (435) 679-8665.

## PETS AND KENNELS

No pets are allowed below the rim. They are allowed on leash on rim trails, but not on shuttle buses. A kennel is available at the South Rim near Maswik Lodge. Advance reservations are recommended; call (928) 638-0534. There is no kennel at the North Rim. Ginger's LUV'N Touch offers the closest services in Fredonia, Arizona, 76 miles northwest of the North Rim; call (928) 643-7377.

*Chapter 6*

# LOW-IMPACT AND SAFE HIKING AND CAMPING

## PLANNING A SAFE TRIP

Each year the inner Canyon, with its steep, rugged terrain, extreme temperatures, and limited shade and water sources, kills a few hikers and forces the evacuation of many more at their own considerable expense. Hikers who create unsafe conditions for themselves or others are subject to citation and/or arrest. Clearly, you don't want to fall into these categories. Planning and good decision making are crucial to the success of your trip; your life may depend on it.

## TERRAIN

The Grand Canyon offers some of the most rugged terrain on the planet (Photo 33). By its very nature, hiking there is grueling: a long, pounding descent followed by a steep, continuous climb with increasingly thin air and tired legs. *Do not attempt to hike from the rim to the river and back in one day.* As you hike, keep a slow, steady pace; you should be able to talk normally. If you are near water, soak your hat, bandana, or shirt often. Take frequent rests, at least one 5-minute break per hour. Relax, put your feet up, and take the opportunity to eat, drink, savor the views, and learn more about Grand Canyon geology.

## TEMPERATURE EXTREMES AND EMERGENCIES

Summer and winter temperatures are often extreme in the Grand Canyon. During the summer, inner Canyon temperatures consistently exceed 100°F. The temperature in the Inner Gorge usually exceeds the rim by 20° to 30°F, and there is very little shade. Hike during the coolest hours of the day, before 10 A.M. and after 4 P.M. Bring along a headlamp to hike at night, if necessary. Avoid excessive solar radiation; wear a hat and long, loose-fitting clothing. Monitor your food and water intake. Consider hiking along the cooler rim trails, or plan your visit for a cooler time of year. During the winter, temperatures often drop below freezing. Backpackers must be prepared for conditions that can vary from warm and sunny one day to cold, windy, and snowing the next.

Temperature- and weather-related emergencies include hypothermia, heat exhaustion, and heat stroke.

**Hypothermia** is caused by exposure to cold, windy, or wet conditions. To prevent hypothermia, stay dry. Most hikers prefer synthetic fabrics; clothing made of cotton is not recommended. Be sure to pack adequate raingear, which doubles as a wind layer. Symptoms of hypothermia include shivering, slurred speech, lack of coordination, exhaustion, and poor judgment. Should someone in your group exhibit these symptoms, get out of the cold weather. Get him into a tent, dry clothing, and a sleeping bag. Provide the victim with food and warm drinks. If symptoms are advanced, place bottles of warm water in the victim's sleeping bag, or share the bag. Severe hypothermia is a life-threatening condition demanding advanced care. In such cases, seek help immediately.

**Heat exhaustion** usually develops while exercising in the heat. To prevent it, don't hike during the heat of the day and be sure to drink and eat adequately. Symptoms include a headache, weakness, dizziness, clammy skin, rapid pulse, nausea, and vomiting. Should anyone in your group exhibit these symptoms, wet down her clothing and have her lie down in the shade, prop up her feet, drink a sports drink, and eat a salty snack. In most cases, these steps will alleviate the symptoms, but in severe cases you should seek help quickly.

**Heat stroke** is a life-threatening condition in which the victim's body overheats during exertion. Symptoms include a very high core body temperature; dry, hot skin; sudden confusion; hallucinations; seizures; and even unconsciousness. Should anyone in your group exhibit such symptoms, you must immediately cool him off to lower his body temperature. If possible, immerse him in water. Have him lie down in the shade, sponge him off, and fan his body. Get help immediately.

## WATER AND FOOD INTAKE

Hikers should always carry water with them, even on the Corridor trails where drinking water is available. Experienced backpackers carry at least 1 gallon of water, or 1.5 to 2 gallons each when hiking to a dry camp. Water intake requirements are based on the season and temperature, the time of day, and the distance and vertical elevation you are traveling.

Be very careful to avoid dehydration, which occurs quickly in the desert. Remember that if you feel thirsty, you are already dehydrated. Drink plenty of water each day before starting and sip frequently during your hike. On average, people walking during the heat of the day sweat 0.5 to 1.5 quarts of water per hour. You should therefore consume at least 0.5 quart per hour. To tell if you are drinking too little or too much, monitor your urine; the amount and color should remain normal.

Be sure to balance your water intake with sufficient food and salts (electrolytes) to maintain your strength and avoid water intoxication, an electrolyte imbalance caused by drinking too much water relative to food intake. Drink sports drinks and eat salty snacks often. While hiking you should consume at least twice as many calories as normal, mostly in the form of complex carbohydrates. If you don't feel hungry or thirsty because of the heat, rest until you do.

## ISOLATION AND EMERGENCIES

Even prepared backpackers can experience serious problems. Broken bones, sprains, and other injuries can create dangerous situations in the isolated canyon environs. Because help may not reach an injured hiker for days, it is important to travel in groups on all but the well-patrolled Corridor trails. Group members should stay together; never leave a slower person behind. If a member becomes debilitated, leave at least one person behind to care for her. Study the exact location where you are leaving the members, and mark a large X on the ground using bright-colored equipment, such as tents. Carry a signal mirror, and use it to flash passing aircraft and/or people on the rim. Carry a hiker's first-aid kit, including an ankle wrap. In addition, remember to leave a copy of your itinerary with someone you trust to initiate a search should you be overdue. To report an overdue hiker, call (928) 638-7888 and dial 2.

## DANGERS AND ANNOYANCES

The Grand Canyon hosts an incredible variety of plants and animals. Only a few of these have cause to concern backpackers. While not inherently dangerous, thorny plants and prickly cacti should obviously be avoided (Color Plate 6).

Rattlesnakes are frequently seen, but bites rarely occur. Rattlesnakes are not generally aggressive, but you should never try to handle one. Pay attention to where you place your hands and feet, especially when stepping over obstacles. Scorpion stings are more common in the Canyon. While extremely painful, most scorpion stings are not life-threatening. Their stings occur in self-defense, usually when a hiker steps on or touches one. Scorpions are nocturnal creatures, hiding under rocks during the day. Inspect rocks before you pick them up, and wear shoes (not sandals) around camp. Look before you sit down, and sleep in a tent. Take care to shake out shoes, clothes, and sleeping bags before using them. Spider and centipede bites can be avoided using similar precautions. While frightening-looking, tarantulas are not dangerous. Ant bites can also be painful. Avoid camping near anthills and avoid dropping food scraps that will attract ants.

## LIGHTNING, FLOODING, AND THE COLORADO RIVER

When selecting at-large campsites, be careful to avoid washes that could quickly become raging torrents should severe thunderstorms occur. This is particularly true during the summer monsoon season. Remember that it does not need to be raining or even overcast where you are for the wash to flood. Avoid high points during lightning storms. Never try to swim in the Colorado River. Even excellent swimmers are no match for its very strong currents and frigid (approximately 48°F) temperatures.

*Photo 19. Cryptobiotic soil helps to stabilize the Grand Canyon's delicate ecosystem.*

## LEAVE NO TRACE ETHICS

It is the challenge and responsibility of all hikers to leave no trace of their passage through the Grand Canyon. Besides damaging or destroying fragile resources such as water, plants, or wildlife, you can create aesthetic eyesores that can be seen from as far away as the rim. Despite their seemingly enduring nature, rocks, the descriptive building blocks of the Grand Canyon's history in stone, can also be damaged. To protect this unique environment, Grand Canyon hikers follow the Leave No Trace ethics described below.

## CRYPTOBIOTIC SOIL

Large areas of soil in the Canyon are covered with a gray/black, lumpy surface called *cryptobiotic soil* (Photo 19, sidebar "Binding the Earth" in Hike 1). This protective layer is a living crust that protects the soil from wind erosion and helps retain moisture. A single footstep can destroy this crust, which takes decades to develop. Where cryptobiotic soil exists, walk only on a developed trail or on slickrock or sand. Never set up camp on cryptobiotic soil.

## HUMAN WASTE

Human waste decomposes very slowly in the desert. When possible, use toilets provided. Otherwise, human waste must be buried at least 200 feet from campsites, trails, and water sources. Please be careful to avoid cryptobiotic soil (Photo 19) when looking for an appropriate site. Choose a spot with darker, organic soil and dig a hole 6 to 8 inches deep, covering the waste with soil. Do not bury or burn your toilet paper! Pack it out in plastic bags along with your other trash.

## LITTER

Everything that you carry into the Grand Canyon must also be packed out. No litter should be left behind, placed in toilets, or buried, including cigarette butts and toilet paper. Food scraps attract pests such as rodents and ants to campsites and should also be removed.

## CAMPSITES

In many backcountry areas of the Canyon, campsites are scarce. Rocky terrain, desert plants, and cryptobiotic soils greatly limit where you can set up your tent. In Threshold and Primitive zones, where you camp at large, careful campsite selection is important. All campsites should be located at least 200 feet from water sources to prevent pollution and allow wildlife access. Choose a previously used site, concentrating your impact. Where possible, camp on slickrock or sandy areas, not on organic

*Century plants bloom in lower Nankoweap Canyon.*

soil. Be particularly careful to avoid camping or treading upon cryptobiotic soil. Do not make "improvements" such as rock shelters or trenches, and do not remove any vegetation; it has a difficult enough time growing in this harsh environment!

## FIRES
Open fires are not allowed in Grand Canyon National Park. Use backpacking stoves for all your culinary needs.

## TRAIL AND OFF-TRAIL USE
Wherever they're provided, remain on developed trails. Passing feet can quickly create a lasting trail that can be seen from as far away as the rim (Photo 44). Don't take unnecessary shortcuts; these contribute to erosion and destruction of fragile desert soils and vegetation. When traveling off-trail in a group, spread out to avoid concentrating your impact. Walk on slickrock or through washes and other sandy and unvegetated areas, and please don't step on cryptobiotic soil.

## PROTECTING WATER SOURCES
Protecting the Grand Canyon's scarce water resources is essential for wildlife and backpackers alike. Small sources of water (potholes, springs, and sluggish streams) are particularly susceptible to contamination. Be careful not to use too much water from a limited source, which could deprive wildlife and other hikers of a much-needed drink.

For bathing and washing, take water only from larger streams and the Colorado River. Wash and discard your wastewater at least 200 feet from the source. Use biodegradable soap, but never use soap directly in the water. When you're near the Colorado River, urinate directly into it. The river is so large that it quickly dilutes it. After passing dishwater through a screen or bandana, you can also discard it directly into the Colorado. However, all food scraps should be packed out with the rest of your garbage.

Purify all water before drinking or cooking with it. You can filter it, add iodine, or boil it. Be aware that water from the Colorado River is so silty that it will quickly clog your filter. Either bring extra filter cartridges or allow the water to stand for a time, letting the silt settle out before treating it.

## PROTECTING CULTURAL RESOURCES AND NATURAL FEATURES
Do not disturb or feed any wildlife. Avoid spilling food, and be sure to suspend all food items above the ground, away from any vegetation or structures. Never pick any vegetation, including flowers. Desert plants can take many years to grow back if they are damaged. Plants such as the century plant bloom only

once in their lifetimes, after 15 to 25 years; take a photo and leave them for other explorers to enjoy.

*Do not remove any objects, including rocks, cultural artifacts, or plants. All of these are protected by law and add to future visitors' enjoyment.*

Most of the Grand Canyon's trails have evolved from primitive routes used by ancient inhabitants. As you explore, you are likely to encounter archaeological and historical ruins and artifacts. These cultural resources are protected by law. Ultimately, however, the preservation of these artifacts depends on each of us. Never walk on stone walls; walk carefully around the slopes supporting them. Don't rearrange the sites, even for a photograph. Because they're so fragile, avoid eating or camping at such sites. Rodents attracted to your crumbs may decide to nest inside the ruins. Avoid touching pictographs; many of these are hundreds of years old, and touching them may cause them to flake off. Respect these sites for the window they provide into the lives of the Canyon's earliest inhabitants, and in deference to the wishes of the Native Americans who are their modern descendants.

## A NOTE ABOUT SAFETY

Safety is an important concern in all outdoor activities. No guidebook can alert you to every hazard or anticipate the limitations of every reader. Therefore, the descriptions of roads, trails, routes, and natural features in this book are not representations that a particular place or excursion will be safe for your party. When you follow any of the routes described in this book, you assume responsibility for your own safety. Under normal conditions, such excursions require the usual attention to traffic, road and trail conditions, weather, terrain, the capabilities of your party, and other factors. Because some of the lands in this book are subject to development and/or change of ownership, conditions may have changed since this book was written that make your use of some of these routes unwise. Always check for current conditions, obey posted private property signs, and avoid confrontations with property owners or managers. Keeping informed on current conditions and exercising common sense are the keys to a safe, enjoyable outing.

*The Mountaineers Books*

*An approaching storm along the Hermit Trail.*

**Hike 1**

# TANNER TRAIL

## A Fault's Work Is Never Done

*Revel in unusual and dramatic views of the Colorado River, the Palisades of the Desert, and Marble Canyon, while you learn how these stunning features all result from repeated activity on the Butte Fault, the Canyon's most important fracture.*

LENGTH ■ 9 miles

ELEVATION CHANGE ■ 4660 feet

TIME ■ 1–2 days each way

DIFFICULTY ■ Very difficult; remote, very steep, and rocky tread

BACKCOUNTRY ZONING ■ Primitive; at-large camping (BB9)

WATER AND TOILETS ■ Only at Colorado River

EMERGENCY SERVICES ■ Nearest ranger station at Desert View

MAP LIST ■ 1, 3, 4, 8

KEY REFERENCES ■ 1, 22

DAY HIKES ■ 75-mile Saddle (4 miles round trip); overlook atop Redwall Limestone (8.4 miles round trip)

SEASONS ■ Year-round, but very hot in summer and potentially icy in winter

**About the Landscape:** Tanner is the park's easternmost inner-Canyon trail, and it provides vistas unlike any others. The first thing that strikes hikers is how clearly you can see the Colorado River along much of the trail; a long stretch is in plain sight even from the rim. Another scenic spectacular is the intimate view you get of the Palisades of the Desert, the 4000-foot, sheer cliff that bounds the Grand Canyon on its eastern side (Color Plate 14). Finally, because the Tanner Trail reaches the Colorado where Marble Canyon meets the Grand Canyon proper, it offers unparalleled views into spectacular Marble Canyon, a treat normally reserved for river runners.

Although these exceptional scenes seem unrelated, they can all be attributed, directly or indirectly, to the presence of the Butte Fault, the single most important fault in the entire Grand Canyon. The Butte Fault runs immediately east of the Tanner Trail, and its movements have governed the geography of the Grand Canyon region for almost a billion years.

The Colorado River is plainly visible from the rim here because, rather than being confined to the Inner Gorge's dark, narrow slot, the river instead winds its way through the vivid red Dox Formation, part of the Grand Canyon Supergroup (Figures 2, 20). Where a river encounters resistant, hard-to-erode rocks, such as the Inner Gorge's Vishnu Schist and Zoroaster Granite, it directs its fury to slicing down through them, creating a narrow chasm. In contrast, where a river runs over soft, easily eroded rocks, such as the Dox, it prefers

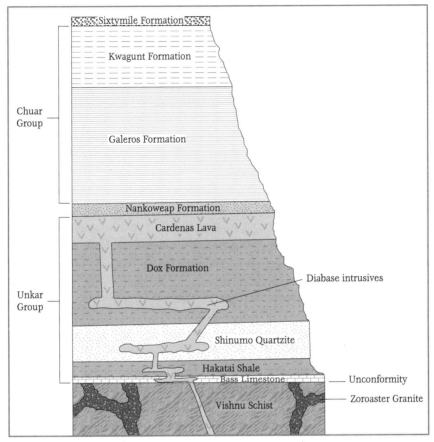

*Figure 20. The Grand Canyon Supergroup.*

to lazily meander from side to side, carving out a wide, gentle valley. The Colorado's lazy, looping meanders as it wanders through the Dox Formation are easily visible along the trail.

Supergroup rocks like the Dox are preserved only on the downdropped sides of a series of normal faults that were active about 750 million years ago (Figure 10, Hike 4), and the Butte Fault was the biggest of them all. Accordingly, it preserved an unusually hearty slice of Supergroup on its west side, including the Canyon's only exposures of the Cardenas Lava, Nankoweap Formation, Chuar Group, and Sixtymile Formation, which together comprise the Supergroup's upper half (Figure 20). Thus, the Butte Fault is responsible for the presence of Dox Formation at river level, and hence the excellent river views here.

The mighty wall of the Palisades, which soars 4000 feet above the river, provides a breathtaking counterpoint to the soft, open terrain at river level. This imposing rock wall is part of the East Kaibab Monocline (Photo 68), the

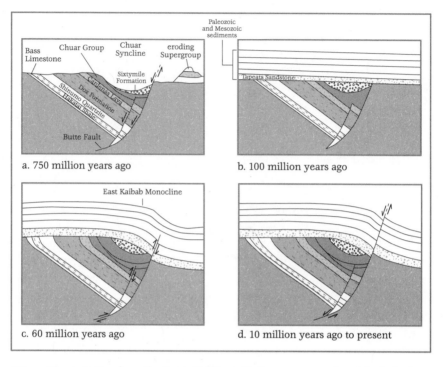

*Figure 21. Activity along the Butte Fault. a. Birth as an extensional fault during the breakup of Rodinia, 750 million years ago. The Chuar Group sediments were deposited in the growing sag, creating the Chuar Syncline. Later, landslides deposited rubble that formed the Sixtymile Formation. b. During 680 million years of inactivity, thousands of feet of Paleozoic and Mesozoic sediments accumulated above the fault. c. Reactivation as a compressional fault during the Laramide mountain-building episode 60–70 million years ago, which formed the East Kaibab Monocline. d. Geologically recent reversal to a normal fault due to stresses related to Basin and Range extension.*

stairstep-like fold along which the Kaibab Plateau formed. The East Kaibab Monocline directly overlies, and owes its existence to, the Butte Fault. After its spasm of activity 750 million years ago, the fault lay dormant for over 680 million years. During this time, thousands of feet of sediment accumulated above the fault, burying it deep below the surface (Figure 21). But old faults never die; they just wait to be reactivated. For the Butte Fault, that reactivation came 65 million years ago, during a mountain-building episode known as the Laramide Orogeny (Chapter 3). During this event, the Colorado Plateau was raised from sea level to a tremendous height, with the unusual characteristic that most of its rock layers remained in their original, horizontal position. The main exception was where old weaknesses in the crust, such as the Butte Fault, were reactivated by the new compression. Although the Butte Fault had started its life as a normal fault, the Laramide compression reactivated it as a reverse fault (Figure 21c). You can see evidence of this reactivation here and along the Nankoweap Trail. As the compression spread upward through the rock layers, the fault's slow movement cracked and offset the lower Paleozoic rock layers. Higher in the stack, the layers didn't crack, but instead buckled into a one-sided fold, or *monocline* (Figure 50), resembling carpet draped over a staircase riser. Because it was formed by the reactivation of the area's largest and most important fault, the East Kaibab Monocline is the biggest and most visible member of a family of monoclines that crisscross the Grand Canyon region.

From its confluence with Nankoweap Creek to Tanner Rapid (at the end of this trail), the Colorado River runs south through Marble Canyon, closely paralleling the East Kaibab Monocline. Is it just coincidence that these two beautiful canyons link up here, next to the largest fault and the biggest fold in the region? Because crucial rock evidence has been eroded away, it is not clear when the Colorado River's modern course through Marble Canyon was established, so the exact cause of the river's location cannot be known with certainty. However, the Butte Fault probably played a crucial role in determining the Colorado's current route. There are two likely ways that the fault may have affected its course. First, the river may have found the downwarped side of the East Kaibab Monocline to be a convenient, low-elevation route to its destination. Alternatively, the river may have exploited weaknesses created by the fault's most recent episode of activity (Figure 21d), which began within the last 30 million years with the onset of extension in the nearby Basin and Range province. The Colorado Plateau is beginning to experience similar extension (Chapter 4), and the Butte Fault is presently reactivating itself as a modest normal fault that may have provided weaknesses that the Colorado River used to establish its course through Marble Canyon.

**Trail Guide:** Follow the East Rim Drive 19.6 miles east of the junction between AZ Highway 64 and the Village Loop Road. Turn left on the signed road to Lipan Point. Park at the Point and walk 50 yards back to the signed trailhead.

After a gentle, 50-yard descent into a small bowl, the Tanner Trail gets down to business, plunging off the rim in earnest. It drops through the Kaibab Limestone in a series of steep, tight switchbacks. The Kaibab is unusually rich in resistant chert here, and much of the chert is tinted various shades of red and yellow, giving you the first hint that these rocks lie along a fault zone.

The vegetation along the rim is dominated by pinyon pines, which remain abundant as you drop onto the shady slopes below the rim, where they share space with moisture-loving Douglas firs. Healthy bushes of buffaloberry, the bush with the silvery, oval leaves, also line the trail in unusual abundance.

Although soil and vegetation obscure the exact *contact* (the place where different rock layers meet), the trail passes from the Kaibab to the Toroweap Formation at a left-hand switchback at mile 0.3 (GPS 36°02.01'N, 111°50.95'W), soon after passing under a long cliff of limestone on a lengthy straightaway. Grand Canyon hikers are used to getting a breather in the Toroweap, whose mudstones and evaporites usually form gentle, vegetated slopes. Here, however, the gradient doesn't let up at all, and you continue to zigzag your way down steep switchbacks under a partial canopy of evergreen trees.

The reason for the Toroweap's unusual steepness here is a change in the formation's rock type. When the Toroweap was deposited, the central Grand Canyon was an arid coastline, accumulating lots of mud, plus salts from the evaporation of seawater. Those sediments later turned into soft, easily eroded rocks. The open ocean lay to the west, with land here, near the Tanner Trail. Sand dunes that once guarded the coastline now form the more resistant sandstone lens-shaped pods that you see in the Toroweap along this hike.

The Toroweap's sandstone is even more evident on the Palisades of the Desert, the massive rampart bounding the river to your right (east). The Palisades owes part of its impressive steepness to the Toroweap's local abundance of sandstone, which is strong enough to prevent the break in slope that normally prevails in the Canyon's uppermost reaches.

Although the Toroweap bears some resemblance to the Coconino Sandstone here, their contact is easy to spot. The Toroweap sandstones exist as small layers and lenses, but the top of the Coconino marks the rim of a several-hundred-foot-tall cliff. The contact lies near a left-hand switchback that provides an open view toward the Palisades (mile 0.6, GPS 36°02.03'N, 111°50.96'W). The blonde Coconino displays its distinctive, large-scale cross-bedding very prominently here (Figure 27). These cross-beds were formed by sand dunes marching across a vast desert that stretched from here to Montana 270 million years ago.

The trail becomes even steeper in the Coconino, and you must clamber over a few boulders, a bit of an effort while carrying a large pack! Where you first reach Tanner Wash, 1.4 miles from the start, your descent through the Coconino is complete (GPS 36°02.24'N, 111°50.96'W). Initially, a pile of Coconino Sandstone blocks litter the slope, mostly obscuring the red Hermit Formation beneath. However, 20 yards later the red outcrop briefly appears, peeking through the rubble in a tributary gully entering Tanner Wash from the right (south).

Less than 100 yards after entering Tanner Wash, the trail exits out its left side. At this point you have crossed from the Hermit Formation to the Supai Group, where you will remain for the next 1.3 miles. Like the Hermit, the Supai is brick red. The contact between these rock units is marked by a significant cliff of red Esplanade Sandstone, the Supai Group's uppermost formation.

As you traverse the slope left of the wash, look across right, where you will see tangible evidence of the fault zone you have been descending. The fault here is broken into two splays, or branches, and each displaces the Coconino-Hermit contact, which is easy to spot because of the dramatic color change from tan to red. The east fork of the fault raised the Hermit-Coconino contact about 90 feet above the equivalent point to the west; the west branch lifted the west side about 60 feet. Between these two fault splays, the downdropped wedge forms a small *graben*. Like most Grand Canyon trails, the Tanner uses such faults as corridors to pass through the major cliff-forming rock layers.

Throughout your descent, the observation tower at Desert View is clearly visible. Its stone turret, designed by architect Mary Colter in 1932, appears to grow right out of the rim and gives you a sense of scale otherwise lacking in this expansive scene.

The trail now begins a descending traverse, winding its way between out-crops of Supai Group on rubbly slopes. En route, you cross from the downdropped to the upthrown side of the fault, neatly cutting out much of the normally endless Supai descent in the process. The trail is never hard to follow, but the rocky tread demands your attention. At mile 1.8, the trail emerges onto a narrow ridge, revealing a spectacular view into Seventyfivemile Canyon. Although most of the nearby drainages flow northward, this canyon runs almost due west along the Seventyfivemile Fault.

From this vista point, the trail drops steeply back into Tanner Wash, which it reaches again at mile 1.9. After following the wash for 100 yards, the trail climbs back out, passing excellent outcrops of interbedded Supai mudstones and sandstones. The Supai was deposited on a low-lying coastal plain, over which the ocean encroached and receded many times in response to sea-level fluctuations driven by the waxing and waning of distant glaciers (Figure 14). Most of the Supai mudstones were deposited in shallow marine conditions when the sea encroached, and the sandstones were laid down in small, coastal dune fields when the ocean retreated.

After a short, angling climb up the side of the wash, the trail reaches Seventyfivemile Saddle, another stunning vista point located at the head of Seventyfivemile Canyon. Two tent sites sit directly on the saddle, offering camping with a view but no water. The saddle is also an outstanding place to visualize the process of stream piracy.

## THE SWASHBUCKLING PIRATE

The process of *stream piracy* occurs when a steep, rapidly eroding stream encroaches on the midsection of another waterway with a gentler gradient. The rapid erosion at the headwaters of the steep stream causes it to extend headward, eventually breaching the ridge separating it from the gentler stream. This breach allows the steep stream to capture the headwaters of the other waterway, "beheading" it and redirecting the entire drainage's flow (Figure 22). At Seventyfivemile Saddle it is easy to visualize how, in the geologically near future, the terrifically steep Seventyfivemile Creek will soon become a swashbuckling pirate, breaching the narrow ridge on which you stand and spiriting away the headwaters of Tanner Creek. This process is constantly at work in river drainage systems, causing streams to swap segments in a mix-and-match way. We tend to think of drainages evolving as a single unit, but standing on Seventyfivemile

*Figure 22. The process of stream piracy, in which a smaller, steeper stream "steals" the headwaters of a larger stream due to more rapid erosion of its headwaters.*

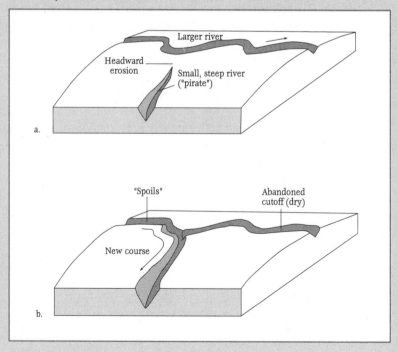

Saddle illustrates that this is not the case. Stream piracy happens on big rivers as well, and the process has played a pivotal role in the formation of the Grand Canyon (Figure 18).

The trail now begins a long but pleasant traverse in the Supai Group, passing huge red boulders and stunted pinyon and juniper trees, as well as many fine, dry campsites. The ground here is covered by a thick, black crust known as *cryptobiotic soil*. This is a living crust that provides crucial functions for the fragile desert ecosystem, so please stay on the trail to avoid trampling it.

## BINDING THE EARTH

Cryptobiotic soil is common along many trails in the Grand Canyon (Photo 19). This "soil" is actually a colony of symbiotic fungi and algae, a living metropolis of small organisms. However, these most modest and inconspicuous of desert organisms play a far larger role in the Canyon's ecology and geology than their small stature implies. Ecologically, they are extremely important sources of nitrogen for plants around them. Nitrogen is a crucial nutrient for all life, and it is the most abundant element in the atmosphere, comprising 78 percent of it. But, in a cruel joke of nature, atmospheric nitrogen is in a form that is useless for most life forms. Luckily, one class of bacteria can convert this atmospheric nitrogen into a form that other organisms can use, a process called *nitrogen fixing*. The cryptobiotic soil houses more of these fixing bacteria than just about any other part of the Grand Canyon ecosystem.

The cryptobiotic soil also plays an important role in the Canyon's geology. It binds together sediment particles that would otherwise be loose in this dry region. The winds that race across the area hungrily pick up loose sand and dust, blowing it many miles away. The cryptobiotic crust prevents such erosion through the cohesion it imparts to the soil. Where the crust has been broken, the loose sediment quickly blows away, removing the soil necessary for organisms to grow. So please don't walk on cryptobiotic soil; just one footprint is enough to break the crust, shutting down the nitrogen-fixing process and giving wind the toehold it needs to carry away the Canyon's sparse soil.

As you continue the Supai traverse, now beneath Escalante Butte, the trail inches closer to the gray Redwall Limestone. At mile 2.8 it finally reaches the Supai-Redwall contact (GPS 36°03.18'N, 111°50.58'W). The trail continues its traverse in the uppermost Redwall, following a large, bowl-shaped amphitheater. At mile 3.1 the trail climbs slightly, crossing back into the Supai as it angles toward the amphitheater's northern bounding ridge. From here you traverse a second, smaller amphitheater directly below Cardenas Butte, finishing with a short climb to another small ridge at mile 3.7. A third, much smaller bowl comes into view here, and the trail descends a bit before also traversing it.

In this final bowl the trail reaches the top of the Redwall Limestone again. On the bowl's north side at mile 4.2 (GPS 36°03.94'N, 111°50.02'W), the trail takes a sharp right turn and drops through the Redwall Limestone. Before taking the plunge, consider detouring 50 yards north to one of the Canyon's best viewpoints. When the weather is cool, fit hikers can use this viewpoint as a day-hike destination, and those willing to haul water can relax at the spectacular dry camp perched on the Redwall Buttress's northern edge (Color plate 14).

The view from here takes in the river from Marble Canyon to Tanner Rapid. To the left, just above the spot where the river disappears, you see the angular unconformity between the eastward-tilting Supergroup and the horizontal Tapeats Sandstone. Black, rubbly cliffs of the Cardenas Lava underlie the Tapeats on the left side, and the red sandstones and mudstones of the Nankoweap Formation (Figure 20) underlie it to the right. More black Cardenas Lava underlies the Tapeats at the base of the Palisades, which confine the eastern side of Marble Canyon.

After soaking up the view, retrace your steps to the spot where the trail descends the Redwall. Although the descent is steep, the limestone has been shattered by the Butte Fault, so the trail manages to navigate through chinks in the cliff's armor. You begin with a series of switchbacks between small cliffs. After the cliffs peter out halfway down, the trail points straight downhill, descending a low, red ridge poking out of the slope. This ridge is composed of Supai blocks transported downhill in a rotational landslide. In such landslides, entire sections of cliff are lowered and rotated as a unit when the soft mudstone layers below them (in this case the Bright Angel Shale) slowly creep downhill (Figure 36d).

From the landslide, a cliff of olive-drab Muav Limestone is apparent below. As you near the Muav, you pass two more campsites tucked in among red Supai landslide boulders (mile 5.1, GPS 36°03.99'N, 111°49.83'W). Fifty yards north of the camps, a patch of purplish rock is evident directly above the Muav's olive cliffs. The purple patch is a lens of the Devonian-age Temple Butte Limestone, which was deposited 374 million years ago in *tidal channels* criss-crossing an intertidal mudflat.

The view to the south encompasses a prominent fold in both the Redwall and Muav Limestones. The layers bend down sharply to the left, part of the East Kaibab Monocline (Figure 21c).

From the campsites, the trail heads down a short slope to a pass between two small hills. From the pass you can see that the left (west) hill is composed of tilted red Supai layers and the right (east) hill is gray Redwall Limestone. Both hills are piles of rubble, part of the same landslide block you have been descending. It is obvious these rocks have been displaced when you consider that the nearest Supai outcrop is up above the river viewpoint, hundreds of feet above your head!

From the pass the trail drops into a steep gully between the landslide debris and the cliff of Muav Limestone. At the base of the Muav cliff, the trail crosses the gully (left turn) and begins a long, northward traverse. Because the Bright Angel Shale grades into the Muav, the exact contact is hard to discern, but it lies near the base of the Muav cliff that you follow for the next 0.5 mile. As you hike, keep your eyes peeled for worm burrows (Photo 86) on the shale's flat bedding surfaces. There are some good examples on the slabs lining the gully at the traverse's start.

As you walk along the Bright Angel–Muav contact, notice that most of the thin mudstone beds are green. This color is a distinctive characteristic of the Bright Angel, and is provided by the mineral glauconite. The shale was deposited 530 million years ago on the bottom of a shallow sea close to shore. The layers accumulated gradually, as mud issuing from nearby streams slowly settled to the seafloor. In contrast, the brown sandstones you see interbedded with the mudstones here were probably deposited suddenly, in a matter of hours, during hurricanes or other storms that periodically raked the area. The storms stirred up sand that lay closer to shore, transporting it into slightly deeper, offshore waters where it covered the slowly accumulating mudstone.

At mile 5.8 (GPS 36°04.29'N, 111°49.85'W) the trail reaches another small saddle, where the traverse ends and another impressive vista of the river appears. A short descent down the saddle's north side lands you on a narrow catwalk of Tapeats Sandstone (mile 6). As you traverse northward along this spine, you get great views of a cliff rising immediately to your west, across an unnamed canyon. The scruffy, black portion of the cliff is composed of Cardenas Lava, and the more orderly bands of red to brown rock above the Cardenas are part of the Nankoweap Formation. These are the best views of the Nankoweap Formation available on any Canyon trail. The formation was deposited about 1000 million years ago along the shore of an inland sea that covered part of the supercontinent known as Rodinia (Chapter 1).

At mile 6.9, the trail descends the eastern side of the Tapeats catwalk, winding its way through more rotational landslides whose layers are tilted toward

the cliffs that spawned them. The landslide debris obscures the Tapeats-Dox Formation contact on the path, but you can tell when you cross it because it is easily visible in the slopes north of the trail (about mile 7.2, GPS 36°04.86'N, 111°49.65'W). The Dox, being mostly mudstone here, appears as a rubbly slope of purplish mudstone chips.

The trail remains in the Dox Formation for the rest of your journey. In places the gradient is gentle, and in others the trail drops surprisingly steeply down the sparsely vegetated slopes. A few grasses and shrubs grow, but even the hearty blackbrush, normally common at these elevations, finds the Dox's shrinking and swelling clays a problematic host. The mudstones' ephemeral nature is graphically illustrated by the many tiny gullies roiling their slopes.

*Photo 20. Ripplemarks in the Dox Formation.*

With so little vegetation, what rain falls washes swiftly and erosively downhill, creating the rivulets.

The trail reaches Tanner Wash at mile 8.5. Left of the wash sits an outcrop of Dox Formation that has been folded into an *anticline* (an archlike fold) by the Butte Fault, which now runs directly under your feet! Tilted *fins* of resistant sandstone protrude from the slopes. These narrow rock slabs display outstanding ripplemarks (Photo 20), well worth the 15-yard detour to see.

The trail then crosses Tanner Wash, dropping through a set of recently formed terraces consisting of flash-flood deposits, then climbing back up them on the wash's east side. At mile 8.7 the trail drops off the higher terrace onto warm, golden sands deposited by the Colorado River. Here you encounter a trail junction. To the right is the Beamer Trail, a 9.5-mile excursion to the Colorado-Little Colorado River confluence. Turn left here to reach Tanner Rapid. Fifty yards beyond is a sign for the toilet, tucked out of sight behind tamarisk and willows. The trail traverses below sand dunes, which are off-limits to hikers because of a revegetation project. The trail ends at Tanner Rapid, 200 yards past the toilet. Fifty yards beyond the mouth of Tanner Wash lie several campsites. The path beyond these camps is the Escalante Route, which winds up and down hills of Dox Formation for 15 miles to a junction with the New Hance Trail (Hike 2).

*Photo 21. View of the Butte Fault. North of Tanner Rapid, the dark cliff (left) consists of Cardenas Lava, capped by lighter Nankoweap Formation. To the right, outcrops of the horizontally bedded Dox Formation are separated from the Cardenas by a nearly vertical gully, which lies along the Butte Fault.*

The impressive cliff directly across the river is particularly interesting from a geologic perspective, because it provides a great view of the Butte Fault (Photo 21). The bulk of the cliff is composed of black Cardenas Lava, above which sit the Nankoweap Formation's layered, reddish-brown sandstones and mudstones. To both left and right, the Cardenas Lava is abruptly cut off against the soft, pastel mudstones of the Dox Formation, which normally lie below the Cardenas. This juxtaposition is due to faults bounding the cliff on both sides, the Basalt Canyon Fault to the left and the mighty Butte Fault to the right. In between, the Cardenas cliff has been downdropped several hundred feet to form the Tanner Graben, whose presence documents the Butte Fault's first life as a normal fault (Figure 21a).

From Tanner Rapid you can enjoy the unusual pleasure of simultaneously soaking your feet in the river and gazing up to the South Rim. This rare river-to-rim view is made possible by the softness of the Dox Formation that surrounds you. Its presence, plus many other unique geologic features you observed along the descent, is brought to you by the never-ending work of the Butte Fault, whose still-active trace runs directly under your soaking feet.

# NEW HANCE TRAIL

## A PERFECT STORM

*Hear the thunder of Hance Rapid echoing off cliffs of ancient beach sand as you cross a fossil graveyard created by a powerful hurricane that wracked the Grand Canyon region 1200 million years ago.*

LENGTH ■ 8 miles

ELEVATION CHANGE ■ 4400 feet

TIME ■ 1–2 days each way

DIFFICULTY ■ Very difficult; remote, very steep and rocky tread

BACKCOUNTRY ZONING ■ Primitive; at-large camping (BD9)

WATER AND TOILETS ■ Perennial water only at Colorado River; seasonal water in Red Canyon. No toilets available

EMERGENCY SERVICES ■ Nearest ranger station at Desert View

MAP LIST ■ 1, 3, 5, 6

KEY REFERENCES ■ 1, 8, 12, 22, 23

DAY HIKES ■ A beautiful view awaits hikers on top of the Redwall Limestone (4.8 miles round trip)

SEASONS ■ Year-round, but very hot in summer and potentially icy in winter

**About the Landscape:** John Hance built the New Hance Trail down Red Canyon in 1894 after a rockslide rendered his original trail, located in Hance Creek, impassable. Red Canyon is appropriately named, as much of it is carved in the brilliant red Hakatai Shale, part of the Grand Canyon Supergroup (Figures 2, 20). Red Canyon's resplendent layers provide both stunning scenery and hidden geologic delights. The trail ends at thunderous Hance Rapid, one of the biggest in the Grand Canyon.

Slashing through the red Hakatai layers are several jet-black dikes (Photo 22) and sills (Photo 23), providing a color contrast that is impossible to miss.

*Photo 22. A dark, diabase dike slashes across the Hakatai Shale at Hance Rapid.*

*Photo 23. A diabase sill in lower Red Canyon forms the small, arched cliff between layers of Hakatai Shale seen in the center of this photo.*

## TYPES OF IGNEOUS INTRUSIONS

Magma rises through the earth in balloon-shaped blobs called *diapirs*. When magma diapirs cool and solidify, they form roughly spherical pods of igneous rocks called *plutons*. The diapirs are under high pressure, so fingers of magma commonly shoot through weaknesses in the surrounding rock (known as *country* rock), solidifying into narrow, tabular rock bodies called *dikes*. Where dikes intrude sedimentary rocks, they commonly inject themselves between weak layers, forming a special kind of parallel dike that geologists call a *sill* (Figure 23).

During their lifetime, 1100 million years ago, these dikes were subterranean conduits feeding magma up to the earth's surface. The resulting lava flows, known as the Cardenas Lava, are exposed east of here, along the Tanner Trail (Hike 1). Because the temperature of the magma was around 2200°F, its intense heat baked the Hakatai layers through which the dike intruded. This alteration, known as contact metamorphism, is apparent at several places along the trail (Photo 24). You can recognize it by a black discoloration of the originally red rock and a welding of the ordinarily crumbly Hakatai into hard, fine-grained rock called hornfels. Asbestos also forms in these contact zones.

In fact, John Hance constructed this trail to access an asbestos mine downriver from Hance Rapid.

The Hakatai Shale and the Cardenas Lava are both part of the Unkar Group (Figure 20), which comprises the lower Grand Canyon Supergroup. Deposited over a span of 250 million years beginning 1250 million years ago, the Unkar

*Figure 23. Types of igneous bodies. Sills are igneous bodies injected parallel to sedimentary layers.*

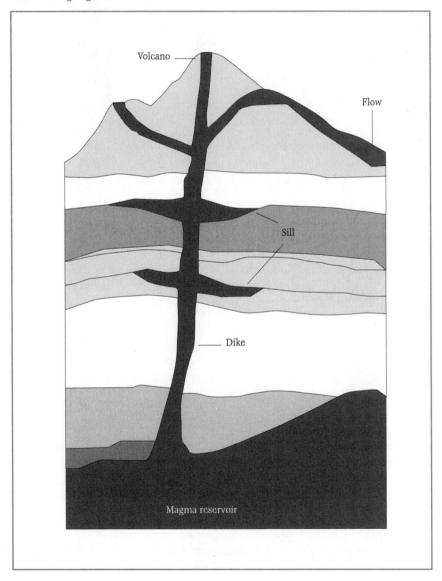

*Photo 24. Downstream of Hance Rapid, a thin white layer is visible where a dark sill touches the Bass Limestone. John Hance's historic asbestos mine lies in this bleached layer, which "baked" into a metamorphic rock when the sill intruded it.*

Group marks the resumption of sediment accumulation after a long period of erosion that removed all traces of an earlier mountain range, leaving behind only a flat, rocky plain lying near sea level (Chapter 1). A shallow sea then approached from the west, depositing the Bass Limestone, the Unkar Group's oldest layer. As this sea withdrew, the muds of the Hakatai were set down along the retreating shoreline. From mudcracks, casts of evaporite salt crystals, ripplemarks, and low-angle cross-beds, geologists think that the sediments were deposited in broad mudflats that frequently dried out. Even the color of the Hakatai is an indication of an arid climate; its intense hues are the result of iron oxidation under dry conditions. Quartz-rich sandstones of the Shinumo Quartzite were later laid down on beaches, deltas, and river channels near the sea shore.

With its bold, pink faces, the Shinumo endows lower Red Canyon with a powerful ambiance. The wash is littered with enormous quartzite blocks that have tumbled from the towering cliffs. Metamorphism of its quartz-rich sands has made the Shinumo one of the Canyon's hardest rock layers, so at Hance Rapid the quartzite hems the river in a spectacularly narrow gorge. The Shinumo is so resistant to weathering that when it was originally exposed on the earth's surface 545 million years ago, it formed rugged hills rising hundreds of feet above the surrounding plain. Encroachment by the sea eventually buried the hills with sediment (of the Tonto Group), but more recent erosion has reexposed them. During your descent of Red Canyon you will cross one such hill of Shinumo that formed an island in a long-departed sea (Photo 25).

The Bass Limestone is the last of the Unkar layers through which the trail passes. It holds more geologic treasure; its 1200-million-year-old layers contain the oldest fossils in the Grand Canyon. At that time, the earth supported no life more complex than single-celled bacteria. Quadrillions of these bacteria formed a living carpet on the shallow seafloor. Generations of bacteria grew atop each other, creating crinkly laminations in the rock known as *stromatolites* (Photo 79). Although stromatolites are visible in the Bass on several trails, their presence here in a most unusual *conglomerate* layer (a sedimentary rock composed of large particles) is something special. A quick examination of the conglomerate reveals that every fragment is a stromatolite (Photo 26)! When viewed edge-on, you see that every stromatolite fragment is flat, making this a flat-pebble conglomerate. This rock formed when a particularly violent storm hit the region one fateful day 1200 million years ago. The wind whipped up huge waves that scoured the seafloor, violently ripping up the bacterial crust. The stromatolite fragments were tumbled in the crashing waves and carried out into deeper water, where they settled to the bottom, lying lengthwise, as the storm's fury waned. The storm's violence wiped out the region's living community, and the devastation has been preserved for a mind-boggling 1200 million years.

**Trail Guide:** The trailhead sits at the bottom of the hill between Buggeln Picnic Area and Moran Point, but parking is not allowed there. Follow the East Rim Drive 13.6 miles east of the junction between AZ Highway 64 and the Village Loop Road. The trailhead is at a small pullout marked with two "No Parking" signs. Park 0.6 mile west of here on the south side along a dirt fire road. Please do not block the gate.

Unlike most rim-to-river trails, the New Hance begins in a nondescript patch of pinyon-juniper forest rather than at a spectacular vista point. The trail's first 0.2 mile entails a pleasant, nearly flat stroll through this woodland along an old dirt road. This gentle beginning is deceptive, though, because once it drops off the rim, the New Hance Trail becomes one of the most challenging of the Canyon's established trails.

You reach the rim at mile 0.2. The Kaibab Limestone here is discolored, with lots of reds and yellows speckling its normally drab shades of gray. This discoloration indicates that you are entering the Canyon along a fault, as you do on so many Grand Canyon trails. Here it is the Hance Fault, one in a family of northeast-trending fractures that includes the more prominent Bright Angel Fault. Activity along these *reverse faults* first began 1100 million years ago as the area was squeezed by a continental collision occurring in west Texas (Chapter 1). Although such collisions mainly compress the crust, some local areas can actually stretch. Such stretching in the Grand Canyon area 1100 million years ago (Figure 7) created weaknesses through which magma flowed to form the dikes and sills you see along the New Hance Trail today.

Shortly after dropping off the rim, the trail executes a prominent 180-degree left-hand switchback. Several trees lining the trail beyond this switchback are white firs, easily spotted by their white bark and flat needles. These normally high-elevation trees are rarely found on the South Rim; they thrive here only because of the cool, moist microclimate.

The trail meanders down a series of switchbacks between cliffs of Kaibab Limestone that exhibit a mottled, lumpy texture. Many of these lumps are fossils of brachiopods, crinoids, and other marine creatures now encased in durable nodules of chert (Figure 29). Most of the fossils are not well preserved, but there are a few jewels to discover.

The Kaibab Limestone ends at mile 0.4, where its final 200-foot-high cliff is adorned with blocky overhangs. Below this cliff, a left switchback at a patch of red soil marks your passage onto the Toroweap Formation (GPS 35°59.66'N, 111°56.31'W). Because of its soft composition, the Toroweap forms a smooth, vegetated slope below. To your west, the rock layers of the Sinking Ship (Photo 27) are noticeably tilted to the east. This tilt, which inspired the butte's name, marks the Grandview-Phantom monocline.

The Toroweap's upper portion provides a long, gentle southwestward traverse, but below that lies a series of tight switchbacks down steeper slopes littered with tumbled Kaibab boulders. At the base of these switchbacks (mile 0.6), you cross a small wash and then, using your hands, scramble down a 5-foot-high limestone layer. After negotiating another switchback, you begin a northeastward traverse in the lowermost Toroweap, with the stark, white cliffs of the Coconino Sandstone visible below. At mile 0.7 you pass a U.S. Geological Survey benchmark, a silver disk attached to the cliff at shoulder level. Ten yards beyond the benchmark is a left switchback that marks the Toroweap–Coconino contact (GPS 35°59.76'N, 111°56.23'W). Here the Coconino Sandstone has a yellow hue and is speckled with black desert varnish. The varnish is more erosion-resistant than the sandstone, so the varnished bits protrude as knobs from the rock surface.

The descent through the Coconino is typically steep, negotiated along a tight series of switchbacks. Keep a sharp eye out for cairns, as the tread is obscured in places by rubble. At mile 0.8 you pass beneath a 100-foot sandstone cliff pockmarked by *tafoni*, a weathering texture consisting of circular cavities. The lower part of the cliff is red instead of the usual tan or white. The yellow and red coloration reminds you how close you are to the Hance Fault; mineral-charged waters that percolated through the fault zone deposited these coloring agents.

At mile 1.1 in a small wash you reach a 5-foot drop down a resistant sandstone layer. Two tree roots provide welcome handholds through this slippery passage. Once down, the trail veers left out of the wash onto a pleasant, grassy meadow below the Coronado Butte-South Rim saddle. Soil covers all outcrop here, obscuring the contact between the Coconino Sandstone and the underlying Hermit Formation. The point where these two rock units meet lies somewhere near twin ponderosa pines, one now dead (mile 1.2), that tower over the more abundant Gambel's oak, pinyon, and juniper trees. The trail exits the meadow at mile 1.3, where it drops into the west branch of Red Canyon wash. There is still no outcrop, but this is roughly the contact between the Hermit Formation and the underlying Supai Group.

The trail hugs the wash for the next mile, alternately crossing from bank to bank. Your hands are useful in spots where the trail descends piles of Supai boulders. At mile 2.1 the trail enters the wash from the right at the brink of a 10-foot pourover. A false trail crosses to the wash's left bank, but the actual trail, marked by cairns, descends the pourover at a pile of boulders. The trail then continues down the wash another 200 yards before climbing back up the right bank, where it splits into several strands, all of which rejoin shortly downstream.

At mile 2.2 you pass a campsite; 0.2 mile below it you reach the brink of a 400-foot-tall Redwall Limestone cliff (GPS 36°00.30'N, 111°56.11'W), where the trail turns abruptly right. This spot makes a particularly scenic dry camp. A mile-long Supai traverse begins at the right bend, first contouring around a deep tributary canyon, whose axis you cross at mile 2.5. The trail is easy to follow but makes for slow walking as you weave around tumbled blocks. The path contours around several minor drainages before reaching a prominent right turn on the west flank of the next significant tributary, 3 miles from the rim. A small campsite with a big view is perched on the ridge here.

The trail reaches the axis of this tributary and a noteworthy geology stop at mile 3.1. The tributary forks into two smaller gullies below a large Supai cliff to the right (southwest). To the left, the wash plunges through a narrow slot canyon in the Redwall. In the recesses of this slot lurks an outcrop of the elusive Surprise Canyon Formation (Figure 13). From the nose of the small ridge separating the wash's forks (GPS 36°00.44'N, 111°55.77'W), look at the slot canyon's left wall for the layered, purple to maroon rock filling a gap between two pillars of massive, gray Redwall Limestone. The Surprise Canyon Formation was deposited in a marine estuary 315 million years ago. It also filled sinkholes, like this one, created in the Redwall Limestone by harsh, tropical weathering after it was exposed by a drop in sea level (Chapter 2, Hike 3). After the Surprise Canyon was deposited, another fall in sea level eroded most of the formation, resulting in its present patchy exposure.

This Surprise Canyon outcrop is one of the best visible from the Canyon's trail system. More of it lies immediately below the trail here, in the form of a *breccia* composed of angular limestone fragments surrounded by maroon mud. The limestone pieces are bits of Redwall that fell into the sinkhole, which was later filled in with the maroon mud of the Surprise Canyon Formation.

The trail leaves this ancient sinkhole to continue its northeastward traverse of the Supai, crossing two minor gullies before descending to a tent platform perched above an amazing fin of Redwall Limestone at mile 3.5 (GPS 36°00.64'N, 111°55.79'W). This narrow rock slab is isolated from the main cliff by two deep slots, themselves separated by a narrow saddle that provides passage onto the fin. From the saddle, the trail picks its way down the fin's northwest face, taking advantage of a pile of landslide rubble resting against the cliff.

Outcrops of Redwall protrude through the landslide rubble, and at mile 3.7 you pass to the left of one cliff pockmarked by cavities filled with perfect calcite crystals several inches long. In places along this descent, the layers are discolored, fractured, and even kinked into small folds. All of these features are signs that you are walking along the Hance Fault here. The trail traverses a cone of landslide debris on an ever-easing slope, passing through a maze of large boulders, including red blocks of Supai that have been transported far downslope, at mile 3.9.

At mile 4.2 you pass three clustered tent sites set amidst sparse junipers (GPS 36°00.84'N, 111°55.81'W). This spot roughly coincides with the Redwall-Muav contact, although landslide debris obscures it. This is also a good place to observe the unbroken, mile-long wall of rock forming the northwest side of Red Canyon. Below the prominent Redwall cliff lie the drab, yellow to olive layers of the Muav Limestone. In the center of the wall, these two formations are separated by a lens-shaped pod of thin, purplish Temple Butte Limestone.

The Bright Angel Shale forms the green-gray slopes under the Muav. Below that, however, things get more complicated. On the left side of the wall, a massive cliff of brown Tapeats Sandstone lies beneath the Bright Angel, just as you would expect (Figure 2). However, as you follow this cliff of Tapeats to the right, it gets progressively thinner, until it ends at a cliff of Shinumo Quartzite tilting down to the east (Photo 25). The tilted red beds to the left, below the Tapeats, are Hakatai Shale. The contact between these tilted Supergroup rocks and the overlying, horizontal Tonto Group layers is the *Great Unconformity*, here representing 600 million missing years (Chapter 1).

*Photo 25. An ancient island. As you follow the cliff of horizontally layered Tapeats Sandstone from lower left to right, it gets progressively thinner, until it ends against some right-angling beds of Grand Canyon Supergroup. These Supergroup rocks once formed an island that rose above the waves of the sea in which the Tapeats was deposited.*

The Hakatai outcrops to the left rest directly below a particularly tall Tapeats cliff. The Tapeats is especially thick there because it fills a 100-foot-deep channel cut into the soft Hakatai when it was exposed 545 million years ago. In contrast, the erosion-resistant Shinumo formed an island that escaped burial by the Tapeats beach sands. The island wasn't covered until the sea deepened and the Bright Angel muds were deposited, hence the disappearance of the Tapeats at the contact between the soft Hakatai and the hard Shinumo.

At mile 4.5 the trail passes a large Redwall boulder whose top has been sculpted into an ornate spire. Ten yards beyond this distinctive boulder, you reach a narrow ridge providing the first overlook into the east fork of Red Canyon. To the south this ridge consists of a Muav Limestone outcrop folded into another monocline.

The trail heads straight down the narrow ridge, passing a few lonely pinyons and junipers. Almost immediately you begin to see small outcrops of green mudstone interbedded with thin, brown sandstones, revealing that you have crossed onto the Bright Angel Shale. From this narrow ridge you get impressive views into Red Canyon. To the right you see the Hakatai's red slopes overlain by a cliff of Shinumo. Straight ahead the Hakatai Shale forms the slopes above the confluence of Red Canyon's two forks; from here you can see black diabase dikes, the conduits through which the Cardenas Lava traveled, cutting the Hakatai.

A tent site straddles the ridge at mile 4.7, where several knobs of hard Shinumo protrude above the rubble-covered crest. Because of the ancient island, the Tapeats is missing here (Photo 25), so you pass directly from the Bright Angel to the Shinumo (GPS 36°01.12'N, 111°55.80'W). At mile 4.9, the trail bends sharply right to begin its final descent into the east fork of Red Canyon. As you round this corner, the tan trail tread abruptly turns red, signaling your passage from the Shinumo to the Hakatai. Many Shinumo boulders litter the red slopes, and a number of them display slickensides, yet another sign of the Hance Fault.

The Hakatai Shale provides an inhospitable substrate for plants, so few grow here. Because the trail becomes faint on the barren slopes, a maze of trails made by wandering hikers descends the northeast slopes of the ridge. They all reunite at mile 5.25, where the trail reaches the east fork of Red Canyon. The trail crosses the wash 20 yards above a series of slickrock ledges composed of Bass Limestone. It is absolutely worth the 20-yard detour to examine this magnificent outcrop (GPS 36°01.21'N, 111°55.72'W), the flat-pebble conglomerate filled with stromatolites discussed earlier. The wash has polished the tops of the stromatolites, revealing their individual layers of bacterial deposition as concentric rings (Photo 26). The view is similar to that of a cabbage head cut in half! The edges of the wash provide a cross-sectional view that reveals the flat, two-dimensional nature of the particles, demonstrating that they formed a mere surface crust before they were ripped apart by the hurricane that left this graveyard.

*Photo 26. Concentric layers in each cobble reveal their origins as ancient mats of bacteria known as stromatolites.*

103

The trail exits the wash on its right side, directly opposite its entry point, and quickly climbs a short slope onto tilted layers of bright red Hakatai. Some of the bedding surfaces here are crossed by webs of ancient mudcracks. To the left, on the far side of the wash, a 6-foot slab of Bass is covered with excellent ripplemarks. At mile 5.3 the trail approaches a black dike, never quite reaching it but instead crossing dark, surprisingly hard layers of Hakatai Shale baked during contact metamorphism.

At mile 5.4 the confluence between the two forks of Red Canyon is visible to your left. There the beds of Bass Limestone, which were nearly flat upstream, are now tilting steeply down to the northwest, another example of a monocline. Downstream of the confluence, a diabase dike is visible on the wash's far wall, where it slices through the Hakatai and the overlying Shinumo. Another zone of dark, baked Hakatai lies to the dike's right on the red slope. The trail now gradually descends the southeast flank of Red Canyon. At mile 5.6 the rubble-covered slope changes for a few yards from red to dark green. This change marks where you cross the diabase dike (GPS 36°01.36'N, 111°55.86'W). A second branch of the dike is apparent 100 yards farther on.

The trail reaches Red Canyon wash at mile 6, very near the Hakatai-Bass contact. Slabs of sandstone immediately left of the trail here sport excellent examples of ripples and mudcracks. Good campsites on the banks of the wash are shaded by cottonwood trees. If you arrive during the spring, you may see water in the creek and showy pink blossoms on the beavertail cacti that dwell here. One hundred yards downstream, you encounter the first of many tamarisk trees. Introduced as ornamental plants, these Asian migrants quickly found the lower Colorado River to their liking. They have marched farther and farther up the river and its tributaries, squeezing out much of the native riparian vegetation.

The trail now follows the wash's sandy bottom, with the path becoming less distinct. Occasional shortcuts on the banks are marked by cairns. At mile 6.5 the canyon narrows as the cliffs of Shinumo Quartzite close in around you. The abundant, house-sized blocks of Shinumo littering the wash are a testament to the process of *scarp retreat*. Flash floods quickly eat away at the soft slopes of Hakatai Shale, undercutting the overlying Shinumo cliff. Blocks break away in huge landslides, effectively widening the valley (Color Plate 18). A fairly recent landslide scar is apparent on the left bank, made obvious by the scar's lighter color (due to less desert varnish). The gorge is narrow here because erosion only recently exposed the Hakatai, leaving much less time for the scarp to retreat.

At mile 7 you begin to hear the roar of Hance Rapid. At mile 7.1, where the wash is littered with particularly large blocks of Shinumo, the path moves onto the right (east) bank to avoid two pourovers created by the boulders. The path rejoins the wash 0.25 mile downstream, and it stays there the rest of the way to the river.

Soon after returning to the wash, at mile 7.4, you encounter a beautifully exposed diabase sill on the wash's right bank (GPS 36°02.29'N, 111°55.22'W). Water coursing down Red Canyon has polished the greenish intrusion. The edges of the sill are especially green and are composed of smaller crystals than those in its center. This is an example of a *chilled margin;* where the magma met the cold wall rocks, it cooled quickly, resulting in smaller crystals. The Hakatai Shale surrounding the sill has a zone of contact metamorphism similar to the ones you observed earlier. You can trace the sill for 50 yards downstream, where it disappears below the wash. Just as you lose sight of this sill on the wash's right bank, another, wider one appears on the left bank. This one is higher on the slope, and it undulates in a series of gentle folds along with the layers of Hakatai that enclose it (Photo 23).

At mile 7.8 the Colorado River comes into view, as does another diabase dike, this one slashing up and right across the Hakatai on the north side of the river (Photo 22). You reach the river and the powerful Hance Rapid, which was created by debris flows surging down Red Canyon, at mile 8.

Twenty yards upstream lie several good camp spots tucked around a mesquite tree, and another tent site is situated in the sand dunes 20 yards downstream. The Escalante hiking route passes the upstream campsites, and the Tonto Trail begins at the dune campsite. From the top of these dunes, the view downstream is impressive. The walls of the gorge consist of Hakatai Shale and Bass Limestone, all angling upriver, toward you. An 80-foot-thick diabase sill that was injected between Bass layers forms the prominent black cliff north of the river. At both the sill's upper and lower contacts, the Bass has been bleached white, another example of contact metamorphism (Photo 24). John Hance's asbestos mine can be spotted on the north side of the river as a cone of white debris raining across the black sill at its downstream end. Hance and his partners used this trail to access the mine, crossing the Colorado in canvas boats downstream from Hance Rapid.

This spot is unique in the Grand Canyon, as it is the only place where the vertical cliffs of Shinumo Quartzite reach the banks of the Colorado. The result is a gorge as narrow and steep as any found in the crystalline rocks of the Inner Gorge, but with an ambiance all its own. As the deep roar of the rapid thunders off the towering walls, it is easy to conjure in your mind's eye some of the violent geological episodes that produced and shaped the rock you've passed through. From the injection of 2200°F magma, to crushing landslides and debris flows, to the perfect storm that created a stromatolite graveyard 1200 million years ago, the New Hance Trail gives you a taste of just how stormy geology can be!

# GRANDVIEW TRAIL

## OF MINES AND MONOCLINES

*Relive the Grand Canyon's mining heyday at the Last Chance copper mine, located on the Grandview monocline, a flexure in the earth's crust that formed during the Southwest's last great episode of mountain building.*

LENGTH ▪ 3.1 miles to Horseshoe Mesa

ELEVATION CHANGE ▪ 2500 feet

TIME ▪ 5–6 hours round trip

DIFFICULTY ▪ Difficult; very steep and exposed

BACKCOUNTRY ZONING ▪ Threshold; camp only in designated area on Horseshoe Mesa (BF5)

WATER AND TOILETS ▪ Perennial water at Page Spring, 400 vertical feet below Horseshoe Mesa. Toilet at camping area

EMERGENCY SERVICES ▪ Nearest ranger station at Grand Canyon Village

MAP LIST ▪ 1–3, 5, 6

KEY REFERENCES ▪ 1, 8, 12, 22–25

DAY HIKES ▪ Coconino Saddle (2.2 miles round trip)

SEASONS ▪ Spring through fall. The upper trail is notoriously icy during winter

**About the Landscape:** Nowhere is the Grand Canyon's mining legacy more visible than in the shafts of Pete Berry's Last Chance copper mine. Berry and several partners staked the Last Chance claim on Horseshoe Mesa in 1890. The mine was worked on and off until 1916, producing about $75,000 worth of copper. The ore was rich; a nugget assayed at a remarkable 70 percent copper won first prize at Chicago's 1893 Columbian Exposition, but the cost of shipping the ore from such a remote location ensured that the mine was never a financial success. Instead, Berry and his partners made their money shepherding tourists down the Grandview Trail, an ancient Native American path that they improved and maintained. Berry's Grandview Hotel, situated at the trailhead, was the Canyon's leading tourist destination from the time of its construction in 1897 until 1901, when the completion of the railroad shifted the tourist epicenter to Grand Canyon Village.

The Last Chance Mine extracted copper ore from the Grandview *breccia pipe*, a rubble-filled tube formed by the collapse of overlying rock layers into a limestone cavity (Figure 24). One of thousands that dot the Grand Canyon region, the Grandview breccia pipe formed above either a limestone sinkhole or cave that developed in the Redwall Limestone during a period of karst erosion about 320 million years ago. At that time, the Grand Canyon lay at tropical latitudes, and a pronounced drop in sea level exposed the recently deposited

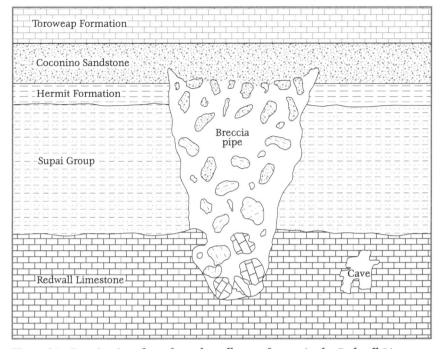

*Figure 24. Breccia pipes form from the collapse of caves in the Redwall Lime-stone. Debris from overlying layers tumbles into the cave, disrupting the layers.*

Redwall Limestone to millions of years of harsh, tropical weathering. A system of caves and sinkholes then developed, particularly along the trends of Precambrian faults, which provided easy pathways for the flow of limestone-dissolving groundwater.

Over the next 100 million years, as thick piles of sediment were deposited on top of the Redwall, they slowly sagged into the eroded openings, creating the breccia pipes. For millennium after millennium, the pipes served as conduits, allowing large volumes of groundwater to flush through the loose rubble that filled them. At least twice, first about 260 million years ago and again 200 million years ago, that groundwater became saturated with a variety of metals, including copper and uranium. These metals probably came from dissolving the volcanic ash that then blanketed the landscape. The chemical conditions in the Grandview and other breccia pipes were just right for the metals to crystallize out of the groundwater, thus forming pockets of copper ore minerals such as chalcopyrite and cuprite, as well as uranium ores like uraninite. Berry's Last Chance was strictly a copper mine, but a study in 1952 showed that it also has elevated uranium levels. The highest-grade uranium ore ever produced in the United States came from the Orphan Lode Mine, situated just 10 miles west of Horseshoe Mesa in the Orphan breccia pipe (Photo 46).

*Photo 27. The layers of the Sinking Ship plunge down to the left along the Grandview-Phantom monocline.*

Running beneath Horseshoe Mesa is the Precambrian-age Cremation Fault, whose presence helped to channel groundwater flow and thus to form the Grandview breccia pipe. In addition to its contribution to the Canyon's human history, the fault is also responsible for much of the Grandview area's dramatic scenery. The Cremation Fault was born 750 million years ago during the breakup of the Rodinian supercontinent (Photo 33), but following this thrilling birth, it lay dormant for almost 700 million years. Just 65 million years ago, the fault stirred from its slumber as plate compression off the coast of California was felt in the Four Corners region. This compression triggered a major mountain-building episode, known as the Laramide Orogeny (Chapter 3), which uplifted the modern Rocky Mountains of Colorado and New Mexico. Because the Grand Canyon region occupies especially strong crust, the area resisted full-scale mountain building. Instead, the Laramide compression reawakened a handful of Precambrian faults, including the Cremation Fault. Reverse motion on these structures created "kinks" in the overlying sedimentary rocks, forming one-sided folds known as *monoclines* (Figure 50). Monoclines are characterized by nearly flat-lying layers that abruptly plunge at almost vertical angles, then quickly bend again at the bottom, once again approaching horizontal. Because the Grandview Trail descends the Grandview-Phantom

monocline's plunging beds, it is a particularly spectacular and scenic trail.
**Trail Guide:** The trail begins at Grandview Point. Follow the East Rim Drive
8.7 miles east of the junction between AZ Highway 64 and the Village Loop
Road. Turn left on the signed road to Grandview Point.

From Grandview Point, the trail leads north along a ridge, quickly descending through the Kaibab Limestone via a series of switchbacks. The trail soon passes a 70-foot Kaibab cliff that has beds studded with white chert nodules. Immediately beyond this cliff, a right-hand switchback provides an excellent view southeastward to the tilted layers of the fancifully named Sinking Ship (Photo 27). The eye-catching tilt of the Sinking Ship's layers is due to its position astride the axis of the Grandview-Phantom monocline.

Fifty yards beyond, the trail crosses the nose of the ridge falling away from Grandview Point, passing through a narrow gap between two Kaibab outcrops. Now on the ridge's eastern flank, the trail enters a steep, tight series of timber-reinforced switchbacks that convey you quickly through the remainder of the Kaibab Limestone. About 0.15 mile from the trailhead you pass beneath a final overhanging cliff and cross onto the slopes of the Toroweap Formation, dotted with pinyon pine and Gambel's oak. Little Toroweap outcrop is exposed due to the soft nature of its evaporites and mudstones, which were once deposited near an arid shoreline. However, 0.5 mile from the trailhead, you reach a 25-foot-tall cliff of limestone. This was deposited during a brief interval when the Toroweap Sea encroached far enough to provide the deeper waters necessary to deposit limestone.

Beneath this outcrop, the trail bends to the right, providing a view to the east. There you can see a matching Toroweap cliff across the linear gash created by upper Grapevine Creek. This cliff clearly lies below you, revealing the presence of a small normal fault along the creek. The fault's east side has dropped down about 40 feet, and the presence of the fault accounts for Grapevine Creek's linear character.

A short distance farther, 0.6 mile from the rim, you reach the Toroweap–Coconino Sandstone contact (GPS 36°00.00'N, 111°59.11'W). The point where these two rock units meet is easy to recognize because the trail's tread suddenly changes to tilted white sandstone beds. The tilt is due to the Coconino's cross-bedding (Figure 27), relicts of the steep lee sides of giant sand dunes that occupied this region 270 million years ago. A couple of young Douglas fir trees have taken advantage of this spot's shady, moist nature to begin their life amidst the more abundant pinyons.

One hundred yards beyond the contact lies the narrow saddle at the head of Grapevine Creek. Here you are standing directly on the fault, and as you step eastward off the saddle, you cross from the Coconino back into the Toroweap on the fault's downdropped side. The trail soon encounters the

Toroweap-Coconino contact again at mile 0.8, where the path takes a sharp left bend and drops steeply down a section of cobblestone trail.

After 1.1 miles you reach Coconino Saddle, which forms the divide at the head of Cottonwood Creek. This impressive notch lies at the contact between the Coconino and the underlying Hermit Formation. The contact couldn't be more obvious on the cliff south of the saddle. The tan, cross-bedded Coconino forms the bulk of this cliff, but its lower 30 feet are composed of the horizontally bedded, brick-red Hermit.

As you leave the saddle, you enjoy more good views of the Coconino-Hermit contact in the cliffs across Cottonwood Creek. Along the trail, the soft Hermit Formation is poorly exposed because it is so easily eroded. At 1.2 miles you pass one good Hermit outcrop that lies 15 vertical feet below the contact with the Coconino. Thirty yards beyond this outcrop, you pass a U.S. Geological Survey benchmark, which reveals that you have already descended 1216 feet from the South Rim. To the north is an excellent view of Horseshoe Mesa, and you can clearly see the two Redwall Limestone arms that give the mesa its name. In the base of the U rises a small butte capped by Supai Group rocks.

The long straightaway that follows passes mostly across vegetated slopes. It ends at mile 1.4 at a series of steep, cobblestone switchbacks. At the second switchback, which bends to the right, you are standing at the approximate Hermit-Supai contact, although no outcrop here reveals this fact. Instead, you must look toward the northwest, where the highest sandstone cliffs of the Supai are visible at about the same elevation.

Below the switchbacks you begin a long, descending traverse through the Supai Group, angling across the eastern flanks of Cottonwood Creek. The cliff-slope-cliff nature of the Supai is readily apparent, as squat, red sandstone cliffs alternate with soil-covered mudstone slopes (Photo 13). Along this stretch, you get great views down Cottonwood Creek. Of special note is a cliff of Redwall Limestone on the creek's left (western) flank. Here the Redwall displays a prominent kink in its beds, defining the Grandview monocline (Photo 28). Just where the beds tilt eastward, a large, triangular divot filled with rubble occupies the cliff top. This feature is likely a sinkhole created 320 million years ago during the great karst episode that formed the Redwall's abundant caves and sinkholes.

The traverse continues to mile 2.3, where a 4-foot-thick limestone band laced with red chert indicates that you are nearing the base of the Supai Group. At 2.5 miles from the rim, the slope of Supai rocks to your right falls away as you emerge onto a tilted mesa top. Beneath a thin veneer of red Supai rubble, polished gray Redwall Limestone forms the mesa's surface (GPS 36°00.98'N, 111°58.53'W). Here you are standing directly on the axis of the Grandview monocline, marked by the northeast tilt of the mesa top, which faithfully follows the Supai-Redwall contact. The tilted beds are even more apparent as you look both to the left, toward the kinked Redwall beds (Photo 28), and to the

*Photo 28. Redwall Limestone layers bent along the Grandview-Phantom monocline. The triangular depression at the kink is probably a 320 million-year-old sinkhole.*

right, where a long ridge of Supai rocks across the next wash angles down to the northeast.

To the right of the trail at mile 2.7, several discolored knobs of Redwall Limestone protrude above the mesa's surface. On the far side of these knobs lies a rusted cable spool, an artifact from the glory days of the Last Chance Mine (Photo 29). The spool lies near the entrance to one of the old mineshafts, but

*Photo 29. Rusted mining equipment left behind at the Last Chance copper mine.*

please don't visit any shafts on Horseshoe Mesa, as they are unstable and could collapse without notice.

The discoloration of the limestone here is due to the passage of mineral-rich fluids, and it marks your arrival at the Grandview breccia pipe. It is just this sort of discoloration that caught the eyes of the prospectors as they explored Horseshoe Mesa in the late 1800s. At mile 2.8, a tall, shallow shaft lies immediately right of the trail. The excavated rocks littering the ground contain beautiful streaks of green malachite (Color Plate 11) and sky-blue azurite, two copper-bearing minerals.

Fifty yards past this shaft, a sign marks the turnoff to Miners (also called Page) Spring (Photo 18). Emerging at the base of the Redwall, this lovely spring provided the only perennial source of water for the miners, as it does for Horseshoe Mesa campers today. Bear left at this junction to continue on the Grandview Trail.

At 3.1 miles from the rim you reach a narrow neck of land. From here a marked trail veers left and drops down into Cottonwood Creek. The Grandview Trail continues straight ahead, reaching the remains of Pete Berry's cabin 20 yards later. A short spur trail leads right (east) from the cabin to the camping area and the toilet. The group camping area lies 100 yards farther down the main trail at another signed junction.

Veer left at the group camp sign to hike out the west arm of the mesa to a magnificent overlook of the Inner Gorge. The trail skirts the western flank of a butte capped by Supai Group rocks. Although the lower slopes you are crossing appear to be Supai as well, they are actually part of a much rarer unit, the Surprise Canyon Formation. It is only exposed in a few scattered, lens-shaped outcrops (Figure 13). Most are far from trails, so the formation is rare to see. It was deposited 315 million years ago in estuaries that formed here as the sea returned after the karst erosion ceased. The caves and sinkholes formed in the Redwall by that event were filled with Surprise Canyon Formation, as were the fingers of the large estuary. The outcrop you are traversing was deposited in this estuary, whose geography can be reconstructed by "connecting the dots" between the patchy modern outcrops. The estuary finger on which you now stand extended west to Lyell and Pattie buttes and east to the New Hance Trail.

The trail crosses back onto the Redwall Limestone at mile 3.6. A faint trail branches west from here to the Cave of the Domes.

---

## CAVE OF THE DOMES

Cave of the Domes is one of thousands of caves initially carved by karst erosion 320 million years ago. Like the nearby estuary, the cave was then filled with Surprise Canyon Formation sediments, but it was reexcavated during more recent erosion. The cave was discovered by the cook at the Last Chance Mine, and it soon became a tourist destination. Unfortunately, these early visitors vandalized the cave, breaking off stalactites and scrawling their names on the scars. Historical photos show that the caving trophies were displayed on the front porch of the Grandview Hotel. This is one of the more accessible Grand Canyon caves, so it provides an excellent introduction to the geological wonders of karst topography. If you do visit the cave, please leave the few remaining decorations for others to enjoy.

The entrance lies on the western edge of Horseshoe Mesa about 400 yards from the main Grandview Trail. Veer left where the trail steps off the red-brown Surprise Canyon Formation onto the gray Redwall. Follow the faint trail down a wash that soon tumbles over an edge, where a short, northward traverse leads you to the cave's two entrances.

The first entrance is almost completely blocked by a pack rat midden and by sandstone layers of the Surprise Canyon Formation. The second access, just 20 yards beyond the plugged entrance, is the one you want. The entrance arch is decorated with a few "soda straws," thin tubes created as limestone crystallizes from individual water droplets dripping from the cave ceiling.

The first domed chamber lies within reach of the entrance's faint light. The cave leads eastward from here through a series of narrow passages that open up into more domed chambers. You will see the names of tourists written on the ceilings, some dating back as far as 1898. Stalactites and soda straws decorate the ceiling, and cave "bacon" ripples across some walls. A few stalagmites also remain. The cave's several passages extend about 0.5 mile into the depths of Horseshoe Mesa. If you decide to explore, be sure to bring a light and spare batteries, and do not proceed past the first chamber unless you have previous caving experience.

---

At mile 3.9 you reach the edge of the Redwall escarpment and an unmarked trail junction. Follow the left branch, which stays near the mesa top. You reach the tip of the horseshoe's west arm at mile 4.25, where a magnificent view of the Inner Gorge unfolds. Straight ahead rise steep, black walls of Vishnu Schist intruded by rosy Zoroaster Granite and capped by horizontal Tapeats Sandstone. Tracing the wall of rock to the right reveals an abrupt change. The vertically foliated Vishnu Schist is replaced by eastward-tilted sedimentary layers of the Grand Canyon Supergroup. The bright orange slopes in the middle of the stack are the Hakatai Shale. The bold cliff above is Shinumo Quartzite and the smaller, brown cliff below consists of Bass Limestone. A scruffy black slope below the Bass consists of a diabase sill injected between Bass layers 1100 million years ago (Photo 23).

Leaving Horseshoe Mesa, retrace your steps past the many mineshafts left from the Canyon's Wild West days, when the local geology lured rugged prospectors into probing the recesses of the Grandview monocline.

Hike 4

# SOUTH KAIBAB TRAIL

## A CONTINENT TORN ASUNDER

*Hike across the faults of a geologic "grave" that tell the story of a supercontinent's destruction.*

LENGTH ■ **7 miles**

ELEVATION CHANGE ■ **4740 feet**

TIME ■ **1 day each way**

DIFFICULTY ■ **Difficult; smooth tread but very steep**

BACKCOUNTRY ZONING ■ **Corridor; camp only in Bright Angel Campground (CBG)**

WATER AND TOILETS ■ **Water only at trailhead and Bright Angel Campground (treated); toilets at Cedar Ridge, Tonto Platform, and the campground**

EMERGENCY SERVICES ■ **Emergency phone on Tonto Platform near toilet; ranger station at Phantom Ranch**

MULE TRIPS ■ **Available uphill as part of a round trip down Bright Angel Trail**

MAP LIST ■ **1–3, 7**

KEY REFERENCES ■ **1, 7, 8, 10, 11, 26**

DAY HIKES ■ **Cedar Ridge (3 miles round trip); Tonto Trail junction (8.8 miles round trip); Phantom Ranch to Tonto Trail junction (5.2 miles round trip from river)**

SEASONS ■ **Year-round, but very hot in summer and potentially icy in winter**

**About the Landscape:** Unlike many of its sister trails, the South Kaibab doesn't sneak into the Grand Canyon along a side stream. Instead, it tackles

114

the Canyon head-on, plunging down narrow Cedar Ridge and providing hikers with unrivaled vistas. Because the ridge is nearly clear of ground-masking debris, you are treated to exceptional views of the Canyon's Paleozoic rock layers. But the South Kaibab's rocks save their most exciting story for the end: the geologic epic of a supercontinent ripped asunder.

Where the trail tumbles into the Inner Gorge, the three lowermost formations of the Grand Canyon Supergroup—the Shinumo Quartzite, Hakatai Shale, and Bass Limestone—are sliced by four normal faults into a feature known as the Cremation Graben (*graben* is the German word for grave). About 750 million years ago, movement along the two outermost faults dropped this chunk of Supergroup down into the graben while simultaneously heaving the adjacent blocks skyward. Erosion later beveled the landscape, erasing all traces of the Supergroup from the uplifted blocks (Figure 10). However, by protecting this segment of Supergroup, the "grave" effectively hid it from the ravages of erosion long enough to be preserved by a blanket of Paleozoic rock layers. The much more recent carving of the Grand Canyon reexposed these layers and, consequently, the epics they have to tell.

These normal faults bear witness to one of the most profound events to shape North America. During the deposition of the Unkar Group, to which the Shinumo, Hakatai, and Bass formations belong (Figure 20), the great supercontinent of Rodinia was forming (Figure 7). By 1100 million years ago, Rodinia included virtually all the world's continental area. The ultimate fate of all supercontinents is to be ripped into wandering fragments, torn apart by the heat the continent traps beneath it (Appendix C). By 800 to 900 million years ago the outer fringes of Rodinia began to tear off; by 750 million years ago, Rodinia was split apart along a jagged line crudely traced by modern Interstate Highway 15 from Las Vegas to Montana (Figure 8).

Geologists have hotly debated the identity of our former continental neighbor to the west, but many now agree that it consisted of Australia and eastern Antarctica, which were then welded together. It is believed that the east coast of Australia-Antarctica butted up against today's North American west from central British Columbia to Death Valley.

Whether it was the Australian or the Antarctic portion that shared a border with Arizona and southern California is an ongoing discussion in geological circles (Chapter 1), but whichever segment it was, its departure splintered the Grand Canyon region and created the faults you observe today along the South Kaibab Trail. When continents part company, the stretching first forms a narrow ocean basin, like the Red Sea or the Gulf of California, which then evolves into a great ocean, such as the modern Atlantic (Figure 49). But the stresses of rifting emanate across the margins of the newly divorced continents, creating swarms of normal faults in regions hundreds of miles from the infant ocean. The Grand Canyon lay in this broad zone. Consequently normal

Photo 30. *Layers in the Toroweap buckled by the flow of evaporites within the formation.*

faults uplifted some of its blocks, while simultaneously tilting and downdropping others into grabens (Figure 10).

**Trail Guide:** Parking is not allowed at the trailhead. The free Yaki Point shuttle bus (green line) from Canyon View Information Plaza stops at the trailhead, situated on a marked spur 200 yards west of the Yaki Point road.

The well-maintained South Kaibab Trail is the shortest of the rim-to-river trails, so it accomplishes its task with an especially steep gradient. The trail gets down to business right away, steeply zigzagging through the Kaibab Limestone. As you wind your way down, note the numerous white and yellow chert nodules scattered throughout the more abundant limestone. These nodules owe their existence to sponges that dwelt here in shallow ocean waters 260 million years ago. The sponges contained stiffening *spicules* made of silica, which provided the material that formed these nodules. Fossils of these sponges, along with brachiopods, are visible at switchback 5 (Figure 29).

After about 0.3 mile (GPS 36°03.25'N, 112°05.02'W), the trail leaves the switchbacks to begin a long, descending traverse through the rubbly, vegetated slopes of the Toroweap Formation. The Toroweap was deposited 265 million years ago when the eastern Grand Canyon lay along an arid coastline. In the areas above low tide, seawater regularly evaporated, thus depositing abundant evaporite minerals (called *evaporites*) such as table salt and gypsum. Today you can observe these evaporites as soft, chalky, green-and-white beds within the Toroweap. Evaporites are less dense than most other rocks, so later, after the Toroweap was buried beneath a thick pile of sediment, these layers began to rise, seeking a stability relative to their buoyancy, just as a helium balloon rises in the heavier atmosphere. These rising evaporites fracture and buckle overlying layers, forming small domes. One such dome is visible at mile 0.5 (GPS 36°03.44'N, 112°05.11'W) as a 2- to-3-foot-high, teepeelike structure contorting a bed of white limestone above it (Photo 30).

The Toroweap's softness and malleability cause it to creep slowly downhill. As it does so, it carries loose blocks of the overlying Kaibab Limestone down with it. These blocks end up leaning against the stable Kaibab cliffs, much like the book at the end of a shelf tilts onto its companions for stability. In the Southwest, such tilted blocks, known as *Toreva blocks*, are common where a resistant layer overlies a softer one. On your right (east), immediately down the trail from the salt dome, lies a textbook example of a Kaibab Toreva block tilting toward the rim (Photo 31).

At mile 0.8 you pass the contact between the Toroweap and the underlying blonde Coconino Sandstone (GPS 36°03.63'N, 112°05.17'W). The trail resumes its winding ways through the Coconino cliff, treating you to outstanding examples of the sweeping, steeply inclined cross-beds that reveal this layer's origin as a sand dune (Photo 35). You soon reach the brick-red mudstones of the Hermit Formation at mile 1.3 (GPS 36°03.80'N, 112°05.30'W). A west-trending straightaway makes short work of the Hermit, but be sure to watch for several lens-shaped pods of sandstone embedded within its finer-grained mudstone layers. These sand lenses mark the channels of ancient streams meandering their way across vast floodplains that dominated the Grand Canyon landscape in late Permian time.

You cross from the Hermit Formation to the Supai Group just below the Cedar Ridge Resthouse (mile 1.5, GPS 36°03.85'N, 112°05.32'W), which consists of a toilet perched on a pleasantly flat expanse of red stone dappled with juniper trees. Before you leave, take a minute to visit the glass-covered display of fern fossils in the stone shelter 50 yards northwest of the outhouse (Figure 25).

Fern imprints, terrestrial animal tracks, and marine fossils are all found in

*Photo 31. A Toreva block. The block of Kaibab Limestone over the hiker's right shoulder has leaned toward the cliff, carried by the slow, downhill creep of the underlying Toroweap.*

*Figure 25. Permian-age fern fossil (©2004 by Dona Abbott).*

the Supai Group, revealing that the Grand Canyon area alternated between land and sea during Supai time. The Supai's distinctive variation between sandstone cliffs and mudstone slopes results from the region's rapidly changing shoreline, which alternately deposited silt in near-shore mudflats, then sand in low coastal dunes (Figure 14).

The next section of trail traverses Supai Group outcrops along O'Neill Butte's eastern flank (Photo 7). Tucked against the butte's northern tip at mile 3 (GPS 36°04.53'N, 112°05.49'W) lie some interesting polygonal cracks resembling floor tiles (Photo 32). A white pillar of breccia crossed by webs of calcite veins lies 15 yards west of the trail. These clues reveal the presence of a *breccia pipe* (Figure 24), a feature formed when a buried cave collapses, leaving a debris-filled cavity that is later filled in by sediments.

A half mile farther (GPS 36°04.88'N, 112°05.36'W) at Skeleton Point, the trail abruptly shifts from gentle to precipitous, and you depart the Supai Group for a rollercoaster ride down the massive cliff of Redwall Limestone, deposited in a vast, shallow sea that covered most of the North American west during the Mississippian Period. As you descend several switchbacks, observe the numerous caves riddling the walls. Near the bottom of the cliff, at mile 3.8, you reach a sharp, right-hand switchback with a softer, purplish rock visible on the left (GPS 36°04.92'N, 112°05.17'W). Note how this rock forms a lens, widening to the north (away from the trail) for about 30 yards before quickly pinching out. This is a scrap of the Temple Butte Formation, a rock that is only exposed as isolated lenses in the eastern Grand Canyon. This is because the formation, composed mostly of dolomite, was deposited in a series of tidal channels that drained Persian Gulf-like mudflats here 374 million years ago. The open ocean lay to the west, where thicker deposits accumulated. A later drop in sea level led to erosion of the mudflats, forming a *disconformity* (a gap in the rock record) and removing all traces of the Temple Butte except where it hid in the bottoms of the deepest tidal channels (Figure 46). To either side of the purple lens, the Mississippian-age Redwall Limestone rests directly on the much older Cambrian Muav Limestone.

Beyond the Temple Butte outcrop, the trail again switches back before temporarily straightening out. As you pass outcrops of Muav Limestone along this straightaway, keep your eye out for ripplemarks and worm burrows (Photos

*Photo 32. Breccia pipe. The polygonal cracks at the hiker's feet formed when this area slowly buckled into a breccia pipe after a buried cave collapsed.*

20, 86). You cross the Muav–Bright Angel Shale contact 3.9 miles from the rim as you drop onto the mercifully gentle Tonto Platform. For the next 0.5 mile, you pass small outcrops of green-hued Bright Angel Shale. However, most of the rock on the platform is covered by a thin soil supporting a near monoculture of blackbrush.

You reach a toilet, emergency phone, and the Tonto Trail junction at mile 4.4. Bear straight ahead to descend into a small valley with 10-foot-high, brown sandstone walls composed of Tapeats Sandstone, the Canyon's lowermost Paleozoic layer. As you follow this valley, look at the blocks of Bright Angel that have been used to line the trail, as many of them display excellent worm burrows, the tubular bumps protruding from the stones (Photo 86).

At mile 4.6 (GPS 36°05.51'N, 112°05.36'W), the trail reaches "The Tipoff," where it enters the steep Inner Gorge. At the first left-hand switchback you cross from brown sandstones and thin, green mudstones belonging to the Tapeats onto extremely hard, reddish purple Shinumo Quartzite. With a single footfall, you step 550 million years back in time! This amazing gap in the rock record is marked by an *angular unconformity* (Figure 45), which is spectacularly illustrated northeast of your perch (Photo 34). There the layers in an isolated outcrop of brown Tapeats Sandstone are horizontal, but the bright orange layers of Hakatai Shale below tilt noticeably to the right. This evidence tells us that a tectonic event tilted the Hakatai before the Tapeats was deposited. That event was the rifting of Rodinia.

You have stepped into the Cremation Graben, a narrow slice of Supergroup rocks underlying the Tonto Group (Figure 2) on both sides of the river. From this vantage point, you can see the boundaries of the "grave." Looking upstream at the wall of rock across the river, no tilted Supergroup rocks are found between the horizontal, brown Tapeats cliff forming the rim of the Inner Gorge and the underlying, dark Vishnu Schist with its vertical foliation. These rocks lie on the opposite side of the Cremation Fault, on the side uplifted during Rodinia's breakup. The Supergroup rocks were thus eroded there before the

*Photo 33. The South Kaibab Trail zigzags down the Cremation Fault, which offsets the Bass Limestone (center left). A second normal fault also offsets the Bass above and right of the trail.*

*Photo 34. Angular unconformity. Beds of Hakatai Shale angle down to the right beneath a cap of horizontally layered Tapeats Sandstone.*

Tapeats was laid down. The same juxtaposition of rocks occurs on the far side of the tributary canyon to your west. These rocks lie on the opposite side of the Tipoff Fault, which bounds the Cremation Graben on its southwest side.

From this panoramic perch, the trail winds through the Shinumo, in which you can observe low-angle cross-beds created when these sediments were beach sands. The trail angles east below a growing cliff of Shinumo, which abruptly ends at mile 4.7 (GPS 36°05.51'N, 112°05.30'W) at a rubble-covered slope with scruffy bands of orange Hakatai Shale. These bands end against the Shinumo cliff. A normal fault separates the Shinumo from the Hakatai here. This is the western of two small faults internal to the Cremation Graben. The fault dropped the Shinumo, which normally lies above the Hakatai, to the same elevation.

The trail winds its way down slopes of Hakatai to a narrow neck of land dividing two tributary valleys (mile 4.8; GPS 36°05.62'N, 112°05.29'W). This neck is one of the best vantage points for viewing the handiwork of the two faults that lie within the graben (Photo 33). Looking back up the trail, you get a great view of the fault you just crossed. To your east stands another bold cliff of Shinumo Quartzite. In front of it and at the same elevation lies more orange Hakatai Shale, identical to what you are standing on. The near edge of the cliff marks the eastern of the two internal faults. The block of Hakatai Shale between these faults, which is the block on which you are standing, was uplifted. Corresponding Hakatai outcrops lie at lower elevations to either side, below the Shinumo cliffs on the downdropped sides of the faults.

In addition to ancient faults that broke apart the supercontinent, this neck of land holds yet another fascinating geologic tale. Just 70 yards north of you lies the horizontal outcrop of Tapeats Sandstone that you earlier observed overlying the angular unconformity (Photo 34). All around this outcrop lie giant boulders of Tapeats rubble that toppled from the cliff as it was undermined by erosion. Many of these boulders contain breccia layers composed of jagged blocks of sparkling pink Shinumo Quartzite surrounded by Tapeats sand grains (Color Plate 10). The best example is on the boulder teetering atop a small pillar of Hakatai Shale 40 yards northeast of the trail. The chunks of Shinumo embedded in the Tapeats tumbled from a cliff of Shinumo Quartzite very similar to the ones you see today. However, the earlier cliff rose straight out of the Tapeats Sea. About 545 million years ago, waves crashing against the cliff periodically unleashed rock falls, which were then covered by beach sands that later hardened into the Tapeats Sandstone.

From the neck, the trail passes west of the Tapeats cliff before bending east around its northern nose, where there is another spectacular view of the river and a great lunch spot. The trail then begins to drop into the steep gully east of the Tapeats outcrop, crossing the gully's axis at mile 5.2. The eastern of the graben's two internal faults runs through this gully before crossing a low rib of land into the next gully to the east. Throughout this section the trail traverses Hakatai outcrops. Keep your eyes peeled for mudcracks and ripplemarks; both are abundant in the formation. As you reach the axis of the second (eastern) gully at a left-hand switchback (mile 5.3; GPS 36°05.81'N, 112°05.10'W), you step abruptly from layered Hakatai onto hard, crystalline rocks: dark Vishnu Schist cut by pink bands of Zoroaster Granite. This switchback sits astride the Cremation Fault, which bounds the graben on its northeast side.

As the trail completes this switchback it bends westward, back into the Hakatai Shale. A short distance below, the trail passes underneath a room-sized boulder of Shinumo Quartzite, then negotiates a right switchback. After a short straightaway, the trail bends 90 degrees to the right at a panoramic overlook on the brink of a cliff of Bass Limestone. This overlook is at the Hakatai-Bass contact (mile 5.5). Below the overlook the trail passes under a second house-sized Shinumo boulder, then negotiates two more switchbacks. To your left at the second switchback (a right) stands a 4-foot-high outcrop consisting of limestone bands separated by orange mudstone layers (mile 5.6; GPS 36°05.87'N, 112°05.18'W). Look at the resistant limestone layer on the right (northwest) side of this outcrop for a series of wavy laminations. These are *stromatolites*, fossilized bacterial mats that grew along the edges of the Bass Sea 1200 million years ago (Photo 79), making them the oldest fossils found in the Grand Canyon.

More stromatolites are visible in the 2-foot-high cliffs lining the right side of the trail 15 yards beyond the switchback. After walking an additional 15 yards, you again encounter Zoroaster Granite and Vishnu Schist along the Cremation Fault. These crystalline rocks stay by your side for the remainder of the hike.

At mile 5.8 the trail crosses a wash whose channel consists of breccia composed of modern talus cemented together. Grand Canyon groundwater is loaded with calcium carbonate dissolved from the limestone layers through which it travels. The cement holding this breccia together is calcite precipitated from such groundwater during the geologically recent past. Be sure to watch for bighorn sheep and deer along this section of trail; we regularly see them in this area.

When you reach the junction with the River Trail at mile 6, bear right for 0.3 mile. A few switchbacks later, you reach the black bridge across the Colorado. Just upstream of the bridge on the north side of the river is an outstanding outcrop of pink Zoroaster pegmatite with a large, black inclusion of Vishnu Schist tucked in it. This outcrop graphically illustrates the molten state of the Zoroaster as it shoved its way into cracks and seams in the solid Vishnu, occasionally breaking off dark blocks that sank into the molten granite, where they froze in place as the granite cooled.

From the north side of the bridge, the trail heads west another 0.4 mile to Bright Angel Campground. Phantom Ranch and ice-cold lemonade await you a flat 0.3 mile beyond. From this little patch of civilization set amidst the grandeur of a primeval-looking world, you can sip your lemonade and admire the soaring walls of rock that witnessed the sundering of a supercontinent.

### Hike 5

# BRIGHT ANGEL TRAIL

## ROSETTA STONES

*Turn the geologic clock back 60,000 years with each step as you envision the tropical seas, lazy rivers, and desert dunes that alternately occupied this very spot in times past.*

LENGTH ■ 9.7 miles

ELEVATION CHANGE ■ 4400 feet

TIME ■ 1–2 days each way

DIFFICULTY ■ Difficult; a long trail with a smooth tread

BACKCOUNTRY ZONING ■ Corridor; camp only at Indian Garden (CIG) and Bright Angel (CBG) Campgrounds

WATER AND TOILETS ■ Treated water year-round at both campgrounds and seasonally at 1.5-Mile and 3-Mile Resthouses. Toilets at all but 3-Mile Resthouse

EMERGENCY SERVICES ■ Emergency phones at 1.5-Mile, 3-Mile, and River Resthouses. Ranger stations at Indian Garden and Phantom Ranch

MULE TRIPS ■ Available to Phantom Ranch and Plateau Point

MAP LIST ■ 1–3, 7, 8

KEY REFERENCES ■ 1, 3, 8, 21–23, 27

DAY HIKES ■ 1.5-Mile Resthouse (3 miles round trip); 3-Mile Resthouse (6 miles round trip); Indian Garden (9 miles round trip); Plateau Point (12 miles round trip); Phantom Ranch to Indian Garden (9 miles round trip)

SEASONS ■ Year-round, but the upper trail is usually icy during winter

**About the Landscape:** The Bright Angel Trail boasts a scenic and geologic splendor worthy of being the Grand Canyon's most popular trail. It is an excellent hike to acquaint yourself with the stories behind the brightly colored horizontal layers emblematic of this geologic wonder. All of these layers were deposited during the Paleozoic Era between 545 and 245 million years ago. This is the first era when rocks contained abundant fossilized organisms, which look very different from most modern organisms and so were given the name Paleozoic, meaning "ancient life."

Below Indian Garden, you pass into the dark, forbidding, and spectacular Inner Gorge, where you are surrounded by craggy, black rocks called the Vishnu

Schist. Twisting their way through the schist are sparkly pink ribbons of Zoroaster Granite. These crystalline rocks are over 1700 million years old, so as you descend from the Bright Angel Lodge to the Colorado River, you pass through almost 2 *billion* years of the earth's history! With each footstep, you transport yourself an average of 60,000 years back in this incredible journey through time.

The Canyon's sedimentary layers each possess distinctive characteristics that allow you to quickly and easily identify them. The passing of stormy seas, raging rivers, and desolate deserts all left their marks, allowing you to reconstruct while you hike the sweeping changes this landscape has witnessed. Curious hikers can use these rocks as their Rosetta Stones, the keys to deducing the amazing landscape transformations this area has undergone over the course of geologic time.

## LOQUACIOUS LAYERS

Once you learn to speak their language, all rocks tell colorful tales of the events they have witnessed, but sedimentary rocks are especially loquacious. Sedimentary rocks are consummate storytellers, weaving intricate tales complete with vivid details about the land and its inhabitants, such as whether the climate was humid or arid, what types of plants and animals lived there, the direction of prevailing winds, or the location of the area relative to the coast, mountain ranges, rivers, glaciers, or deserts. For those of us curious about the Canyon's history, it is fortunate that this grand chasm was cleaved primarily through a layercake of sedimentary rocks.

Many of the stories these rocks have to tell are clearly visible and easy to understand, such as the footprints impressed in the Hermit Trail's Coconino Sandstone (Photo 51). These tracks bear silent witness to the passage of a kitten-sized animal whose journey 270 million years ago paralleled the one you can take today. Other tales are reserved for readers who want to dig deeper. Clues as subtle as the thickness, grain size, and orientation of individual sediment layers can tell us that 270 million years ago, the prevailing wind direction in the Grand Canyon was from the north. Other signs speak of the passage of a hurricane over the then-coastal New Hance Trail 1200 million years ago, or testify to the violent shaking the denizens of the Clear Creek Trail endured one day 1100 million years ago when the Bright Angel Fault rumbled to life. Knowledge of a few basic words from the rich language of sedimentary rocks will help you to visualize what the area you are traversing looked like so many years ago when these rocks were born.

**FIGURE 26:** CLUES TO ANCIENT ENVIRONMENTS IN SEDIMENTARY ROCKS

| CLUE | INDICATOR | PALEOENVIRONMENT |
|---|---|---|
| Sediment size | Energy of transport | Coarse grains: Swift current. Fine grains: Little or no current. |
| Sediment shape | Distance of transport | Angular: Transported short distance. Well-rounded: Transported long distance. |
| Frostiness of quartz | Impact during transport | Frosted: High-velocity impacts during wind transport. Not frosted: Cushioned impacts during water transport. |
| Sediment composition | Type of environment | Predominantly quartz and feldspar: Near-shore deposit such as a beach or terrestrial deposit. Predominantly limestone: Tropical ocean or lake. Predominantly evaporite: Shallow ocean or lake in an arid climate. |
| Cross-bedding | Type of environment | Large-scale and steep: Sand dunes. Small-scale and gentle: River, beach, delta. |
| Fossils, trace fossils | Marine vs. land Environment, paleoecology | Land plants and animals: Onshore environment; types indicative of climate. Marine organisms: Ocean environment; types indicate water depth, salinity, proximity to land. |
| Bed thickness | Sediment availability Rate of sedimentation | Thick beds: Rapid deposition/high availability. Thin beds: Slow sediment accumulation/limited availability. |
| Grain sorting and size | Transport agent, environment | Well-sorted: Desert dunes, lake or ocean bottom, beach. Moderate sorting: River, delta. Poorly sorted: Landslide, debris flow, glacial deposit. |

Sedimentary geologists rely on a basic principle known as *uniformitarianism,* a principle often summarized as "the present is the key to the past." If you find a match between the properties of an ancient sedimentary rock and a modern environment where sediments are accumulating, it is a good bet that the area covered by that rock layer resembled the modern environment when the rock was deposited.

Making these interpretations is a fun, trailside exercise in deduction requiring only three simple steps. First, carefully observe every feature visible in the rock layer before you. Second, let your mind roam to every place you have ever visited, seen in a travel magazine, or yearned to go. Visualize a pristine beach in the Bahamas, a mighty Alaskan glacier, the placid waters of a Canadian lake, Saharan sand dunes, the Mississippi River meandering through a Louisiana bayou, and the silent depths of the ocean floor. Think about what processes produce and move sediment grains in those landscapes, and what features the leftover piles of sediment would possess. The clues sedimentary geologists rely on most are (1) fossils and trace fossils; (2) the size, composition, and shape of individual sediment grains; and (3) the thickness, angle, and size-sorting of sedimentary layers (Figure 26). The final step is simply to match the features you see in the

*Photo 35. Cross-bedding. The Coconino Sandstone's crazily tilted beds attest to its deposition in enormous desert sand dunes.*

rock layer with the features you have seen or would expect to see in a particular environment. Run through all the possibilities, and the one with the best match likely represents what your trail looked like when that layer was accumulating.

Let's try to interpret the depositional environment of the Coconino Sandstone as an example of the technique. In places, the Coconino contains tracks resembling the ones made today by scorpions on desert sand dunes. This clue might lead you to hypothesize that the Coconino was deposited as sand dunes in an arid climate where scorpions thrived. You would then examine other aspects of the Coconino to see if this makes sense. Outcrops of this layer on the Bright Angel Trail consist of pure sandstone, with grains of uniform size. Are these characteristics consistent with our dune interpretation? A look at modern dunes reveals similarly excellent grain-size sorting (Figure 26).

This sorting makes sense if you think about the mechanism for sand dune creation: wind. Only strong winds can move sand. Only rare, extreme winds like tornadoes can pick up gravel, and even they can't move it very far, so you never see gravel dunes. On the other hand, strong winds do pick up a lot of dust (silt and clay-sized particles), but modern sand dunes generally do not have silt and clay. That's because dunes are formed where strong winds encounter some sort of obstruction that slows their velocity, causing the sand-sized particles to drop to the ground. All of the smaller, lighter silt and clay particles continue to be carried with the wind, to be deposited elsewhere. So, wind as a transport mechanism is very good at creating well-sorted sand layers, which is exactly what we observe in the Coconino.

Another distinctive characteristic of the Coconino is its large-scale *cross-bedding*, which is easily seen along the trail. Although the formation itself rests horizontally, many of its individual beds are inclined at angles up to 30 degrees (Photo 35). If our sand dune interpretation is correct, it must explain this characteristic. In fact, modern sand dunes display cross-beds just like this, which they acquire as windblown sand tumbles over the steep lee side of the dune (Figure 27). With all of these independent lines of evidence in agreement, we conclude that the Coconino was deposited as a series of sand dunes. Because geologists have discovered similar dune deposits of identical age from the Grand Canyon to Montana, we can conclude that this desert was vast, rivaling the Sahara in scale. But the

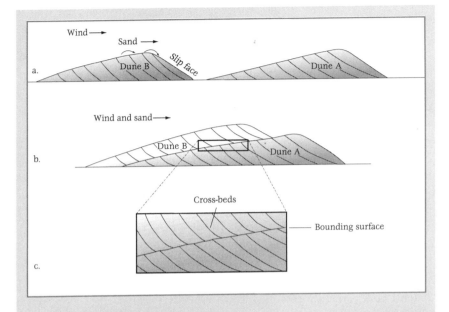

*Figure 27. Movement and preservation of sand dunes. a. High-angle cross-beds form when sand grains tumble down the dune's steep lee face (the slip face). b. When a second dune encroaches on the first, stacked cross-beds are separated by a low-angle bounding surface (c) and preserved in the rocks.*

rocks can tell us even more. Because the steep side of modern dunes lies downwind, we can use the cross-beds to deduce the prevailing wind direction in the 270-million-year-old Coconino desert. Along the Bright Angel Trail and elsewhere, most Coconino cross-beds tilt down to the south, indicating that the wind blew from the north, off an arid upland that lay in that direction.

Had you visited Grand Canyon Village 270 million years ago, the vista would have resembled the one you see today in Egypt. If you had come to the Canyon at other times in its history, it would have physically resembled Tibet, the Texas Gulf Coast, the Pacific Northwest's Cascade Mountains, the Bahamas, and Nevada's Basin and Range. The stories of these fantastic changes in the Canyon environment, each of which has left its indelible imprint on the scenery we enjoy today, are all told by the rocks you pass on your way from rim to river (Chapters 1–4). If you employ some keen observation, imagination, and trailside detective work, you too can listen to the testimonies of these enduring witnesses to history.

**Trail Guide:** The trailhead is located 300 yards west of the Bright Angel Lodge in Grand Canyon Village, just above the shuttle stop.

This historic path was constructed in 1891 by miners, who improved an ancient Native American route that exploited a break in the massive cliffs rendered by the Bright Angel Fault. The vertical offset of rock layers caused by fault movement is immediately apparent from many locations along the trail.

About 130 yards after leaving the rim, you encounter the first of the trail's many switchbacks, followed by a long straightaway lined with excellent outcrops of Kaibab Limestone. The rocks you pass between this switchback and a tunnel at mile 0.15 provide a window into the landscape of the Grand Canyon region about 260 million years ago. At that time the area lay beneath a shallow, tropical sea inhabited by brachiopods, crinoids, bryozoans, horn corals, and sponges (Figure 29). The rock here is mottled, with many bulbous chert nodules protruding from the more abundant limestone. The brainlike patterns found in some of the nodules are sponge fossils. Most of the animals inhabiting this sea secreted shells of calcium carbonate (the material that makes limestone), but the sponges had spicules made of silica, which later turned into chert, an extremely resistant material. These nodules are of tremendous significance because the chert has armored the Kaibab Limestone against erosion, providing the hard rim for this fantastic canyon.

After you pass through the tunnel, look up to the left about 30 feet above the trail to see some red pictographs left by ancient Puebloans who inhabited this area 1250 to 850 years ago, a mere blink in geologic time!

Beyond the tunnel, the long straightaway continues another 0.25 mile. Near its end, you reach the Kaibab-Toroweap contact (GPS 36°03.51'N, 112°08.75'W). The point where these two rock units meet is subtle, but you will know that you have reached it when the cliffs that have dominated the trail thus far gradually give way to more subdued, vegetated slopes.

The switchback at the end of the straightaway (0.4 mile from the trailhead) is a great place to examine the Bright Angel Fault, which you have just crossed. Look downstream along Garden Creek Canyon, which you are in, and you will see the arrow-straight canyon of Bright Angel Creek descending from the North Rim and pointing right at you. Both Garden and Bright Angel Creeks are located along the Bright Angel Fault, explaining their mutual alignment and their impressive linearity. The movement that occurred along the fault is also visible from here. If you look above you to the left (west), you can see the lowest cliffs of the Kaibab Limestone above you, but looking down and to the right (east) reveals that the Kaibab cliffs extend well below your present elevation. The southeast side of the fault dropped about 200 feet relative to the upthrown northwest side, accounting for this mismatch.

Below this second switchback the trail begins a 0.3-mile-long straightaway. Two hundred yards beyond the switchback, the trail crosses Garden Creek, which is dry here. Because you find yourself back among 15-foot-tall cliffs of Kaibab Limestone, you know that you have once again crossed the Bright Angel Fault. A short distance later, you leave the Kaibab for good.

The best exposures of Toroweap are found at the next switchback, about 0.7 mile from the trailhead. This switchback is the first of a pair in quick succession, and it is overhung by Douglas fir boughs, testifying to the cool, moist microclimate established in this shady canyon. The Toroweap is composed of alternating layers of gray limestone, which produce small cliffs, and brown mudstone mixed with green-gray evaporites, which comprise the soft, decomposing slopes. The mixture of limestone, mudstone, and evaporites is the legacy of a fluctuating, shallow sea, whose coastline lay near the Bright Angel Trail 265 million years ago. Seawater evaporated in the arid climate of the time, leaving behind the Toroweap evaporites.

About 0.9 mile from the trailhead, you encounter a second tunnel (GPS 36°03.55'N, 112°08.64'W). Just before you enter it, the rock to your left is Toroweap Limestone, but the tunnel

Photo 36. Coconino-Hermit contact. The smooth, upper cliff of Coconino Sandstone contrasts starkly with the lower cliff of dark Hermit Formation. The light-colored, tabular areas piercing the Hermit are ancient mudcracks that filled with Coconino sand as dunes began to blow across the landscape.

itself has been hewn from tan Coconino Sandstone. Note a thin zone of sheared green rock on the left as you enter, as well as the web of white calcite veins shooting through the tunnel's roof. All of this geologic diversity in such a small area is caused by the Bright Angel Fault, which runs directly through the tunnel. Fault movement crushed the rock, allowing water to percolate through and precipitate the calcite veins. It also juxtaposed the Toroweap and Coconino Formations due to uplift of the fault's northwest side. This vertical movement is clearly displayed here, where a cliff of Coconino Sandstone towers above you to the west, but the same cliff lies well below you to the east.

As you exit the tunnel, the tan cliff of Coconino Sandstone before you displays sweeping cross-beds tilted down to the left at a rakish angle. Note how the cross-beds are separated into groups by horizontal lines known as *bounding surfaces* (Figure 27). Each group of cross-beds was formed on the steep, lee side of a giant sand dune that blew south across the landscape 270 million years ago.

The trail now quickly plunges through the Coconino in a dizzying series of switchbacks. There is little outcrop exposed along this section because you are descending landslide debris that covers it up. As you round the seventh switchback after the tunnel (a right-hand bend at GPS 36°03.60'N, 112°08.62'W), you draw even with the Coconino-Hermit contact to your left. It is marked by the distinctive transition from the tan Coconino above to the brick-red Hermit Formation below (Photo 36). Although you will cross more Hermit, its mudstone is so easily eroded that it is mostly covered by soil and vegetation, so this is the best place to examine it. The Hermit mudstones were deposited by a network of lazy, meandering rivers crossing a vast floodplain that covered the region 275 million years ago. The rivers flowed from the east, where they drained an ancestral Rocky Mountain range. This flow direction is revealed by larger particles in the Hermit and contemporary rocks east of the Grand Canyon.

The top of the Hermit here is marked by several 15-to-20-foot-deep gashes filled with blonde sandstone derived from the overlying Coconino Formation (Photo 36). These are huge mudcracks formed on the Hermit floodplain as the climate dried out. No sediment was deposited for a time while these mudcracks were forming, creating an *unconformity*, or gap, in the rock record (Figure 45). Eventually, enough sand accumulated to form the Coconino dunescape.

After completing the series of switchbacks, the trail begins a descending eastward traverse to the appropriately named 1.5-Mile Resthouse. An emergency phone is located in the first of two rock shelters, and 100 yards beyond is a toilet. The toilet conveniently lies near the contact between the Hermit Formation and the Supai Group, which was deposited from 310 to 285 million years ago. At 1000 feet, the Supai Group is the thickest of the Paleozoic layers. It is composed of four separate formations; the distinctive Esplanade Sandstone is on the top. The Esplanade is characterized by a large cliff of cross-bedded, red sandstone, which you encounter a short distance below the toilet.

The trail zigzags its way through the Supai layers all the way to 3-Mile Resthouse, crossing the Bright Angel Fault several more times en route. The most notable feature of the crimson Supai Group is the distinctive alternation between sandstone cliffs and mudstone benches. Using your deductive reasoning, can you guess what events transpired to create these? A mixture of plant, animal, and marine fossils found in the Supai in other locations suggests that the Grand Canyon area then lay along a coastal plain. During this period, sea level fluctuated frequently, triggered by repeated advances and retreats of glacial ice sheets caused by a great southern continent, known as Gondwanaland, straddling the South Pole (Figure 14). As the glaciers advanced, sea level would drop, and the arid Grand Canyon coastal plain would be covered by sand dunes that later formed the Supai's prominent cliffs. As the glaciers later retreated, sea level would rise again, covering the plain with a shallow sea in which many of the Supai mudstones accumulated. In this way, the existence of glaciers half a world away created the pattern of cliffs and rubbly slopes characterizing the Supai Group you are traversing.

At mile 2.8 the trail again reaches Garden Creek wash (GPS 36°03.89'N, 112°08.28'W), where you can gaze down on its polished gray, slickrock floor. This is the top of the Redwall Limestone on the upthrown, western side of the Bright Angel Fault. The 3-Mile Resthouse is visible to the northeast, 120 feet below you. It is built just above the Redwall on the downdropped, eastern side of the fault, making this another good place to observe the offset of layers.

An excellent destination for day hikers, the 3-Mile Resthouse provides an emergency phone and seasonal water. Immediately below the 3-Mile Resthouse, the trail embarks on another series of tight switchbacks known as Jacob's Ladder. These switchbacks descend the Redwall Limestone, which you encounter a short distance below the resthouse. Look for fossils in the Redwall,

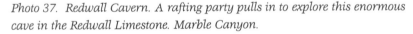

*Photo 37. Redwall Cavern. A rafting party pulls in to explore this enormous cave in the Redwall Limestone. Marble Canyon.*

which show that the rock is composed of the fragmented remains of literally trillions of brachiopods, corals, bryozoans, sponges, and crinoids (Figure 29). These creatures all lived in a shallow, tropical sea that covered the region 350 million years ago. As you marvel at the sheer, 450-foot-tall cliff, notice how it is pockmarked with huge, shallow caves. Groundwater, which is slightly acidic, has percolated through this limestone, dissolving the rock along its path and creating the openings. Limestone dissolves more easily than any other rock type; it is for this reason that most of the world's great caves are found in limestone, including several large ones in the Grand Canyon (Photo 37). The Redwall contains more caves than other Grand Canyon limestone layers because, unlike the other formations, it began dissolving immediately after it was deposited (Chapter 2).

John Wesley Powell named the Redwall for its obvious red cliffs lining the river throughout the Canyon. He recognized that the limestone itself is gray; its red color comes from Supai mud dripping over the Redwall cliff during storms. Notice how the isolated Redwall spires, which have lost their Supai cap to erosion, are gray instead of red.

At 3.3 miles from the trailhead, the path weaves its way through a series of switchbacks surrounded by large blocks of Redwall Limestone that have tumbled from the cliffs above. Many of these boulders display thin, discontinuous beds of red chert interspersed with the limestone.

The trail reaches the bottom of the Redwall just before entering an eastern tributary to Garden Creek, where it crosses the pipeline delivering water to the South Rim from Roaring Springs (Hike 15). The Cambrian-aged Muav Limestone lies beneath your feet here, but the Redwall-Muav contact is completely obscured by rubble. As you cross the boundary between the 350-million-year-old Redwall and the 530-million-year-old Muav, you step across another of the Canyon's major unconformities.

The book of the Canyon is missing several pages here, so our story will be forever incomplete. The pages detailing events during the Ordovician and Silurian Periods (505 to 408 million years ago) have been torn out completely, but a fragment of the Devonian page still exists in the form of a small outcrop of Temple Butte Limestone. This outcrop is not easy to spot, but it is visible high on the cliff to the east (right) as you walk from here to Indian Garden. It forms a 35-foot-thick lens of purplish rock located about 200 feet up the wall, sandwiched between the massive cliff of Redwall Limestone above and the more broken, olive-colored Muav Limestone below.

The Temple Butte Formation was deposited on an intertidal mudflat 370 million years ago. It occurs only in isolated patches throughout the eastern Grand Canyon because soon after it was deposited, erosion removed all but a few scraps that lay in the deepest tidal channels (Figure 46).

The trail now starts a long, relatively flat straightaway on its path to Indian Garden, still nearly a mile away. The bedrock in this section is Muav Limestone, but very little of it is exposed along the trail because it is covered by sediments recently deposited by Garden Creek. The sediments form the flat-topped terraces above the trail. These terraces possess fertile soils in which the Havasupai Indians grew crops while living at this desert oasis.

At mile 3.9 the trans-Canyon water pipe, supported by rock pillars, spans a tributary wash. About 0.2 mile farther, the trail drops below the terraces into a tiny gorge cut by Garden Creek. The Muav Limestone peeks out from under its sediment cover here, revealing hundreds of thin, drab-colored limestone layers.

The Muav and the underlying layers of Bright Angel Shale and Tapeats Sandstone together make up the Tonto Group (Figure 2), a package of rock layers deposited during Cambrian time by a sea that slowly encroached upon the region from the west. As the sea crept eastward, the sandy shoreline, represented by the Tapeats Sandstone, was covered by fine muds (the Bright Angel Shale), which were finally overlaid by limestones deposited in still deeper waters (the Muav Limestone) (Figure 12).

A short distance below the small gorge, the trail crosses from the Muav to the Bright Angel Shale, but this contact is also obscured by the terraces. At 4.4 miles from the trailhead, you reach Indian Garden. You soon pass the campground and reach a composting toilet and a drinking fountain, which provides potable water year-round from the trans-Canyon pipeline. A sign here marks the trail to Plateau Point, a spectacular overlook of the Inner Gorge that is an outstanding day hike from Indian Garden (see Hike 11).

The towering cottonwood trees that provide such welcome shade owe their existence to a spring that lies along the Bright Angel Fault. Garden Creek has been dry up to this point, but because it is fed by the spring, the cheerful babble of flowing water will now accompany you as the trail hugs Garden Creek. Just beyond the sheltering shade of the riparian cottonwoods lies a parched plain covered by desert blackbrush and Mormon tea, a graphic reminder of how precious water is in the desert.

Although the entire Indian Garden complex is built on the Bright Angel Shale, very little of this formation is exposed to view. The soft, crumbly green shale that dominates the formation is quickly eroded and then covered by sediment and soil. The green color comes from the mineral glauconite, which was precipitated directly out of the seawater in which the shale was deposited.

The signed junction with the Tonto East Trail lies almost at the contact between the Bright Angel Shale and the underlying Tapeats Sandstone. Beyond it, you quickly drop into a Tapeats gorge, which gets progressively more spectacular as Garden Creek carves ever deeper. The Tapeats' resistant brown sandstone layers protrude as a series of ledges that are each undercut by erosion of much softer, tan to maroon mudstone layers, giving the cliffs a ragged outline. The Tapeats sandstones are composed almost exclusively of coarse, well-rounded quartz sand. In which settings could such consistent rounding occur? Some of the best-rounded modern sediments occur on beaches, the product of incessant, back-and-forth washing of the grains. This texture is thus another clue that the Tapeats was deposited as a beach sand 545 million years ago.

As Garden Creek and the trail veer to the right, you leave the last of the big cottonwood trees behind. About 0.3 mile after you enter the Tapeats gorge, a pile of rockfall debris comes into view 10 yards right of the trail. This debris lies at the Great Unconformity, the magic line marking the boundary between the 545-million-year-old Tapeats Sandstone above and the 1700-million-year-old Zoroaster Granite below (Photo 6). A 15-yard detour to the rock pile's downstream end reveals the contact itself. The brown, horizontally layered Tapeats slightly overhangs the decomposing, unlayered Zoroaster Granite sitting at knee level. Here you can place your finger over the contact, which spans a mind-boggling 1200 million years of missing history. Fortunately, some of this missing record has been preserved elsewhere in the rocks of the Grand Canyon Supergroup.

The trail crosses the Great Unconformity immediately below the rockfall, and the path stays on the crystalline Zoroaster Granite and Vishnu Schist for the rest of the journey to Phantom Ranch. About 0.1 mile past the rockfall, pink pegmatite dikes cut the light gray Zoroaster rocks. A short distance farther, much of the outcrop becomes darker in color, and a vertical pattern is readily apparent. These darker rocks are part of the Vishnu Schist, and the vertical pattern is the *foliation* that identifies them as metamorphic (Figure 40). The Vishnu Schist was originally deposited as mud and volcanic ash layers from a series of active volcanoes that rose out of the ocean here about 1750 million years ago. The Zoroaster Granite marks the solidified magma chambers that fed those volcanoes. The subduction zone that gave birth to these volcanoes terminated 1700 million years ago when these volcanic islands collided with an approaching continent, in the process metamorphosing the muds and ash layers into schist and gneiss (Figure 5).

The trail continues to follow Garden Creek for the next 0.5 mile, crossing it twice en route. About 1.5 miles beyond Indian Garden the trail abruptly leaves the creek, turning right to avoid a steep, narrow slot canyon through which the creek plunges (GPS 36°05.39'N, 112°06.82'W). The view from this point is spectacular! Looking to the right (southeast), you see a dizzying series of switchbacks ahead of you, known as the Devil's Corkscrew. The switchbacks convey you to the floor of Pipe Creek.

As you descend the Pipe Creek gorge (Photo 38), you pass several times beneath powerlines that provide electricity to the pumps pushing water through

*Photo 38. Hikers stare at Grand Canyon Supergroup layers throughout their descent of Pipe Creek gorge.*

the trans-Canyon pipeline. Garden Creek rejoins the trail at mile 7.25, greatly increasing the flow of Pipe Creek. Below this point the water has polished the outcrops of Vishnu Schist, providing beautiful lunch spots with great opportunities to examine the details of folding and metamorphism within the rocks.

About 0.2 mile below the Pipe Creek-Garden Creek confluence, two old mineshafts are visible above the path. In 1890 Ralph Cameron and Pete Berry filed numerous mining claims in the vicinity of the Bright Angel Trail, quickly gaining control of thousands of acres of land, including Indian Garden. The mines produced virtually no valuable ore, but Cameron and Berry maintained their claims so they could operate the trail as a "toll road" for tourists, charging each customer $1. In 1903 Cameron built a hotel on the rim near the trailhead, but in 1905 the Santa Fe Railroad built the El Tovar Hotel at the head of their rail line, and the battle was on for Canyon tourist dollars. In 1906 Berry's toll road franchise expired, and Coconino County took over the trail. The original Devil's Corkscrew reached the floor of Pipe Creek near these mineshafts, but after the Grand Canyon became a national park in 1919, the Park Service rerouted this section to avoid Cameron's mining claims.

Soon after you pass the mineshafts, the noise of the Colorado River begins to echo off the walls of the Pipe Creek gorge. At mile 7.75 you see a rock shelter just across Pipe Creek. The shelter provides an emergency phone and a great view of the Colorado River's swirling waters. A hundred yards beyond the shelter there is a signed trail junction, with the left fork leading 200 yards to the Pipe Creek beach. The right fork continues on to Phantom Ranch, paralleling the Colorado River on what is called the River Trail.

The River Trail quickly climbs onto a tiny shelf hewn out of Vishnu Schist high above the Colorado. The tread is surprisingly smooth given that it clings to a steep cliff of hard rock. This is because the shelf was blasted out by the

*Photo 39. Near Phantom Ranch, yuccas thrive along the Colorado River.*

Civilian Conservation Corps in 1933. It now hosts the trans-Canyon water pipe, which lies just below the trail. Occasional access ports stick up through the trail tread, looking like the covers of suburban water meters terribly out of place.

The vista along this section of trail is awe-inspiring. Dark walls of Vishnu Schist criss-crossed by pink Zoroaster Granite soar over 1000 feet above the trail. Across the river the crystalline rocks form a shorter cliff capped by brown sedimentary layers tilting downstream. These belong to the Bass Limestone, the oldest formation in the Grand Canyon Supergroup (Figure 20). Above the Bass lie more Supergroup layers, the orange Hakatai Shale, the pink cliffs of the Shinumo Quartzite, and the chocolate-brown ledges of the Dox Formation (Photo 38). These layers occupy a *graben*, a downdropped region between two faults, that was active about 750 million years ago. The presence of these same layers on the South Kaibab Trail gives it a very different atmosphere and geologic history. Consider returning to the rim along the South Kaibab to complete an incomparable geologic tour de force.

After 0.6 mile clinging to the side of the cliff, the trail enters an open, sandy area studded with tall yuccas announcing your arrival in the Mohave life zone (Photo 39). Plants of the Mohave Desert to the west have used the gorge of the Colorado to migrate hundreds of miles east of their normal location, basking in the warmth of the low-lying river bottom.

At 9 miles from the trailhead you reach the silver bridge. Phantom Ranch lies 0.75 mile beyond. The River Trail continues upstream another 0.5 mile to its junction with the South Kaibab Trail. Soon after crossing the bridge, you encounter the Phantom Ranch ranger station. Bright Angel Campground lies another 0.1 mile and Phantom Ranch another 0.4 mile down the path.

Your observations of the Rosetta Stones you passed along the trail have transported you through a dizzying array of landscape changes, from volcanic islands to stark deserts to tranquil seas. Here, gazing at the spectacular and utterly foreign landscape of the Inner Gorge, it is easy to imagine that you truly have walked back in time, traversing 1700 million years of the earth's history in a mere 9.7 miles.

# CLEAR CREEK TRAIL

Hike

6

## ISLANDS IN A CAMBRIAN SEA

*Touch the 1200-million-year gap of the Great Unconformity, along which topographic bumps were once islands in a Cambrian sea.*

LENGTH ■ **9 miles**

ELEVATION CHANGE ■ **1900 feet**

TIME ■ **1 day each way**

DIFFICULTY ■ **Difficult; relatively flat and smooth but remote**

BACKCOUNTRY ZONING ■ **Threshold; at-large camping (AK9)**

WATER AND TOILETS ■ **Water only at Phantom Ranch (treated) and Clear Creek. Toilet located above the Clear Creek floodplain**

EMERGENCY SERVICES ■ **Nearest ranger station at Phantom Ranch**

MAP LIST ■ **1–3, 7**

KEY REFERENCES ■ **1, 7, 8**

DAY HIKES ■ **Phantom Overlook (2.2 miles round trip) has excellent views of Phantom Ranch; Tonto Platform (4.2 miles round trip) offers great views of Colorado River and the Great Unconformity**

SEASONS ■ **Year-round**

**About the Landscape:** The hike along the Clear Creek Trail is an encounter with an ancient Cambrian shoreline, where the Grand Canyon region lay at the edge of a vast sea. This hike provides a rare opportunity to sketch the area's changing geography and surface conditions in such detail that we can still observe individual islands that protruded from this sea some 545 million years ago.

Along 0.5 mile of the Clear Creek Trail you walk near the contact between the Tapeats Sandstone and the crystalline rocks below. Dubbed the Great Unconformity by John Wesley Powell, this line represents a 1200-million-year gap in the rock record (Photo 40). In most places the underlying crystalline schists and granites are black and pink and very hard, forming steep cliffs. However, along the Clear Creek Trail, where the top 10 to 20 feet below the unconformity are exposed, these rocks are uncharacteristically soft, discolored, and sugary in texture. About 740 million years ago, they lay at the earth's surface, exposed to the elements during an extended period of weathering that continued for 200 million years until the area was flooded by the Cambrian sea.

As the sea encroached from the west, most of the low-lying coast was covered by Tapeats beach and near-shore sands. However, bits of resistant rock standing above the generally flat landscape created locally hilly terrain. These knobs were temporarily able to keep their heads above the rising tide, causing the lowermost Tapeats beds to lap around, but not cover, them (Figure 28).

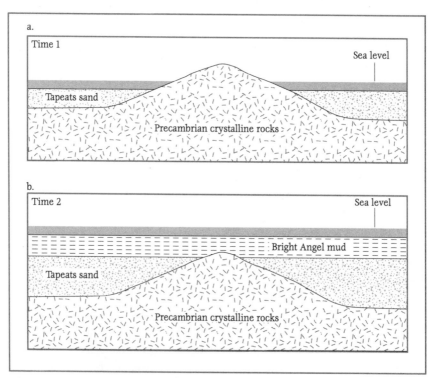

*Figure 28. a. A hump in the Precambrian rocks forms an island in the Cambrian sea. The island is fringed by Tapeats beach sands. b. A later rise in sea level drowns the island, covering it with Bright Angel mud.*

*Photo 40. The Great Unconformity along the Clear Creek Trail. The rocks tell us that 545 million years ago, this hump of unbedded Zoroaster Granite (lower left) was once a small island in an encroaching sea. The layered Tapeats beach sands built up slowly around the island and soon covered it entirely.*

However, as the water continued to rise, the lower knobs were drowned and were later draped by more layers of sand (Photo 40). Some taller islands continued to jut out and were not drowned until the sea was deep enough to deposit the mud of the Bright Angel Shale over them. In these places, the Tapeats Sandstone is missing entirely. These islands were composed of two rock types tough enough to withstand millions of years of weathering: Zoroaster Granite and the Grand Canyon Supergroup's Shinumo Quartzite.

When you reach Clear Creek, you will see tight, swirled patterns in the Shinumo Quartzite that tell of earthquakes that shook this region 600 million years before the Cambrian islands would even form. These features mark the first stirrings along the Bright Angel Fault, which is followed by Bright Angel Creek, along which this hike begins.

**Trail Guide:** Access is via the South Kaibab, Bright Angel, and North Kaibab Trails (Hikes 4, 5, and 15).

From Phantom Ranch, begin by walking north along the North Kaibab Trail for 0.5 mile to the Clear Creek Trail junction. From here, the Clear Creek Trail heads east, climbing steeply up the east flank of Bright Angel Canyon in a series of well-graded switchbacks. If you look behind you toward the west wall of Bright Angel Canyon, you can observe an inverted triangle of bedded sedimentary rocks between buttresses of schist and granite. These beds belonging to the Supergroup (Figure 20) occupy a small graben (Figure 10) like the one along the South Kaibab Trail.

At mile 1.1, you arrive at Phantom Overlook, marked by a stone bench. From here you can look west over the buildings of Phantom Ranch and south into the Inner Gorge of the Colorado River. Twenty feet beyond the bench, a spur trail leads 40 feet around a pegmatite dike and up a couple steps to an even more spectacular view of the river. This is a great place to examine the pegmatite's large, pink potassium feldspar and clear quartz crystals. Look at its edge, where the pegmatite intruded the surrounding schist, and you can see that most of the crystals are smaller here. This is an example of a *chilled margin*. The crystals cooled more quickly, so they are smaller near the contact with the colder surrounding rock. In contrast, the crystals near the center of the dike had room and time enough to grow large.

From Phantom Overlook, the trail continues to switchback up slopes of schist and granite, soon approaching the cliffs of Tapeats Sandstone above. At mile 1.6 the trail rounds another point, and suddenly the Inner Gorge is displayed at your feet. The trail then bends left and traverses the slope to the east, paralleling the Colorado River. At this point, the Tapeats lies only 30 feet above you.

As you round the point, the unconformity itself is covered in rubble, but 200 yards farther, it is exposed along the trail. Look for the change in the rock as the vertical foliation of the Vishnu below gives way to the horizontal bedding of the Tapeats above. At this spot, you can touch a gap in time that spans one-quarter of the earth's existence!

The Great Unconformity is your close companion over the next 0.5 mile as the nearly level trail traverses around two large amphitheaters. With so many great views of the unconformity, you can begin to see more subtle aspects of its nature. Pay special attention to the character of the schists and granites below the unconformity. Here you can observe how the top 10 to 20 feet are unusually soft and sugary, indicating the 200 million years of weathering they endured before the Tapeats reburied them. They remained hidden for another 500 million years until the geologically recent cutting of the modern Grand Canyon reexposed them. The type, thickness, and style of weathering at this contact provide one of the few clues we have to the geography and surface conditions of the Grand Canyon area 550 to 600 million years ago.

The first of the amphitheaters that the trail traverses is broken into two smaller amphitheaters by a small ridge, whose nose you reach 2 miles from Phantom Ranch (GPS 36°06.38'N, 112°05.10'W). From here, look back at the excellent exposure of the Great Unconformity you just traversed. You can see a hump in the crystalline rocks, with layers of Tapeats Sandstone pinching out against either side of that hump (Photo 40). This was one of the resistant knobs that stood above the sea 545 million years ago as the long period of weathering and erosion drew to a close. At first, the knob remained above water, causing the lowermost beds of the Tapeats to lap around it (Figure 28). Soon, however, the knob was drowned and layers of Tapeats draped right over its top.

At mile 2.4, the trail completes its traverse of the second amphitheater and begins its ascent through the Tapeats onto the Tonto Platform, the large, relatively flat plateau that is prominent even from the rim (Photo 56). As it traverses the platform for the next 5.5 miles, the trail is easy to follow except near mile 4.7, where it heads up a wash for about 200 yards. The trail leaves the wash at a distinctive red boulder crowned by a large cairn. Although most of the Bright Angel Shale along the platform is obscured by debris that has rained down from the cliffs above, good exposures are visible in places, especially where the trail cuts across dry washes. The Bright Angel's distinctive thin, green shales and interbedded brown sandstones are apparent in these cuts. Keep your eyes out for trace fossils (mainly worm burrows, Photo 86) and ripplemarks (Photo 20) along this section of trail.

To the right of the trail at mile 5.2 (GPS 36°05.86'N, 112°03.00'W), two hills separated by a dry wash are visible. The hills are both composed of Zoroaster Granite. To the left of the hills you can see horizontal layers of the Bright Angel Shale at the same height. What is absent in this scene is the Tapeats Sandstone, which normally lies between the Bright Angel and the Zoroaster. What could

*Photo 41. Ancient granite islands. Two dome-shaped humps of Zoroaster Granite (arrows) bulge above the horizontally layered Tapeats Sandstone. They formed larger islands in the Cambrian sea and were not drowned until the water was deep enough to deposit muds of the Bright Angel Shale over their tops.*

have happened to it? Three possibilities exist. First, a fault could slice between the rock units, cutting the Tapeats out of the picture. However, close examination of this exposure by geologists has shown that no such fault exists here, plus, you can see Tapeats layers fringing the far side of the Zoroaster knobs (Photo 41). A second possibility is that the Tapeats was deposited here but was later eroded, prior to deposition of the Bright Angel Shale. While this could also be the explanation, it doesn't fit the facts on the ground. Erosion generally strips geologic layers wholesale from a large area, and the nearby outcrops of Tapeats indicate that no such regional stripping occurred here. Also, close examination of the contact between the Tapeats and the Bright Angel has convinced geologists that both units were deposited in a continuous sequence by a steadily rising sea, with no erosion in between. Instead, the evidence supports the third possibility, that the Tapeats was never deposited here. These bedrock hills were islands in the Cambrian sea, islands that were tall enough to remain above sea level until they were finally buried by the mud of the Bright Angel Shale about 530 million years ago (Figure 28).

Beyond these ancient islands, at mile 5.6, the trail curves to the northeast as it enters the drainage of Zoroaster Creek. Half a mile farther, a narrow gorge of Zoraster Granite comes into view. It is an impressive slot that is worth the 20-yard detour (GPS 36°06.08'N, 112°02.31'W) to gaze over the lip. From this vantage point, you can see that this gorge was carved out of Zoroaster rocks that formed another island in the Cambrian sea. As at the double hill of mile 5.2, no Tapeats lies between the Zoroaster and the Bright Angel Shale. You can see horizontal layers of Bright Angel lying to both the left and the right of the gorge, *below* the highest hump of granodiorite. Above this, you can see a resistant sandstone band in the Bright Angel that arches up and over the top of the granodiorite. This island was bigger than the double hills, but eventually, it too was swallowed by the rising Cambrian sea.

The trail crosses Zoroaster Wash at mile 6.5 and continues along the Tonto Platform until mile 7.5, where you get your first look into the Clear Creek gorge. By this point, you've left the area of the Cambrian islands, and the Tapeats is back, forming a prominent cliff at the rim of the gorge. Below it lie northward-tilted layers of the Grand Canyon Supergroup that form an angular unconformity (Figure 45) with the Tapeats. From left to right, layers of pink, cliffy Shinumo Quartzite, red, slope-forming Hakatai Shale, and a black diabase sill (Photo 23) sequentially butt up against the Tapeats.

The trail turns left (north) and parallels the canyon of Clear Creek until mile 8.2, where it starts its final descent. As you drop off the rim and into a tributary canyon, the Tapeats has once again disappeared, and the rim is made of Bright Angel Shale. A few hundred yards farther (GPS 36°06.77'N, 112°00.90'W), you come to a cliff of tilted Shinumo Quartzite. Where the trail crosses a small wash about 30 feet before it reaches the cliff, horizontal layers of sandstone and shale, rich with worm burrows, demonstrate that you are standing on Bright Angel Shale. But these layers end against the Shinumo because its cliff marks yet another island in the Cambrian sea.

The trail descends in a series of switchbacks along the base of the Shinumo cliff and then down steep red-orange slopes of the Hakatai Shale. At mile 8.9 it crosses a black-to-dark green diabase dike cutting through the Hakatai. As the trail approaches Clear Creek, a cliff of Shinumo Quartzite looms over the left side of the wash the trail is descending. Here it is difficult to pick out individual beds in the quartzite, and the rock is heavily fractured. This tributary wash lies along a fault, and the fractured nature of the Shinumo is one of the records of its activity.

The trail ends at mile 9, where it reaches the welcome oasis of Clear Creek. Three beautiful campsites lie under the cottonwood trees, just yards from the perennial creek. These camps make an excellent base for exploring 5 miles down Clear Creek to the Colorado, or 4 miles upstream to Cheyava Falls, the tallest waterfall in the Grand Canyon.

Even if your plans don't include an extensive hike, consider exploring the geology near camp. The middle campsite lies next to a 30-foot-thick diabase dike that slashes up and right through the Hakatai Shale. This is a lower portion of the same dike that you crossed 200 yards before reaching Clear Creek. About 0.25 mile downstream, the route drops through an outcrop of Hakatai on the right side of the creek. Look along the flat bedding surfaces for impressive ripplemarks and mudcracks.

*Photo 42. Marblecake bedding. Swirled, contorted beds in the Shinumo Quartzite formed when an earthquake shook them 1100 million years ago, when they were not yet solidified into rock.*

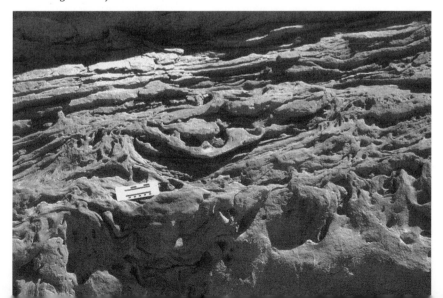

Immediately above the highest campsite, Clear Creek enters a mini-gorge of Shinumo Quartzite. About 50 yards upstream, a room-sized boulder of Tapeats Sandstone has landed with its flat bedding surface exposed, displaying a surface crisscrossed with spectacular mudcracks (Color Plate 13).

Looking upstream, just to the left of this boulder, is a cliff of white Shinumo Quartzite. The layers in this quartzite are contorted in a tight, swirled pattern (Photo 42) that geologists call *marblecake bedding* (geologists often name features after food!). A few feet behind the boulder, the same cliff is cut by a resistant dike, but this is a dike of sandstone, not of once-molten diabase or other igneous rock. As you walk 0.25 mile up the mini-gorge, a network of white veins, more dikes, and marblecake bedding are visible everywhere. These features tell us that a series of earthquakes occurred here about 1100 million years ago, when these rocks were still a pile of loose sand. They lay below the groundwater table, so every pore was filled with water. At this time, the Bright Angel Fault was beginning to come to life (Chapter 1), and earthquakes along this fault shook the water-saturated sediments, liquefying them into quicksand. This same property of water-filled sediments is seen in modern earthquakes and is a primary factor in the extent of earthquake damage. As the earth shook here 1100 million years ago, the soft sand layers crumpled and twisted to form the marblecake bedding. Streams of water shot through the sediments and precipitated their load of dissolved minerals to form the veins. In places, the high water pressure ruptured the layers, and a slurry of sand and water shot up through them to form the sandstone dikes. This phenomenon is also seen in modern earthquakes, where "sand blows" are common.

The hike back to the trailhead retraces the same route, giving you another opportunity to island-hop your way along an ancient Cambrian shoreline, pausing on rocky islets you might have stood upon to watch the sun set over the ocean 545 million years ago.

## Hike 7 SOUTH RIM TRAIL

### DESERT SHIELD

*Stroll across the Kaibab Limestone, the fossil-rich resistant rock shield to which the Grand Canyon owes its very existence.*

LENGTH ■ 4.7 miles from Mather Point to Hopi Point

ELEVATION CHANGE ■ 260 feet

TIME ■ 2–4 hours one way

DIFFICULTY ■ Easy; a pleasant stroll

SPECIAL NOTE ▪ Paved from Mather to Maricopa Points and wheelchair accessible from Mather Point to Bright Angel Lodge

CAMPING ▪ None en route; camp only at Mather Campground

WATER AND TOILETS ▪ Available at drinking fountains and lodges in Grand Canyon Village

EMERGENCY SERVICES ▪ Available in Grand Canyon Village

MAP LIST ▪ 2, 3, 7, 8

KEY REFERENCES ▪ 1, 8, 13, 18, 23, 24, 25

SEASONS ▪ Year-round

**About the Landscape:** Along this entire hike, the rock beneath your feet is the Permian-age Kaibab Limestone (Photo 15, Color Plate 4). Thousands of feet of younger rocks used to overlie the Kaibab here, but millions of years of erosion have stripped all but a few scraps away (Figure 31). Plate tectonics and sedimentation together produced the rocks from which the Grand Canyon was carved, but it was the forces of weathering and erosion that did the actual cutting (Photo 43). Without these twin artists, the Grand Canyon would be nothing more than a high-elevation plateau, indistinguishable from the nearly flat expanses that surround it. Although it took almost 2000 million years to assemble the Canyon's rocks, weathering and erosion carved them into a masterpiece in a mere 5 million years (Chapter 4).

*Photo 43. Weathering and erosion continue to carve the Grand Canyon into a masterpiece. South Rim Trail.*

## SCULPTORS OF A MASTERPIECE:
## WEATHERING AND EROSION

Weathering is the breakdown of rock material, and erosion is the process of relocating this weathered material. Together, these twin sculptors have excavated approximately 800 cubic miles of rock (about 8 trillion tons!) from the Grand Canyon (Color Plate 18). Weathering comes in two varieties: physical and chemical. *Physical weathering* is the mechanical breakdown of rock via abrasion and related processes. Even in the Canyon's desert climate, water is the main agent of physical weathering. Water in the Colorado River drags sediment along the channel, abrading its bottom, and sediment carried by flash floods down usually dry tributaries erodes and expands them.

*Chemical weathering,* as its name implies, is the chemical alteration of minerals when they are exposed to solvents. Water is a fantastically efficient solvent, and given enough time, it can break down virtually any mineral or rock. Rainwater combines with carbon dioxide in the atmosphere to make carbonic acid. The presence of this weak acid further enhances rainwater's dissolving properties. Groundwater can become even more acidic by incorporating various organic and inorganic acids during its journey through soils, sediment, and rocks.

Most rocks are formed of minerals belonging to the *silicate* group, meaning they have both silicon and oxygen in their chemical structure. Water, especially slightly acidic water, reacts chemically with most of these silicates, dissolving elements into the water (known as *ions*) and altering the original mineral into a new, and often softer, product. The most common of these *alteration products* are clays. The clays that enrich soils in nutrients all come from the chemical weathering of feldspars and other common rock-forming minerals (Figure 39). Another important alteration mineral is hematite, which is, quite literally, rust. The chemical weathering of common iron-bearing silicates such as biotite, pyroxene, and olivine produces hematite and a couple of related minerals, which together produce the red and orange hues so common in Grand Canyon rocks.

Limestone is the Canyon's major rock type that is not composed of silicate minerals. Instead, it is mainly composed of the mineral calcite, which is a combination of calcium, carbon, and oxygen. Water dissolves calcite, and hence limestone, entirely, and it does so much more rapidly than it dissolves silicates. Dissolving limestone creates caves and sinkholes, which are abundant in the Canyon's widespread Kaibab and Redwall Limestone layers (Photos 37, 75).

The only common mineral that is nearly impervious to the ravages of chemical weathering is quartz. While other common rock-forming minerals are being chemically transformed into mud, physical weathering processes simply pry quartz from the rock to make sand. Thus, most of the sand found on the beaches of the Colorado River (and elsewhere) is quartz.

In the time since the powerful Colorado River carved through the Kaibab Limestone, other erosive processes have made but little headway against this resistant rock, so the Kaibab now forms the rimrock of the entire Grand Canyon. The Kaibab's great resistance to erosion stems from two facts: (1) it is a limestone sitting in the desert, and (2) it contains an abundance of chert. Although limestones often dissolve away in more humid regions, they usually form resistant cliffs in desert climates. This is because limestones are very resistant to abrasion and other forms of physical weathering but are easily dissolved by chemical processes. In the desert, the water necessary for extensive chemical weathering is lacking, so limestones typically form cliffs there. However, enough water exists to pockmark those limestones with caves and sinkholes, and the Kaibab is no exception (Photo 75).

Even for a limestone, the Kaibab is especially tough due to its bounty of chert nodules. *Chert* is a collection of microscopically small quartz crystals so, like quartz, it is extremely resistant to both physical and chemical weathering. Most of the chert in the Kaibab Limestone was derived from the spicules of billions of sponges that lived in the warm, shallow Kaibab Sea 260 million years ago. When these sponges died, the spicules that stiffened their soft bodies fell out like needles from a rotting pincushion to litter the seafloor. These spicules are composed of opaline silica, which also forms opal gems. As sediment accumulated above them, groundwater began to dissolve the spines. The water consequently became full of dissolved silica, forcing it to deposit chert a short distance away. The bodies of sponges, other fossils, and burrows provided ideal cores around which the relocated silica accumulated, thus causing chert nodules to encircle many of these features. Unlike the opaline silica that formed the original spicules, the chert is exceptionally hard to dissolve, so the presence of millions of chert nodules helps to shield the Kaibab Limestone from erosion. Who knows? Had sponges not inhabited the area 260 million years ago and left behind a desert shield, the Kaibab Limestone and the softer layers beneath it might already have eroded away, leaving us with a much less impressive canyon to hike.

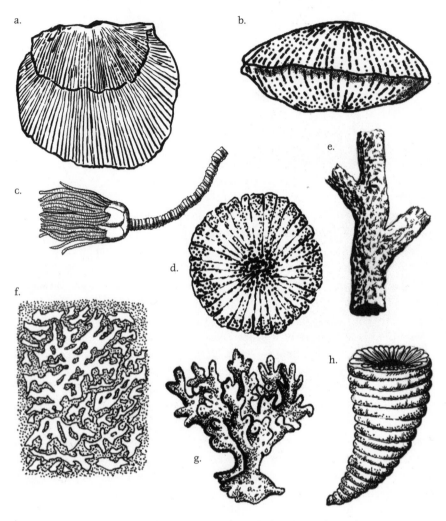

*Figure 29. Common Grand Canyon fossils: a–b. brachiopods; c–d. crinoids; e. bryozoan; f. fossil sponge; g. living sponge; h. horn coral (©2004 by Dona Abbott).*

In addition to sponges, the Kaibab Sea supported a rich invertebrate fauna that included brachiopods, crinoids, bryozoans, and solitary horn corals (Figure 29). The fossilized remains of these animals abound along the Rim Trail. By comparing these fossils with their nearest living relatives, paleontologists have interpreted the conditions under which these organisms thrived and have concluded that the Kaibab Sea was warm and shallow across much of the Grand Canyon region. However, near Desert View, the Kaibab contains fewer of these fossil types and more mollusks, which resemble living cousins that today thrive

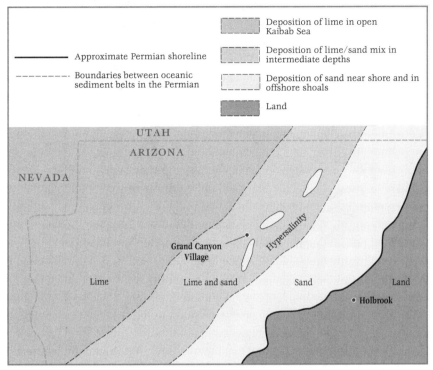

Deposition of lime in open
Kaibab Sea

———————  Approximate Permian shoreline

Deposition of lime/sand mix in
intermediate depths

– – – – – –  Boundaries between oceanic
sediment belts in the Permian

Deposition of sand near shore and in
offshore shoals

Land

*Figure 30. Geography of the Grand Canyon region during deposition of the Kaibab Limestone. Offshore sand shoals restricted water flow in the easternmost Grand Canyon, causing hypersalinity there.*

in very salty marine environments. The proportion of sandstone intermixed with limestone also increases to the east, suggesting that land, and its abundant sand supply, lay in that direction. In fact, the Kaibab Limestone disappears entirely east of Holbrook, Arizona, where it is replaced by a terrestrial sandstone layer. Consequently, based on these fossils combined with the rock record, we can reconstruct the geography and climate of the Grand Canyon area 260 million years ago (Figure 30). The shoreline then lay to the east of the Grand Canyon, somewhere near Holbrook. The eastern Canyon was a restricted arm of the Kaibab Sea, unable to efficiently exchange water with the open ocean that lay to the west. Because the climate was hot and arid, rapid evaporation caused the salinity of this restricted arm to exceed that of normal seawater, making it an inhospitable place for brachiopods, sponges, and many other species, but allowing salt-tolerant mollusks to thrive. Such hypersalinity is common in modern bodies of restricted water, such as the Red Sea and the Persian Gulf, which lie in hot, dry climates.

Fossils are also less abundant in the uppermost portion of the Kaibab Limestone, and where present, they consist of the salt-tolerant mollusks. The upper Kaibab also contains gypsum and other salt deposits, indicating that extensive

*Photo 44. Bright Angel Canyon. The arrow-straight line of Bright Angel Canyon (right) is due to its location along the Bright Angel Fault. The trail to Plateau Point is visible on the flat Tonto Platform (lower middle part of photo).*

evaporation took place in an arid climate. Gypsum from the upper Kaibab is mined in the hills west of Las Vegas for use in sheetrock. This combination of salts and high-salinity fossil species indicates that late in its life, the Kaibab Sea was retreating, its shoreline migrating westward.

Straight-as-an-arrow Bright Angel Canyon (Photo 44), home to the famous Phantom Ranch, is omnipresent on this hike. The reason for its incredibly straight nature is that it lies along the Bright Angel Fault, which was first active 1100 million years ago (Chapter 1). It has had several additional periods of activity, and a handful of small earthquakes that have occurred along it in historic times indicate that it is even moderately active today. Because faults grind and pulverize the rocks along them, fault zones are usually susceptible to erosion. As a result, it is common to find canyons and valleys lining up along faults. Bright Angel Canyon is a particularly graphic example of this phenomenon, one common throughout the Grand Canyon. A quick examination of a topographic map will reveal numerous strikingly linear tributary canyons, many with a twin that runs along the same line on the opposite side of the Colorado River. Almost all of these tributaries lie along faults.

**Trail Guide:** Park at any Grand Canyon Village parking area and ride the blue shuttle bus to the Canyon View Information Plaza. After your hike, catch an eastbound red shuttle to the stop 200 yards west of Bright Angel Lodge, near the Village parking areas.

**Mather Point to Yavapai Point (0.6 mile).** Signs at the Canyon View Information Plaza direct you to Mather Point, a 200-yard stroll to the north. Despite the plaza's name, Mather Point actually offers you the first glimpse of the Canyon, and this view is breathtaking. The North Rim lies a mere 9 miles, but 3 hard days' hike, away. To your right (east) is the amphitheater at the head of Pipe Creek Canyon, and just beyond that lies Yaki Point. The South Kaibab Trail traverses the ridge below Yaki Point, and from here you can see it descending through the Toroweap and Coconino Formations. The Toroweap forms the wide, tree-covered slope stretching from the base of the uppermost Kaibab cliffs to the very large, sheer, white cliff of Coconino Sandstone below (Photo 14).

From Mather Point, follow the paved trail west about 0.6 mile to Yavapai Point. The historic observation tower here hosts a bookstore and a small fossil exhibit. The prominent trail that you see in the Canyon on the flat Tonto Platform ends at Plateau Point, a marvelous viewpoint into the Colorado River's somber Inner Gorge (Photo 44).

**Yavapai Point to the Bright Angel Lodge (1.75 miles).** From Yavapai Point the trail traverses the eastern flank of Garden Creek's near-vertical amphitheater. Every tributary canyon you circumnavigate on the South Rim Trail has this amphitheater shape to it, and each drops steeply below your feet before flattening out to a gentle gradient on the Tonto Platform below. This amphitheater geometry is typical of tributaries in the arid Colorado Plateau landscape, but it is unusual in other river systems (Figure 32), regardless of whether the landscape is subdued or mountainous. The reason for these steep amphitheaters is a process of erosion called *spring sapping*, which plucks grain after grain of sand away from the rock face where a spring emerges (Figure 33). This plucking causes a hollow to form at the base of the cliff. Eventually, the hollow becomes large enough that the wall above collapses, moving the cliff back a few feet (Color Plate 18). As this process is repeated thousands of times over many millennia, the result is an amphitheater like the one you are traversing.

About 0.3 mile past Yavapai Point is a more subdued promontory called Grandeur Point. From this broad shelf of Kaibab Limestone, you get excellent views of the Bright Angel Trail as it snakes its way down through the layers of Coconino Sandstone, Hermit Shale, and the thick Supai Group (Photos 13, 14). The Hermit is the vegetated band lying below the white Coconino cliff. Where visible beneath the shrubs, the shale is brick red in color. Below it, the numerous red cliffs interspersed with vegetated slopes are all composed of rocks belonging to the Supai Group.

These views of the Bright Angel Trail persist for the next 0.2 mile. Garden Canyon, down which the Bright Angel Trail descends, lies along the Bright Angel Fault. This section of the Rim Trail provides an ideal place to personally examine this major fracture in the earth's crust. Focus on the section of the Bright Angel Trail descending through the steep Coconino Sandstone. Notice that the wall of Coconino west of (behind) the trail rises higher than the cliff in front of the trail (Photo 45). The western wall of Garden Canyon has been uplifted about 200 feet relative to its eastern neighbor; this offset is

concrete evidence of the fault's existence. The Bright Angel Trail shoots the gap in the Coconino cliff by running directly down the fault, where the easily eroded, crushed rock forms a slot that the trail exploits.

At 0.75 mile from Yavapai Point, you intersect a trail coming from the Village's Market Plaza. About 0.5 mile beyond this junction, the portion of the Bright Angel Trail along the flat Tonto Platform comes into view. The Indian Garden Spring is marked by the luxuriant growth of cottonwood trees and other vegetation growing around it, in stark contrast to the scrubby blackbrush that dominates the rest of the platform. Just a few hundred yards farther, you reach Hopi House, the easternmost building of the Village complex, and 0.2 mile beyond is the Bright Angel Lodge, where restrooms and refreshments are available.

**Bright Angel Lodge to Trailview Overlook (0.7 mile).** About 0.1 mile beyond the Bright Angel Lodge stands Kolb Studio. Following a red and white sign that clearly marks the way, the Rim Trail veers left here, up a flight of stairs. At the top of the stairs, stay close to the rim, and within another 0.1 mile you reach the beginning of the Bright Angel Trail. The view to the north graphically illustrates the linear nature of both Garden Canyon, down which the Bright Angel Trail descends, and the North Rim's Bright Angel Canyon, which hosts much of the North Kaibab Trail. Although on opposite sides of the Colorado River, these tributaries lie in a straight line (Photo 44) because both have been eroded in the fault-weakened rocks along the Bright Angel Fault.

Just 50 yards to the west lies the West Rim shuttle bus stop. Immediately beyond this, the South Rim Trail descends five stone steps, which mark the end of the wheelchair-accessible portion of this hike. About 300 yards past the bus stop, the trail reaches the Interfaith Worship Area. For 30 yards in all directions, the Kaibab Limestone has a particularly lumpy texture. Each of these lumps is either a fossil or a trace fossil of an invertebrate organism. They stand out as lumps because hard chert nodules formed around them. At first the fossils may be tricky to spot, so look closely for the ribs of shells (Photo 50). Once you tune your eyes, you will see dozens of excellent brachiopod, horn coral, sponge, bryozoan, and crinoid fossils in these rocks (Figure 29).

About 70 yards beyond the Worship Area, you will immediately notice how, for a short distance, the trail becomes steeper. You are actually stepping across the Bright Angel Fault, climbing up onto its uplifted western side! Over the next 100 yards, watch for outcrops of Kaibab that are tinted orange and in places fractured to form a breccia. These anomalies are both indications that you are walking along a fault zone. The breccia was formed by the fault's grinding action, and the orange color is created by iron and sulfur-bearing minerals

*Photo 45. The Bright Angel Trail zigzags down the Bright Angel Fault, which has displaced the Coconino Sandstone cliff 200 feet here.*

introduced by abundant groundwater percolating through the fault zone's highly fractured and therefore porous rocks. About 0.2 mile beyond the Worship Area, the trail flattens out again as you reach the crest of the uplifted block, which stands a full 140 feet higher than the Bright Angel Lodge. This extra height provides stunning views not just into the Canyon but also of the San Francisco Peaks (Photos 46, 48), a five-headed mini–mountain range that rises above the city of Flagstaff, 50 miles to the south. The San Francisco Peaks are sacred to the Navajo, who have lived for centuries in their shadow. The highest peak, Mount Humphreys, constitutes Arizona's highest point. It towers 5500 feet above you and over 10,000 feet above the nearby Colorado River. Amazingly, though, the peak used to rise still higher! San Francisco Mountain is a stratovolcano, similar to Washington's Mount Rainier and Japan's Mount Fuji. Some 400,000 years ago, San Francisco Mountain was conical, like those peaks. Its collapse soon afterward destroyed its perfect cone shape and erased 3000–4000 feet from its summit.

About 0.7 mile from the Village you reach Trailview Overlook, a good place to survey the Bright Angel Trail's serpentine descent, the lush, green Indian Garden, the fault-imposed linearity of Garden and Bright Angel Creeks, and the impressive amphitheater of upper Garden Canyon.

*Photo 46. The headframe of the Orphan Lode Mine towers above the Canyon rim.*

**Trailview Overlook to Powell Point and Hopi Point (1.6 miles).**
Maricopa Point is a 0.7-mile scenic stroll from Trailview Overlook. From
Maricopa Point the view into the Canyon is particularly impressive because
you get a glimpse into the black depths of the Colorado River's Inner Gorge.

Visible to the west of Maricopa Point is the headframe of the Orphan Lode
Mine, perched on the brink of the Canyon rim (Photo 46). The trail reaches
the mine 0.3 mile past Maricopa Point. Due to safety concerns, the Park Service has closed the mine to visitors. At this point, the pavement ends and a
maze of dirt tracks veers left (south) to detour around the bright orange netting barricade. Keep to the paths closest to the netting for the best views of
the mining paraphernalia.

The Orphan Lode Mine began its life as a copper mine in 1893. Until 1946, a
modest amount of copper and other valuable metals were extracted here, but
the real bonanza came in 1951 with the discovery of uranium ore. Between 1956
and 1969, over 4 million pounds of uranium oxide, with a value of over 40 million dollars, were extracted from the mine. Some of these were the highest-grade
uranium ores ever found in the United States. Mining ceased in 1969, and the
Park Service acquired the mine in 1987.

The ores of the Orphan Lode formed in a *breccia pipe*, an area where overlying rock layers have collapsed into caves previously formed in the top of the
Redwall Limestone (Figure 24). The Redwall (Photo 12) is the massive, pale
red-to-gray cliff below the Supai Group that rivals the Coconino in size and
sheerness. There are thousands of breccia pipes in the Grand Canyon area,
and many of these contain ores of uranium, copper, silver, zinc, and other
important metals. The Orphan breccia pipe extends from the Coconino Sandstone down to the Redwall Limestone, so mineshafts were extended 1600 feet
below the rim to extract the ore.

You complete the detour around the Orphan Lode Mine about 0.3 mile
beyond the first orange barrier, just as you reach the road to Powell Point,
which lies 100 yards down the path. Here a large monument to John Wesley
Powell has been erected to commemorate his dramatic whitewater adventures
and pioneering scientific work. As you traverse the narrow neck of land out
to the monument, look to the left of the trail for more nodular, fossil-rich Kaibab
Limestone similar to that at the Worship Area.

Just 0.3 mile beyond Powell Point is Hopi Point, where eastbound shuttles
depart for the Village. However, if you feel like walking farther, the Rim Trail
continues another 5.9 miles to Hermits Rest, the start of the Hermit and Dripping Springs Trails. As you admire this incomparable Canyon from its erosion-
resistant rim, spare a quick thanks for the unassuming sponges that lived here
260 million years ago and helped create the desert shield along which you are
strolling.

**Hike 8**

# RED BUTTE TRAIL

## THE MISSING PAGES

*Summit an outlying butte whose rocks unveil the Grand Canyon's Mesozoic and Cenozoic history, then ascend an historic fire lookout tower to revel in the spectacular 360-degree view.*

LENGTH ■ 1.2 miles

ELEVATION CHANGE ■ 866 feet

TIME ■ 1–2 hours each way

DIFFICULTY ■ Moderately difficult; short but steep

CAMPING ■ National Forest Ten-X campground, 9 miles north

WATER AND TOILETS ■ None available

EMERGENCY SERVICES ■ Nearest assistance in Tusayan, 11 miles north

MAP LIST ■ 9

KEY REFERENCES ■ 18, 28

SEASONS ■ Year-round. Its high elevation and sheltering trees make this a great summer choice. Potentially muddy or icy in winter

**About the Landscape:** As you hike into the Grand Canyon along any of the rim-to-river trails, you drop through layer after colorful layer of rock—the pages of the area's spell-binding Paleozoic history. The plot covering the most recent 245 million years is equally thrilling, but these pages are missing from the Canyon itself. Fortunately, Red Butte (Photo 47), just a few miles south of Grand Canyon Village, preserves part of this intriguing tale (Chapters 3, 4). It is a peaceful and shady hike offering panoramic views and a distinct change of pace from other Grand Canyon adventures.

Today the Grand Canyon is rimmed by the Kaibab Limestone, deposited during the waning days of the Paleozoic Era 260 million years ago. This, however, has not always been the case. During the Mesozoic Era (245 to 65 million years ago), over 4000 feet of sediment piled on top of the Kaibab and solidified into sedimentary rock. Subsequent erosion removed that entire thickness, leaving the hard Kaibab Limestone to hold up the Canyon rim (see Hike 7). These missing Mesozoic rocks still exist in southern Utah, but only a few shreds remain in the vicinity of the Grand Canyon. These scraps, including Red Butte, are extremely important, because they demonstrate that Mesozoic rocks once blanketed the entire area. These scraps also testify to the amazing power of erosion, a force so slow that its activity is almost imperceptible to the human eye, yet is capable, over millions of years, of the wholesale removal of a pile of rock as thick as today's Canyon is deep. In fact, erosion would have succeeded in entirely removing the Mesozoic rocks from the Grand Canyon landscape if not for some volcanic interference.

*Photo 47. Colorful Red Butte owes its existence to its dark basalt cap.*

## THE SAN FRANCISCO VOLCANIC FIELD

Beginning about 9 million years ago, a pool of magma began to form deep in the crust below present-day Williams, Arizona, 50 miles south of the Grand Canyon. The magma erupted at numerous *basaltic cinder cones,* small volcanoes like Vulcans Throne (Photo 89) or the famous Paricutin, which suddenly appeared one day in 1943 in the middle of a Mexican cornfield!

Bigger, more viscous slugs of dacite and andesite magma (Appendix A) formed a series of taller volcanoes, such as Bill Williams Mountain and the San Francisco Peaks (Photo 48). As the magma plume migrated eastward over time, so too did the cinder cones, ending in the eruption 900 years ago of Sunset Crater, a national monument and the youngest volcano in Arizona.

The result of all this volcanic activity is the San Francisco volcanic field, a collection of several hundred cinder cones and a dozen taller volcanoes forming virtually every hill and mountain in the Flagstaff, Arizona, area. During the eruptions, long rivers of lava traveled up to 15 miles from the cinder cones. The summit of Red Butte is capped by a 9-million-year-old remnant of one such outpouring, which at the time looked very much like Sunset Crater's Bonito lava flow.

*Photo 48. Red Butte's Moenkopi Formation stands in front of the San Francisco Peaks, the remnants of an explosive andesite volcano. The smaller hills are cinder cones composed of basalt.*

Color Plate 2. *A band of pink Zoroaster Granite injected into Vishnu Schist is folded like an accordion, providing a clue to the intense compression these rocks have endured. Monument Canyon, Tonto Trail.*

Color Plate 3. *Desert classic. Zoroaster Temple, capped by resistant Coconino Sandstone, is a classic example of a Grand Canyon spire.*

Previous page: Color Plate 1. *Marble Canyon's sheer limestone walls echo of ancient sea creatures and resourceful ancestral Puebloans.*

*Color Plate 4. Sunrise illuminates a spire of Kaibab Limestone on the Nankoweap Trail.*

*Color Plate 5. Blue-green cascades. Precipitation of travertine along Havasu Creek creates small, sinuous dams. These trap pools of blue-green water and send it tumbling to the next pool in a series of beautiful cascades.*

*Color Plate 6. A prickly pear cactus in full glory.*

*Color Plate 7. Muav Limestone, one of the Grand Canyon's hidden treasures.*

*Color Plate 8. Deer Creek Falls tumble past the Great Unconformity, where one-quarter of earth's history is missing!*

Color Plate 9. Pink ribbons of Zoroaster Granite wind across gray Vishnu Schist. The once-straight dikes were tightly folded 1700 million years ago, during the massive collision that metamorphosed the Vishnu.

Color Plate 10. Sealed in stone. Along the South Kaibab Trail, this boulder reveals how blocks of pink quartzite once tumbled off of sea cliffs onto a sandy beach below.

Opposite: Color Plate 11. Green malachite copper ore streaks across red Supai Group rocks near the Last Chance copper mine on the Grandview Trail.

Color Plate 13. Spectacular mudcracks vividly illustrate previous conditions along the Clear Creek Trail.

Color Plate 14. The sheer cliff dubbed the "Palisades of the Desert" stands watch over the eastern Canyon's Tanner Trail.

Opposite: Color Plate 12. Hiking on the South Kaibab Trail.

*Color Plate 15. Havasu Falls crashes over a plug of travertine along Havasu Creek.*

*Color Plate 16. Dripping Springs. Here the process of spring sapping has undercut the blonde Coconino Sandstone to create an amazing scene.*

*Color Plate 17. Young barrel cacti peek through fragments of dark basalt.*

*Color Plate 18. Scarp retreat. Weathering loosens blocks of rock where a spring or creek has created an overhang. The blocks collapse in a landslide, effectively widening the canyon.*

Opposite: *Color Plate 19. Inviting blue-green waters beckon the backpacker in Havasu Campground.*

*Color Plate 20. Spectacular Thunder River springs to life along joints in the Muav Limestone. Thunder River Trail.*

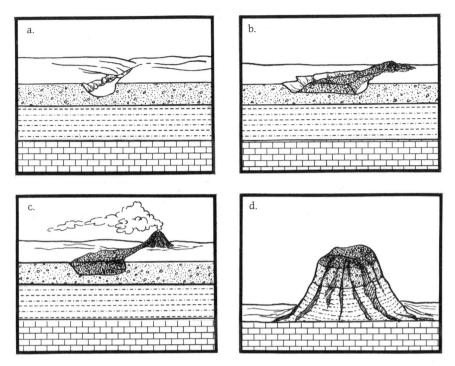

*Figure 31. The evolution of Red Butte through topographic inversion. a. River channel carved in relatively soft Shinarump sandstone. b. Basalt erupted from nearby cinder cone fills channel. c. New channels form at the edge of the basalt because the sandstone is more easily eroded. d. The new channels erode the soft Shinarump and Moenkopi layers except where they are protected by resistant basalt, forming the Butte. (©2004 by Dona Abbott.)*

During this period of volcanism, erosion busily continued to remove the Mesozoic rock layers. When an eruption occurred, basalt lava covered the land surface. The lava tongues, being liquid, tended to flow down the washes and river valleys, filling depressions in the landscape (Figure 31). After each eruption, erosion carried on, but it now found the old washes and valleys plugged with tough basalt. The adjacent plains, formed of soft sedimentary rocks, were easier to wear down, so over the millennia, erosion removed these layers one by one while leaving the basalt flows largely intact. The basalt, which had originally occupied the landscape's lowest areas, soon found itself forming the resistant caps of the higher plateaus.

This process of *topographic inversion* gradually exposed the softer sedimentary rocks on the plateau flanks. Stream undercutting, spring sapping (Figure 33), and overland flooding all began to devour these layers from the side. Blocks of the capping basalt found themselves undercut, hanging over a void of space. Eventually these overhanging blocks gave way to gravity, erosion's best friend, and tumbled down the slope. Through this scarp retreat process (Color Plate 18), the plateaus diminished into mesas, which in turn shrank to the size of buttes. Eventually, most of them disappeared entirely. Red Butte is one of a handful that has yet to be erased by the powerful forces of erosion.

The butte's black cap is easily identified as one of these lava flows, but its name comes from the vivid, red layers the basalt protects. These sedimentary rocks are the Moenkopi Formation and the Shinarump Conglomerate, the first two layers deposited during the Mesozoic Era. About 240 million years ago the mudstones and sandstones of the Moenkopi were laid down by sluggish rivers lazily meandering across a vast plain, much like today's Mississippi River valley. In contrast, the Shinarump contains coarser sandstones and conglomerates. These testify to an episode of mountain building 225 million years ago near present-day Phoenix (Chapter 3). This mountain-building steepened the river courses, allowing them to carry the Shinarump's larger sediment particles toward the Grand Canyon, which then lay downstream.

**Trail Guide:** On AZ Highway 64 drive 11 miles south of Tusayan. At milepost 224 turn left on Forest Road 320. Drive 1.4 miles, then turn left onto Forest Road 340. After another mile, turn right onto Forest Road 340A. Follow this 0.3 mile to its end. Roads 340 and 340A may be impassable when wet.

The trail begins at an interpretive sign at the edge of the parking area. From here, the butte is clearly visible, its right edge consisting of bright red and white cliffs of Moenkopi and Shinarump capped by the black basalt (Photo 47). The trail zigzags across the slope to the left of these cliffs. From the sign the trail ascends, gradually at first, through a pinyon-juniper woodland. Small chunks of basalt fallen from the black cliffs above litter the grass-covered surface, and dark soil covers the Moenkopi Formation, which here comprises the bedrock. When wet, this section of trail becomes a slippery, muddy mess because the Moenkopi's brick-red mudstones rapidly decompose into sticky mud.

About 0.4 mile into the hike the gradient becomes noticeably steeper. The trail begins to zigzag up the butte's southwest flank in a series of switchbacks. At mile 0.5 you reach a short descent to a small saddle, where you get good views of the North Rim. The soil at this point is much thinner, allowing you to more clearly see the red color of the underlying Moenkopi.

*Photo 49. The Missing Pages. The lower cliff of Moenkopi Formation and the upper wall of Shinarump Conglomerate continue the geologic story where the Grand Canyon rocks leave off.*

Less than 100 yards past the saddle you reach a left-hand switchback, where the trail skirts the base of a prominent red cliff. This is the best location to examine the Moenkopi Formation (GPS 35°49.13'N, 112°05.53'W). A 15-yard detour right leads to the outcrop. The Moenkopi cliff consists of red sandstone layers 1 to 10 feet thick separated by much thinner bands of mudstone (Photo 49). The cliff extends several hundred yards to the southeast, and you can see that the mudstones thicken in that direction. The sandstones fill broad, shallow river channels that 240 million years ago crossed expansive, mud-covered floodplains represented by the intervening mudstones. As the channels of these Moenkopi rivers snaked back and forth over time, the floodplain muds and the channel sands were laid upon one another to produce the alternating layers you now see.

Back on the main trail, the path crosses the butte's flank on a rising traverse, reaching its northwest edge and a right-hand switchback at mile 0.65. Another outcrop of red sandstone is visible here, on the butte's north side. It fills a channel carved into the soft mudstones by one of the Moenkopi rivers. From here, you again traverse the butte's flank. At this point, you are on the butte's narrow upper portion, and each traverse is shorter than the last. You reach the southwest edge again at mile 0.7, where you are now above the red Moenkopi cliff you examined below. A mere 10-yard detour at this left-hand switchback provides a good view of the light pink cliff of Shinarump Conglomerate above. Although the Shinarump is composed of conglomerate at many locations, here it consists mainly of sandstone that is coarser than the Moenkopi sandstone below. It is organized into small-scale cross-beds that intersect each other at low angles. Such cross-bedding is characteristic of deposits left by swiftly flowing streams. The Shinarump's soft pink, white, and purple hues are complemented by patches of brilliant orange lichen that have taken up residence on the rock.

The next zig across the butte's flank ends at mile 0.75 with a right switchback. From this turn another red and white Shinarump outcrop is visible on the butte's north side. Next to the trail, blocks of basalt up to 2 feet long dot the slope. They have tumbled from the dark cliffs above in the latest episode of scarp retreat, a process that continues to shrink Red Butte and will eventually erase it from the landscape.

You reach the butte's southwest edge, near the Shinarump cliff, at a left switchback, at mile 0.85. Looking up the slope, you can see the quickly approaching basalt cap, which you reach after 100 yards at the next (right-hand) switchback. The basalt above this switchback is covered with neon-green lichen, which seem to prefer the basalt to the sandstone.

By mile 1, the basalt outcrop becomes continuous and is easily examined from the trail. The rock is compact and contains many tiny, rectangular pits lined with rust. These pits mark the spots where feldspar crystals used to lie. They have since succumbed to the ravages of weathering, leaving only hollow cavities to mark their former existence.

Two final switchbacks in quick succession bring you to the flat surface of the lava flow capping Red Butte. After a short stroll across this tableland, you reach the fire lookout tower, which is listed on the National Historic Lookout Register. Climb up onto the lookout to enjoy the 360-degree views it affords. The Canyon's North Rim is visible to the north. The view to the south is dominated by the volcanoes of the San Francisco volcanic field (Photo 48). The monarch of the field is San Francisco Mountain, the only massif to rise above tree line. It is a 2-million-year-old andesite volcano whose top collapsed less than half a million years ago, leaving a ragged ridge ringing the edge of its former cone. Several peaks crown this ridge, including Humphreys Peak (12,643 feet), the tallest in Arizona. A maze of small, ponderosa-cloaked hills crowd the landscape in front of the mountain. Each hill is a separate cinder cone like the one from which the Red Butte lava flow erupted. A few taller dacite mountains raise their heads above the level of the cinder cones. The prominent peak left of San Francisco Mountain is O'Leary Peak, a neighbor of Sunset Crater. Three similar peaks lie to the right of San Francisco Mountain. From left to right, they are Kendrick Peak, Sitgreaves Peak, and Bill Williams Mountain.

To the southwest lies a smaller, lower range of mountains. These are the peaks of the Mount Floyd volcanic field, a smaller version of the San Francisco field that was active about 8 million years ago. No peaks break the monotony of the flat, grass-covered Kaibab Plateau to the west, right of Mount Floyd, until your gaze reaches the Uinkaret Mountains to the northwest. These, too, are a series of volcanic mountains, with Mount Trumbull their highest peak at 8029 feet. The Uinkarets rise above the remote western portion of the Grand Canyon's North Rim. Geologically recent eruptions from these mountains have repeatedly sent rivers of lava cascading over the North Rim, damming the Colorado River thirteen times within the last 1 million years (Hike 18).

As you survey the world from this lofty perch, it is worth pondering what this spot would look like had you visited it 9 million years ago. Instead of standing on a summit, you would have stood in a shallow wash carved into the Shinarump Conglomerate. Before long, a lava flow issuing from a cinder cone several miles to the south would have filled in the wash with jet-black basalt. That lava flow would ultimately protect this little patch of real estate and its Mesozoic rocks from the erosion that would later lower the surrounding landscape 900 feet, thus preserving Red Butte and a few rare pages from the missing Mesozoic chapter in the Grand Canyon history book.

# HERMIT TRAIL

PATHS OF OUR ANCESTORS

*Track the evolution of life in the Grand Canyon from ancient sea creatures to clawed desert animals to the humans who have explored this beautiful route to the Colorado River.*

LENGTH ■ 8.9 miles

ELEVATION CHANGE ■ 4240 feet

TIME ■ 1–2 days each way

DIFFICULTY ■ Difficult to very difficult; steep, unmaintained trail with marked junctions

BACKCOUNTRY ZONING ■ Threshold; camp only at Hermit Creek Camp (BM7) and Hermit Rapid (BM8)

WATER AND TOILETS ■ Water at Santa Maria Spring, Hermit Creek, and Colorado River. Toilet at Hermit Creek Camp

EMERGENCY SERVICES ■ Phone at Hermits Rest

MAP LIST ■ 1–3, 8

KEY REFERENCES ■ 1, 8, 22, 29

DAY HIKES ■ Dripping Springs Trail junction (3.6 miles round trip); Santa Maria Springs (4.8 miles round trip)

SEASONS ■ Year-round. The west-facing aspect makes it less icy in winter and provides morning shade in summer

**About the Landscape:** The Grand Canyon's rock layers reveal the amazing scope of geologic upheavals that have formed this spectacular landscape, and they also harbor something else just as profound and amazing—fossils of the many ancient organisms that have called this area home. These creatures left behind two types of evidence for modern sleuths: actual fossilized remains, and *trace fossils,* the preserved tracks and trails left by their passage.

The Kaibab and Redwall Limestone formations both contain particularly good fossils of the invertebrate animals that populated the shallow seas covering the Grand Canyon region 260 and 350 million years ago. Along the Hermit Trail, brachiopod, crinoid, coral, sponge, and bryozoan fossils can all be observed in the Kaibab Limestone (Figure 29); some of these are also present in the Redwall. In several other layers, the fossils of the organisms are tougher to locate, but their enduring tracks and burrows are abundant.

By far the most extraordinary trace fossils are individual footprints left by either reptiles or amphibians journeying across the desert sand dunes that covered the area 270 million years ago (Photo 51). Remarkably preserved in the Coconino Sandstone, dozens of trackways, made by several different species, are easily visible without moving a step from the trail. Some of the tracks are merely smudges, but others preserve exquisite detail, right down to the pad prints and pointed claw marks (see photo on dedication page) imprinted by some of the mouse- to cat-sized creatures that passed this way. Trackways a dozen or more prints long afford us an amazingly intimate glimpse into a few moments in these animals' lives as they went about their errands one sunny day so long ago.

Trackways are fairly common in the Coconino, but nowhere are there more abundant or better-preserved ones than along the Hermit Trail, the center of Coconino trackway research since 1918, when a paleontologist named R. S. Lull did extensive work in the area. Researchers have identified the tracks of scorpions, millipedes, and spiders, plus sixteen different varieties of vertebrates. They have also learned that tracks are best preserved when they are made in loose, dry sand that is dampened just prior to burial by additional, protective sediments. Some 270 million years ago, the Hermit Trail lay near the coast at the edge of a vast, Sahara-sized dune field. Periodic coastal fogs, similar to the ones that envelop modern coastal dunes in South America's Atacama and Africa's Namib Deserts, may have provided the moisture necessary to preserve the profusion of tracks present along this trail. Once buried, the tracks were reexposed when erosion removed the layer above, including the individual sand grains that originally filled the delicate tracks.

In addition to this unparalleled prehuman record, the Hermit Trail also embodies a captivating human history. The earliest human occupants to leave evidence of their presence were the Kayenta Anasazi, whose granaries, temporary camps, rock walls, and agave roasting pits are all found in Hermit Basin and along Hermit Creek. In fact, Hermit Camp is built on the site of an old mescal pit.

The first westerners to spend significant time here were mineral prospectors. The Hermit name that adorns so many local features is usually attributed to Louis Boucher, a miner and sometimes hermit who lived at Dripping Springs and tended both an orchard and two mines in Boucher Canyon, just west of Hermit Canyon.

When the Santa Fe Railroad obtained permission to build the Hermit Trail in 1910, human activity exploded in Hermit Creek. By that time the Canyon's tourist trade was booming, and the main trails accessing the river were controlled by miners who charged tolls and restricted visitation (Hikes 3, 5). The railroad wanted unfettered Canyon access for the tourists it brought on its trains, so the Hermit Rim Road (also known as the West Rim Drive) and the Hermit Trail were both constructed between 1910 and 1912. At that time the trail was the finest in the Canyon, and mule trains regularly transported visitors to Hermit Camp, a veritable tent city near the banks of Hermit Creek. Visitors were not deprived of any creature comforts; an aerial tram descended to the camp from nearby Pima Point, supplying the tourists with all the comforts of home. By 1916 telephone service was even available there! The bustle of activity in the Hermit area abruptly ended in 1930, when the Park Service constructed the Kaibab Trail and gained control of the Bright Angel Trail. Their convenient location next to the rim hotels and the rail line doomed Hermit Camp to obscurity, and it was quickly abandoned. Since that time, the Hermit Trail has not been maintained, making this hike a bit more rugged but also quieter than the Bright Angel corridor. Although the tramway and the buildings have been removed, a few reminders of Hermit's tourist heyday still remain. The foundations for some of the Hermit Camp tents are easily seen, and some of the steeper trail sections are constructed of cobblestones, a legacy from an earlier age in which no labor was spared to construct a durable route to explore in the footsteps of our ancestors.

**Trail Guide:** If you have a backcountry permit, drive west along the West Rim Drive to Hermits Rest. If not, take a red shuttle bus, which leaves from a bus stop at the gate blocking the West Rim Drive 200 yards west of Bright Angel Lodge. The trailhead lies at the edge of a dirt parking lot 300 yards west of the gift shop.

Unlike other trails that plunge head-first off the rim, the Hermit Trail sneaks into the Grand Canyon. In fact, the first 0.25 mile heads away from the Canyon toward a small tributary valley as it gently drops down ledges of Kaibab Limestone. Many of the Kaibab outcrops here are stained brown, yellow, and orange by minerals precipitated from water that circulated through the nearby Hermit Fault.

*Photo 50. A fossilized brachiopod in the Kaibab Formation.*

A sweeping right bend at mile 0.25 leads the trail west, where it parallels the small wash for a short distance. In this stretch, watch for outcrops of Kaibab Limestone that exhibit a particularly lumpy texture (GPS 36°03.56'N, 112°12.79'W). These lumps consist of chert that is highly resistant to erosion, so they protrude from the softer, surrounding limestone. Most of the chert lumps have formed around fossils, many of which can still be identified. This is one of the best fossil localities along any Grand Canyon trail and worth spending some time examining. The fossils aren't immediately obvious, but once you tune your eye, you will see them all around. The sponges look like a tangled mass of spaghetti, and the brachiopods resemble clams, with many of them exhibiting a distinct D-shape (Photo 50, Figure 29). The bryozoans come in two varieties: one that looks like finely woven mosquito netting, and the other that looks like a branching twig. The crinoids are small disks, and the horn corals resemble miniature cornucopia. This group of fossils indicates that 260 million years ago, when the Kaibab Limestone was deposited, the Grand Canyon was covered by a warm, shallow, open sea in which these creatures flourished (Figure 30).

A short distance beyond the fossil beds, the trail bends to the north and begins a steeper descent via a series of switchbacks. A view into the impressive depths of Hermit Canyon opens up here. At mile 0.4 a limestone block with six large drill holes sits in the trail, marking your arrival at the Kaibab-Toroweap contact (GPS 36°03.63'N, 112°12.86'W). The outcrops here consist mainly of soft, red and tan mudstones. The trail's gradient lessens, and you begin a series of relatively flat traverses. Along a southwesterly-trending traverse, note how the layers to the left (GPS 36°03.45'N, 112°12.93'W) are gently folded. These rocks were contorted by the upward movement of *evaporite* minerals (such as salt and gypsum) left behind by evaporating seawater along the arid shoreline of the Toroweap Sea 265 million years ago. Evaporites, being less dense than surrounding minerals, tend to migrate upward, distorting the overlying layers in the process (Photo 30).

The lower portion of the Toroweap was deposited in slightly deeper water, where limestones reminiscent of the Kaibab accumulated. The presence of these harder limestones force the trail into another series of switchbacks to navigate the formation's lower reaches. On a switchback at mile 0.9 the trail reaches an obvious transition from brown limestones to the sparkly white, cross-bedded rocks of the Coconino Sandstone (GPS 36°03.38'N, 112°13.08'W). The builders of the Hermit Trail went to great pains to protect this steep, knee-pounding section from erosion by constructing much of its tread out of resistant Coconino cobblestones.

The great, sweeping cross-beds so evident in the Coconino (Photo 35) reveal how it was deposited in a desert the size of the Sahara. *Cross-beds* form

*Photo 51. Tracks that are 270 million years old cross a slab of Coconino Sandstone where they have been exquisitely preserved along the Hermit Trail.*

as sand builds up at the dune's crest, then cascades down the steep lee side. Each thin, inclined sand layer that you see in the Coconino was formed by an individual avalanche of sand grains down a dune's steep face (typically 20 to 30 degrees; Figure 27). Repeated avalanches transfer sand from the upwind to the downwind (lee) side of the dune, so that over time, the dune migrates across the landscape. In many places the trail descends these cross-bed planes. Because these planes once formed the dune's active surface, you should search for vertebrate footprints along these horizons. Keep your eyes peeled during the entire descent, and remember to also scan the flat blocks used to build the trail's low walls.

The highest concentration of tracks is located at mile 1.2 near the end of the Coconino's longest straight section. This west-trending straightaway is cobbled from nearly beginning to end, the most continuous section of cobblestones in the Coconino (GPS 36°03.31'N, 112°13.12'W). Near the end of the straightaway, a set of low rock steps has been constructed immediately left of the trail. From these steps to the 90-degree, right-hand bend 20 yards below, ten long trackways made by animals ranging from mouse- to kitten-size are evident to the left of the trail (Photo 51). Now that you know what you are searching for, you can spot many additional trackways on the slabs below this site. Another concentration lies near the base of the Coconino at mile 1.35, 10 yards before the last (right-hand) bend in a series of six switchbacks.

A particularly good trackway with claw marks and the impressions of foot pads lies on a red-orange outcrop to the left of the trail here (see dedication photo).

Soon after passing these tracks, an abrupt change in rock color marks your passage from the white Coconino to the red Hermit Formation (mile 1.4; GPS 36°03.31'N, 112°13.18'W). The gradient moderates as you enter the broad, gentle valley of Hermit Basin, which was scooped out by erosion of the soft Hermit Formation. The Hermit was deposited by lazy, meandering rivers crossing a flat plain here 280 million years ago. A few sandstone lenses mark the locations of these river channels, but most of the formation is composed of bright red, thin mudstone layers deposited along the rivers' extensive flood-plains. As the trail flattens out, you pass the marked junction with the Waldron Trail at mile 1.5. Another signed junction, this one for the Dripping Springs/Boucher Trails, is reached at mile 1.8. This junction also marks the boundary between the Hermit Formation and the underlying Supai Group. The Hermit Trail takes the right fork, hugging the left side of the wash as it begins a steep, switchbacking descent through the Esplanade Sandstone, the uppermost formation in the Supai Group. Be sure to watch for fossil mudcracks (Color Plate 13) in this area.

The steep descent ends at Santa Maria Spring, a rock resthouse constructed at a trickling spring (mile 2.4). The spring makes a good destination for a day

*Photo 52. Slickensides. The polished surface formed when fault activity heated and melted this rock. Strong minerals later dragged across the surface formed the vertical grooves, which tell us the direction of fault movement.*

*Photo 53. Normal faults slice through and offset Supai Group rocks just left of the shaded slope.*

hike, and it also marks the beginning of a 3-mile-long, nearly horizontal traverse through the Supai Group that is punctuated only by two short, steep descents.

You leave the spring on a gentle, northeastward traverse. New vistas into Hermit Creek open up as you round a series of small points. This section of trail lies near a branch of the Hermit Fault, so many blocks of Supai sandstone littering the area display *slickensides* (smooth, polished surfaces cut by parallel grooves). Slickensides form when movement along a fault creates enough friction to melt a thin film of rock, forming the polished surface. When later fault movement drags strong crystals across the polished face, they score it, creating parallel grooves that indicate the direction of fault movement. To find the slickensides, look for white, polished surfaces on the red sandstone blocks. A particularly good example is found on a 3-foot boulder lying in a dry wash about 0.8 mile beyond the spring (Photo 52).

The first significant descent on this traverse begins about 1.1 miles beyond the spring. Several switchbacks descend through large boulders from an old landslide. The biggest boulder in this pile displays good slickensides on a white and yellow fault surface. Beyond the landslide, the trail resumes its gentle northeastward traverse, following a soft mudstone layer just below a large sandstone cliff.

The traverse's second major descent begins at mile 3.9 (1.5 miles past the spring), where more switchbacks facilitate a drop of almost 400 feet. The trail levels out again as it crosses a flat pass, where the sandstone bedrock has a distinctive orange hue and is cut by numerous thin calcite veins. Both characteristics are calling cards of the Hermit Fault, which passes directly under your feet here.

From the orange pass the trail begins another long, gently descending traverse to Breezy Point, about 1 mile distant. Part of this route runs beneath a tall cliff of overhanging Supai sandstone, on whose underside worm burrows (Photo 86) and mudcracks can be seen. The trail is aiming for a prominent block of shattered and tilted Supai sandstone immediately east of the point (Photo 53). There two subsidiary forks of the Hermit Fault pierce the ridge. The tilted block has been downdropped between these faults, forming a *graben* and causing the distortion of this unlucky rock. The graben's presence becomes much clearer as you near the west-facing amphitheater just south of the point.

As the trail rounds the back of this amphitheater, it weaves between more landslide debris as it descends to the Supai-Redwall contact on the amphitheater's north side (mile 5.3; GPS 36°04.74'N, 112°12.04'W). At this point where the two rock units meet, you are also standing on the eastern of the two fault splays. As you proceed down the trail, you cross into the graben, indicated by the shattered nature of the Supai here. Just 0.1 mile beyond, you bend to the right around Breezy Point, where you cross the western branch of the fault and consequently find yourself back at the Supai–Redwall contact.

*Photo 54. The Hermit Trail's striking Cathedral Spires (along the foreground ridge) formed in fault-weakened blocks of Redwall Limestone.*

From the second contact you can see a saddle 0.2 mile ahead that separates the main ridge from a knob of Redwall Limestone to your left. This saddle marks the end of the long Supai traverse, after which you descend a series of tight switchbacks through the Redwall Limestone. Throughout the descent you stare at a group of small spires adorning the saddle south of Cope Butte. These spires formed because fracturing weakened the rocks along the faults, making them erode more easily. The rock in between fractures is stronger and forms the spires. They resemble cathedral spires and may be the inspiration for this section's name: the Cathedral Stairs (Photo 54).

Because the trail begins its descent along the graben's western fault, you at first see gray Redwall Limestone to your left, but downdropped red Supai Group to your right. Even farther right, a cliff of Redwall towers above the downdropped graben, defining its eastern edge. Just after you round the first right-hand switchback, a 2-foot-long block of limestone with excellent ripple-marks lies to the left of the trail. At the next left switchback, you pass the final block of Supai; the remainder of the descent is solely in the Redwall.

The trail now follows a profusion of switchbacks down the ever-narrowing gully. The first of two significant Redwall fossil localities comes on the ninth switchback below the final red Supai outcrop. It is a sharp, right-hand switchback in the narrow gully at mile 5.9 (GPS 36°04.95′N, 112°11.91′W). By this point, there are no longer any Supai boulders lining the trail. This switchback also marks the end of the cobblestone pavement, although cement covers the straightaway after this bend. Unfortunately, another identifying mark is a bit of graffiti; a few yards below the switchback, the initials "AB" have been chiseled at chest height into a block of limestone to the right of the trail.

The 350-million-year-old fossils at this location have a translucent appearance, and they are slightly darker than the surrounding shiny, gray limestone. Among the many examples here, a few are particularly notable. Above the switchback and to the left of the trail, there are numerous tiny crinoids at head height on either side of a small ash tree overhanging the path. An arm's length up the trail from the "AB" slab, there is an excellent brachiopod specimen at knee height. It is about 2 inches long and has a pronounced D shape, with ridges radiating out from the hinge. Also to the right of the trail, two arm lengths below the "AB" slab, a good cross-section of a crinoid is located at chest level. It is circular, about the size of a nickel, and has septa radiating outward from the center. A palm-sized bryozoan fossil lies to the west of the trail on a straightaway following the next (left) switchback (Figure 29).

From the "AB" slab, five more tight turns lead down to a short, flat section where the trail moves into an even narrower gully to the east. More excellent fossils are found on the outside of the first switchback (a right) below this flat traverse. A ledge at hip height comprises the outside of the bend. Crinoids and bryozoans abound here. The crinoid septa are obvious in both cross-section and in the 1.5- to 2-inch-long longitudinal profiles. The bryozoans resemble mosquito netting, with their gridlike weave of calcite filaments.

Two more switchbacks complete the gully's descent, after which the trail heads northeast across a pleasant tree-filled wash. Two additional switchbacks deposit you at the beginning of a long, northward descent on rubble-covered slopes through the lower Redwall, Temple Butte, and Muav Formations. The trail crosses the Redwall–Temple Butte contact on this rubble near the beginning of the traverse, but the Temple Butte is recognizable in the cliff 40 feet above the trail due to its distinctive purple cast. Farther down, a few small outcrops of Muav Limestone poke out of the rubble to the right of the trail. They illustrate the Muav's typically thin and lumpy beds of gray limestone and are cut by many worm burrows.

The descending traverse ends at the trail's northernmost switchback at mile 6.4. After a short, south-trending straightaway, the trail switchbacks through the lower Muav and upper Bright Angel Shale (Photo 9). The Muav–Bright Angel contact is not exposed on the trail, which descends a rubble-covered slope, but it is evident in the cliff to the north, where the upper limestones give way to thin, green mudstone layers beneath.

The slope moderates as the trail reaches the Tonto Platform, the wide bench that erosion has carved out of the soft Bright Angel Shale in a process similar to the formation of Hermit Basin above. At mile 6.8 the trail reaches a clearly marked junction with the Tonto Trail. The Hermit Trail continues southwestward toward Hermit Creek Camp, now only 1 mile away. For 0.7 mile the route wanders across the platform, past sporadic outcrops of Bright Angel Shale festooned with tubular worm burrows. At mile 7.5 you encounter another signed trail junction. Those bound for the Colorado River and Hermit Rapid should take the right fork; those heading to Hermit Creek Camp should continue straight ahead.

At 0.1 mile past the junction on the way to Hermit Creek Camp, you pass the ruined foundations of the railroad's Hermit Camp. The modern camping area is just 0.2 mile beyond, nestled by the perennial waters of Hermit Creek. You reach the brink of the Tapeats Sandstone directly above the camp, and a short series of switchbacks guide you there through Tapeats outcrops shattered and colored red by fault activity along yet another branch of the Hermit Fault.

**To Hermit Rapid and the Colorado River.** If your destination is Hermit Rapid, take the right fork at the mile 7.5 junction. The trail plunges into an impressive gorge of Tapeats Sandstone before reaching Hermit Creek, which the trail immediately crosses to follow a low terrace on its left (west) side. The route is marked by cairns and the remnants of stonework from the original trail that have survived the flash floods that periodically rake this gorge.

*Photo 55. Pegmatite. This coarse-grained, igneous rock contains dark, rectangular crystals of the mineral hornblende and light, shiny ones of muscovite (white mica).*

The walk along the creek begins in an inspiring gorge of Tapeats Sandstone, passing small waterfalls cascading down the most resistant layers. In places the walls of the gorge are plastered with travertine and salt precipitated by groundwater trickling out at impermeable shale layers. Created by differences in weathering resistance, numerous large overhangs and weirdly shaped cavities adorn the walls, giving the gorge a gothic façade.

After descending a ramp on the left bank, the trail crosses the creek. Almost immediately afterward, the crystalline rocks lying below the Great Unconformity emerge from the creek bed. They are soft and weathered here, making them difficult to distinguish from the Tapeats, but you soon begin to see the Vishnu Schist's vertical foliation as well as vertical granite dikes, all of which stop abruptly at the Great Unconformity below the lowest horizontal Tapeats layer. The walls of Tapeats quickly rise high above you as you hike deeper into the crystalline rocks of lower Hermit Creek.

About 150 yards downstream, the trail crosses back to the left bank and immediately climbs onto a terrace 15 feet above the creek. The trail dips down again before clambering up over a small outcrop, still on the stream's west bank. Here there is an extraordinary pegmatite dike slicing across large outcrops of Vishnu Schist (GPS 36°05.30'N, 112°12.64'W). The pegmatite has exceptionally large crystals of clear quartz, pink potassium feldspar, silver muscovite, and black hornblende (Photo 55). Many of these crystals are several inches long with unusually perfect faces. The great variety of minerals makes this an outstanding place to examine pegmatite.

A short distance below the dike, a major tributary enters from the west. About 0.2 mile farther, the trail again crosses to the creek's right side before returning to the left bank for the duration of the hike. Large clusters of

176

muscovite mica and several pegmatite dikes decorate the walls of Vishnu Schist, which soar ever higher above your head. You reach Hermit Rapid and many good campsites 1.4 miles below the trail junction and 8.9 miles from the rim.

During your journey, you may be lucky enough to catch a glimpse of a bighorn sheep, mule deer, rattlesnake, or other modern inhabitant of Hermit Creek. Part of the modern beauty of this seemingly ancient spot comes from the hard work you endured to get here, following in the footprints, tracks, and burrows of the many creatures who have called this place home.

# DRIPPING SPRINGS TRAIL

Hike 10

### DRIPPING SPRINGS CREATE AMAZING THINGS

*Traverse two of the Grand Canyon's characteristic amphi-theaters to observe first-hand the process of spring sapping that formed them, then rejuvenate yourself by the springs that for years sustained the Canyon's most renowned hermit.*

LENGTH ▪ 3.2 miles

ELEVATION CHANGE ▪ 1480-foot descent and 400-foot climb

TIME ▪ 2–3 hours each way

DIFFICULTY ▪ Moderately difficult; tread is sometimes rocky

BACKCOUNTRY ZONING ▪ Hermit Loop day-use area; no camping allowed

WATER AND TOILETS ▪ Water at Dripping Springs; toilets at Hermits Rest

EMERGENCY SERVICES ▪ Phone at Hermits Rest

MAP LIST ▪ 1–3, 8

KEY REFERENCES ▪ 7, 8, 22

SEASONS ▪ Year-round

**About the Landscape:** Dripping Springs is one of the best day-hike destinations in the Grand Canyon. It requires only moderate exertion but provides a real below-the-rim experience, passing spectacular scenery and a cornucopia of geologic highlights.

One focal point is the unparalleled glimpse of spring sapping, one of the most important erosional processes that carves the Grand Canyon's tributaries. Even a casual glance at a topographic map reveals that the tributary canyons here differ from those in many other landscapes. Instead of being narrow, small-scale models of the main canyon that slowly merge with the hillsides, Grand Canyon tributaries are headed by broad, curving *amphitheaters* whose upstream limits are defined not by a gradual melding with the surrounding landscape but rather by vertical cliffs towering hundreds of feet above small

a.
b.
c.

*Figure 32. The differences between topography created by spring sapping and stream erosion. a. Aerial view of typical steep, amphitheater-shaped Grand Canyon tributary canyons. b. Dramatic amphitheaters created by spring sapping in the Grand Canyon. c. Typical stream-eroded tributaries that merge gently upstream into the hillsides.*

and usually dry washes at their bases (Figure 32). Often, a single tributary will sprout multiple amphitheaters near its head, resembling a bunch of cauliflower on a topographic map. Clearly, some geologic process is dominant here that is of minor importance in most other landscapes. That process is *spring sapping,* the erosion of sediment by springs. However, because springs must emerge from canyon walls, spring sapping could not occur here until the Canyon was carved.

As the Colorado River began to cut the Grand Canyon, it started as a dramatic and narrow slit approximately 2000 feet wide, the distance across the present Inner Gorge. Because this slit was carved into horizontal sedimentary rock layers, it immediately began to widen through another erosional process called *scarp retreat,* the withdrawal of a cliff line through time. This process is triggered by differences in the rock layers' physical strength and ability to transmit water. The Canyon's limestone layers are the most resistant to physical weathering, sandstones are a bit softer, and mudstones such as the Hermit and Bright Angel Formations are crumbly and very easily eroded. When the Colorado reached a soft layer, it eroded back so quickly that the more resistant layers above began to overhang it.

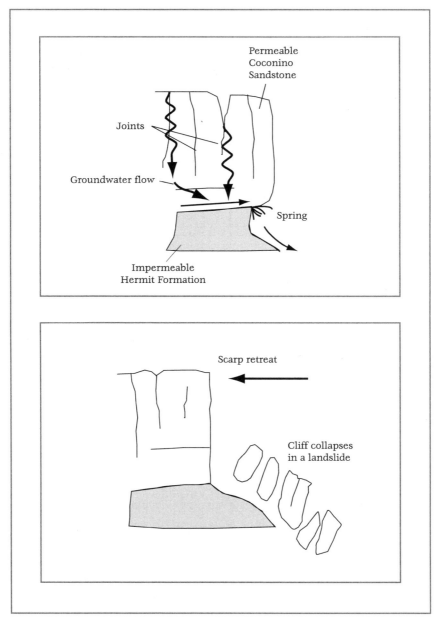

Permeable
Coconino
Sandstone

Joints

Groundwater flow

Spring

Impermeable
Hermit Formation

Scarp retreat

Cliff collapses
in a landslide

*Figure 33. Spring sapping creates overhangs that collapse when joints are undercut, causing scarp retreat.*

All rock layers are criss-crossed by *joints*, cracks caused by tectonic strain or the release of pressure after overlying or adjacent rocks are removed. When an overhang becomes so large that it intersects one of these joints, all support is lost, and it collapses in a landslide (Figure 33, Color Plate 18). In this manner the escarpment retreats over and over again, widening the abyss. Because the wall falls away along a vertical joint, the newly exposed cliff face also tends to be vertical.

In this way, the Grand Canyon was born and began to widen. Once its walls were formed, springs began to issue from them. Much of the moisture that falls on the Kaibab Plateau percolates into the ground, where it slowly wiggles its way down through the rock layers, pulled along by gravity. Its progress is slow but steady through sandstone and limestone layers, but where it encounters a mudstone, like the Hermit Formation, its platy mineral grains block further downward water movement just like shingles do on a roof. Instead, the water flows parallel to the layers until it issues onto the surface as a spring (Figure 33).

The flow of water from a spring slowly plucks individual sediment particles from the rock and carries them downstream. Only a few grains at a time are involved in this "spring-sapping" process, but over tens to hundreds of thousands of years, so many grains are removed that eventually the cliff above overhangs the spring. A classic example of this phenomenon is Dripping Springs, where a cliff of permeable Coconino Sandstone overhangs the soft, impermeable Hermit Formation (Color Plate 16). When the undercut gets large enough to intersect a vertical joint, the cliff collapses in a heap of rubble, effectively lengthening the tributary. As this process is repeated over and over, the tributary can grow very long. The half-mile-wide gorge originally carved by the Colorado River has, through the processes of scarp retreat and spring sapping, expanded to its present width of over 9 miles between the rims!

The process of spring sapping also accounts for the characteristic cauliflower shape of the tributary canyons. Because scarp retreat is fastest where springs are located, an initially straight cliff rapidly (geologically speaking) becomes curved. The mechanics of groundwater movement tend to focus the flow of water into these concave areas, thus increasing the spring's discharge, which in turn accelerates the amphitheater's formation. This positive feedback helps the dominant tributary canyons grow ever larger. Where multiple springs exist, their amphitheaters eventually encroach upon one another, forming a spire (Figure 34, Color Plate 3).

One question regarding this whole process remains. Why does spring sapping not occur in other landscapes? In fact, it does. However, spring sapping is a very slow process. In moist climates, so much water flows down the tributaries that stream erosion dominates, totally swamping any sign of spring sapping. These stream processes result in the upstream-diminishing tributaries so familiar to most landscapes (Figure 32c). In contrast, in the Grand Canyon and much of the Southwest, the arid climate keeps most streams from flowing more

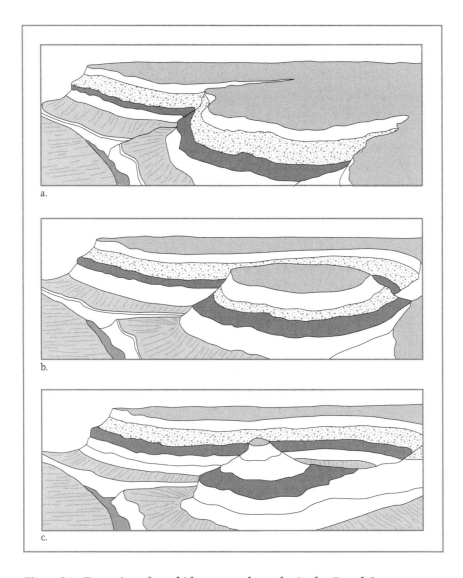

*Figure 34. Formation of amphitheaters and temples in the Grand Canyon.*
*a. Tributaries and springs carve amphitheater-shaped side canyons, which*
*eventually meet, isolating mesas (b). c. Continued erosion of the mesa creates*
*a spire. Modified from Key Reference 39 (see Appendix D).*

than a few days or weeks each year. Spring sapping suddenly becomes an
important force in landscape formation. The result is the impressive series of
amphitheaters you tiptoe around on the Dripping Springs Trail, along with thousands of other amphitheaters dominating the Grand Canyon landscape.

**Trail Guide:** Access is via the Hermit Trail (Hike 9).

Because the first part of this hike repeats the upper Hermit Trail (Hike 9), follow that description to the Hermit-Dripping Springs Trail junction 1.8 miles from the rim. The Dripping Springs Trail takes the left fork at this junction, which is located on outcrops of brick-red Hermit Formation. After a brief climb, the trail settles into a nearly flat traverse through the Hermit Shale. Two miles from the rim, the trail curves left around the nose of a small ridge, and you are treated to a view of the first of two impressive amphitheaters you will contour en route to Dripping Springs. The trail tiptoes its way around the horseshoe on a shelf carved in the Hermit Formation. The walking is easy, but the situation is dramatic. The shelf is perched between a 1200-foot escarpment of Coconino Sandstone, Toroweap Formation, and Kaibab Limestone soaring up to the rim and an equally impressive, if somewhat smaller, 800-foot-high cliff of Supai Group rocks below.

As you travel along the amphitheater's western flank, you are treated to exceptional views of the narrow, vertical slot carved by upper Hermit Creek through the 400-foot-thick Redwall Limestone below. At this point the Canyon walls plunge nearly half a vertical mile across the same horizontal distance. The shelf you are traversing is practically the only respite from this unrelenting drop.

At mile 2.4 you complete the traverse of the first amphitheater at a sweeping left turn around a small ridge end, where the second, equally impressive, amphitheater begins. To negotiate this one, the trail must descend to the thick sandstones of the uppermost Supai Group in a couple of places, but each time it quickly returns to the Hermit Formation. Keep your eye out for ripplemarks and mudcracks on the outcrops here. As the trail swings around the horseshoe's western flank, it has to circumvent the rubble from a small landslide. At mile 2.6 you round another point, completing your journey around the twin amphitheaters. Here you begin a gentle climb up the south side of a small wash.

For the rest of the trip to Dripping Springs, be sure to watch for fossils in the numerous blocks of Kaibab Limestone fallen from the rim. Most of these blocks have a distinctive, lumpy texture formed by chert nodules that protect large numbers of well-preserved brachiopod, bryozoan, sponge, and crinoid fossils (Figure 29). Not far beyond the second amphitheater, the trail has to squeeze left of a prominent white boulder. This boulder contains many brachiopod fossils as well as some lacy bryozoans. Thirty yards farther (GPS 36°03.59'N, 112°14.12'W), a 15-by-10-foot boulder to the right of the trail contains more brachiopods and some fossils resembling twigs, which are branched bryozoans.

At mile 2.7 you reach the signed junction with the Boucher Trail, which heads right on its way to Boucher Creek. Both the Dripping Springs and Boucher Trails were built during the 1890s by Louis Boucher, the miner for whom Hermit Creek was named. He lived in a tent at Dripping Springs, but he regularly commuted down the Boucher Trail to his mining claims in lower Boucher Creek. He also tended a seventy five-tree orchard and a garden there, where he grew oranges, peaches, figs, melons, grapes, and a variety of vegetables throughout the year.

The Dripping Springs Trail continues straight ahead. A short distance beyond the junction, the trail crosses the Dripping Springs wash for the first time. A massive, 30-by-30-foot block of Kaibab Limestone several feet right (north) of the trail is loaded with fossil brachiopods and sponges. After another 100 yards, the trail crosses back to the south side of the wash, then switchbacks twice 0.25 mile beyond the junction. At 200 yards past the switchbacks, a prominent 5-by-3-foot slab of white Coconino Sandstone rests just left of the trail. A set of thumbnail-sized vertebrate tracks ascend the slab face tilted toward you. Claw marks are even visible on some of these 270-million-year-old prints!

You reach Dripping Springs 3.2 miles from Hermits Rest. The springs trickle off the lip of a Coconino overhang that has been undercut by spring sapping (Color Plate 16) along the soft, red Hermit Formation below. Maidenhair ferns and mosses cluster around the springs, and riparian vegetation flourishes in the wash below. A ring of rocks has been constructed beneath the drip to trap the water in a small puddle.

Notice that the Hermit here has weathered in a distinctive pattern of bulbous, rounded blocks. Known as *spheroidal weathering,* this pattern is formed by water that percolates through a gridwork of joints, rounding the edges of the blocks between the joints.

Another interesting feature here is the presence of giant mudcracks in the upper Hermit Formation. Just below the spring, protruding ribs of blonde sandstone in the brick-red Hermit end at the base of the Coconino cliff above (Color Plate 16). These mudcracks reveal the presence of a gap in time, known as a *disconformity,* between the Hermit and the Coconino (Figure 46). After the Hermit was deposited by rivers meandering across a vast plain, the climate began to dry out. Huge mudcracks formed on the floodplain. No sediments were deposited during this time, creating a gap in the rock record. Further drying created sand dunes, which soon marched across the landscape. As these dunes covered the former floodplain, the blonde sand filled in the mudcracks. Today, these sand-filled areas are more resistant to erosion than the surrounding mudstones, so they form the protrusions you see here.

The Dripping Springs Trail continues up to the rim above the spring, but because this route involves a long car shuttle on rough dirt roads, it is rarely used. It is far easier to retrace your steps, giving you the chance to spot more blonde mudcracks as you wind around the double amphitheaters. If, on the way back, your progress seems sluggish, pause and contemplate the incredibly slow chain of geologic events that allow a drip of water to carve a majestic amphitheater and expand the Grand Canyon.

# TONTO TRAIL

Hike 11

JOURNEY TO THE BRINK

*Traverse one of the most impressive portions of the Tonto Platform, viewing rock spires, thundering rapids, and the Canyon's rarest rocks as you tiptoe along the brink of the precipitous Inner Gorge.*

LENGTH ▦ 12.2 miles

ELEVATION CHANGE ▦ 600-foot climb and 1200-foot drop between Indian Garden and the Hermit Trail

TIME ▦ 2–4 days, including detours to Colorado River

DIFFICULTY ▦ Difficult; relatively flat but long and accessed by more difficult trails

BACKCOUNTRY ZONING ▦ Threshold; camp only at Indian Garden (CIG), Horn Creek (BL4), Salt Creek (BL5), Cedar Spring (BL6), Monument Creek (BL7), Granite Rapid (BL8), and Hermit Camp (BM7)

WATER AND TOILETS ▦ Treated water at Indian Garden; perennial water at Monument and Hermit Camps. Do not drink water near Horn Creek due to radiation hazard. Toilets available at all campsites

EMERGENCY SERVICES ▦ Ranger station at Indian Garden and phone at Hermits Rest

MAP LIST ▦ 1–3, 8

KEY REFERENCES ▦ 1, 8, 23, 30, 31

DAY HIKES ▦ Indian Garden to Plateau Point (3 miles round trip); Granite Rapid to the Monument (3 miles round trip from river)

SEASONS ▦ Year-round, but very hot in summer and potentially icy access trails in winter

**About the Landscape:** The Tonto Trail is a pleasant change of pace because instead of descending into or climbing out of the Canyon, it traverses the nearly flat Tonto Platform. In its entirety, the trail is over 90 miles long. The stretch between the Bright Angel and Hermit Trails is the most popular section of this lengthy route because it is easily accessible, it visits some of the most spectacular scenery, and it creates a convenient loop hike with reliable water sources. Beautiful vistas open up at every turn and include some surprises, from The Monument, the area's most impressive monolith, to glimpses of the Canyon's rarest rocks. Although this trail constrains itself to one geologic layer for most of its length, it is anything but monotonous.

The Tonto Platform is the most distinctive bench in the eastern Grand Canyon (Photo 56), a strong horizontal element in a mainly vertical world. It provides a dramatic perspective because Tonto hikers are simultaneously enveloped by the soaring walls above and poised at the brink of the Inner Gorge below.

*Photo 56. The Tonto Platform, cut in the soft Bright Angel Shale, forms the prominent bench in the eastern Grand Canyon.*

The platform owes its existence to the difference in strength between the soft Bright Angel Shale and the hard, underlying Tapeats Sandstone. Like most rivers, the Colorado tends to cut vertically into its bed when it encounters resistant rock layers like the Tapeats. In contrast, when it finds its bed composed of easily eroded materials like the Bright Angel, it begins to meander about, expending more of its energy widening its valley than cutting downward.

As the Colorado River sliced through the resistant Redwall and Muav Limestones, it formed a narrow gorge, similar to the ones upstream in Marble Canyon and downstream near Havasu Creek. Once the river breached the lower Muav, it found itself in the Bright Angel's soft mudstones, where it could lazily meander back and forth the same way that it does today near Tanner Creek, where the riverbed is formed of the equally soft Dox Formation. In the process of meandering, the Colorado would undercut some of its flanking cliffs. Eventually, the weight of the overlying rock would cause the undercut sections to collapse, thus widening the Canyon. Eventually, the river carved its way down into the hard Tapeats Sandstone, where it again formed a narrow gorge. Below the Tapeats it encountered the even harder Precambrian crystalline rocks; the result is the steep and dramatic Inner Gorge. The former river valley in the Bright Angel was left stranded, forming a platform poised above the abyss.

**Trail Guide:** Access is via the Bright Angel and Hermit Trails (Hikes 5 and 9).

This section of the Tonto Trail begins at Indian Garden, 50 yards beyond the toilets. At the junction with the Bright Angel Trail, a sign for Plateau Point directs you to the left. Olive-drab cliffs of Muav Limestone rise to the southwest, but the trail remains in the Bright Angel Shale. The Bright Angel is so soft that erosion easily reduces it to green and tan rubble, so few outcrops are present. The green cast is due to the presence of the mineral *glauconite,* a green, platy mineral that forms in place directly on the seafloor. Its presence reveals that sediments accumulated exceptionally slowly on the floor of the Bright Angel Sea 530 million years ago.

At mile 0.7 the trail reaches a junction with the Plateau Point Trail, which offers one of the Canyon's best panoramic views of the Inner Gorge. If you have the time, it is an excursion not to be missed!

## RIM OF THE WORLD: PLATEAU POINT

Plateau Point is a gentle, 1.5-mile stroll from Indian Garden. It provides a wonderful sunset view for those camping there, and extremely strong hikers can use it as a day-trip destination from the South Rim. There is little geology exposed along the trail because it crosses the flat, rubble-covered bench of the Tonto Platform (Photo 56) the entire way. So instead of examining outcrop, look for lumpy, cylindrical worm burrows (Photo 86) on the small, flat slabs of rock littering the ground around the trail.

Your arrival at the edge of Plateau Point could not be any greater contrast to the flat, brushy plain you crossed to get there! Below your feet, the walls of the Inner Gorge plunge 1300 feet straight down to the Colorado River (Photo 57). Tapeats Sandstone outcrops surround you at the point. The many cylindrical indentations in the rock are the fossilized burrows of worms that rooted through the sandy seafloor here 545 million years ago. *Ripplemarks* (Photo 20) left by waves washing across the beach can also be seen on these rock surfaces.

The Tapeats forms a horizontally layered, 400-foot-tall wall that overlies cliffs of dark Vishnu Schist and pink Zoroaster Granite, which plunge to the river below. On the north side, the Inner Gorge is capped by a group of tilted rocks, including the bright orange Hakatai Shale. These rocks are part of the Grand Canyon Supergroup, a series of Precambrian sedimentary layers absent along the Bright Angel Trail. They lie in an ancient trough left behind when a supercontinent ripped apart here 750 million years ago (Figure 8).

*Photo 57. The Inner Gorge. The horizontal Tapeats Sandstone overlies the foreboding Vishnu Schist and Zoroaster Granite, which plunge to the Colorado River below.*

At the trail junction, the Tonto veers left to begin a northwest-trending traverse across the broad, blackbrush-covered Tonto Platform. Where the trail crosses small washes, outcrops reveal that the Bright Angel consists of numerous paper thin, green shale layers interbedded with slightly thicker, tan- and brown-colored sandstone layers. The shales accumulated through the slow settling of mud to the seafloor. In contrast, each sandstone layer was deposited suddenly by a storm that raked the coast, sending sand streaming down into the quiet, offshore waters where the Bright Angel muds were accumulating.

At mile 1.9, the trail bends to the left (southwest) at the edge of the impressive Horn Creek gorge. The view to the south encompasses soaring rock walls with a prominent metal tower perched on the brink at the South Rim. This is the headframe for the Orphan Lode Mine, which began as a copper mine in 1893. It never turned much of a profit until the uranium boom of the 1950s. The mine then produced over $40 million worth of uranium ore, including the highest-grade ore ever extracted in the United States. The ore formed when uranium- and copper-laden water percolated through a *breccia pipe,* a tube of rock rubble created when an ancient cave in the Redwall Limestone collapsed (Figure 24). When they flow, the waters of Horn Creek have elevated levels of radioactivity because they travel across these uranium ores, both in natural exposures and in the waste rock left from the mine. Because of this hazard, it is important that you heed the warnings and not drink from Horn Creek.

*Photo 58. Ancient island. To the left, the Tapeats Sandstone at the rim of the Inner Gorge stands 200 feet thick, but quickly thins toward the center as it drapes over an underlying knob of granite. This knob once formed a small island in an encroaching sea.*

The trail reaches Horn Creek Camp 2.5 miles from Indian Garden. From camp, the trail climbs out the west side of the wash, then crosses Horn Creek's west fork at mile 2.9. Here the trail reaches the Bright Angel Shale–Tapeats Sandstone contact, but as the trail clambers out the far side of the wash, it passes back into the Bright Angel. At mile 3.3, you can peer down into the gorge you have been traversing and see the confluence of Horn Creek's two branches. They join near the Great Unconformity, the contact between the Tapeats and the underlying, 1713 million-year-old Horn Creek Pluton, part of the Zoroaster Granite.

At mile 3.9 the trail rounds the point separating Horn Creek from a much smaller creek to the west. This is a good place to see an island that once rose above the sea in which the Tapeats Sandstone was deposited (Figure 28). Look to the northeast at the Inner Gorge's north wall. To the left the cliff of Tapeats Sandstone forming the inner rim is about 200 feet thick. However, toward the right, it thins down to only 30 feet as it arches gently over the top of a Zoroaster Granite knob (Photo 58). That knob formed a small island while 200 feet of Tapeats beach sands were deposited around it. Eventually, as sea level rose, the island was inundated and buried by sand, forming the thinner Tapeats cap now covering the knob.

From the point, the trail climbs gradually but steadily to a pass north of Dana Butte. The trail's tread is noticeably green here, thanks to an abundance of glauconite flakes. Numerous worm burrows (short, fat, protruding tubes) riddle the Bright Angel rocks, both in outcrop and in float blocks. The worms formed these burrows as they foraged for food in the mud accumulating on the floor of the Bright Angel Sea (Photo 86).

You crest the pass at mile 4.4 (GPS 36°06.04'N, 112°08.83'W), where a 30-foot jaunt northward to the top of a small knob provides a spectacular view into the Inner Gorge. The view encompasses the usual Tapeats Sandstone rim overlying a rugged ravine of Precambrian crystalline rocks, but this vista also offers something unusual. Look toward the tributary canyon (Ninetyonemile Canyon) due north of this knob, where a small landslide scar is visible just left (west) of the main drainage. At the head of this scar, an outcrop of greenish black, slope-forming rock lies between cliffs of schist with prominent vertical foliation. This green patch is a pod of *ultramafic* rock, one of only half a dozen that exist in the Grand Canyon. These rocks formed when exceptionally heavy, iron-rich crystals settled to the bottom of a magma chamber beneath the Yavapai Arc before the other minerals solidified about 1750 million years ago (see Chapter 1).

At mile 4.75 the trail rounds another point, this one offering exceptional views of Trinity Creek's twisting labyrinth. The Great Unconformity is visible on the gorge's western side. Here, a prominent, 50-foot-thick section of

*Photo 59. The Great Unconformity, representing 1200 million years of missing time, separates the horizontally bedded Tapeats Sandstone above from the darker Vishnu Schist below. The light, rubble-strewn area at the boundary is the top of the Vishnu, which was heavily weathered before deposition of the Tapeats.*

light-colored, slope-forming rock separates the Tapeats from the darker, cliff-forming crystalline rocks below (Photo 59). This light rock is actually the up-permost portion of the crystalline rocks, but it was drastically altered by an extended period of weathering some time between 750 and 545 million years ago, when these rocks sat at the earth's surface. The encroachment of the Tapeats Sea left this heavily weathered and bleached zone sandwiched between the darker, unaltered crystalline rocks below and the newly deposited Tapeats Sandstone above.

From here the trail begins a long, winding traverse along the flanks of two amphitheaters (Figure 32), one carved by Salt Creek and the other by its smaller, eastern companion. This traverse stays in the Bright Angel for 0.5 mile, then drops onto the Tapeats Sandstone at mile 5.4. Sixty yards beyond this contact, you cross a tiny wash. The Great Unconformity, with a 20-foot-thick layer of weathered crystalline rocks below, is visible looking down the wash.

The trail remains in the uppermost Tapeats for 0.5 mile before ascending back into the Bright Angel at the crossing of another tiny wash at mile 5.9. In this wash, look for a large, 10-foot-by-5-foot block of Bright Angel resting next to a 15-foot-high shale outcrop. This block is crisscrossed with especially large, impressive worm burrows up to 0.5 inch wide and several inches long. Ten feet beyond this block is another, south-leaning boulder, this one creased with 1.5-inch-long tubular indentations that are also burrows. Burrows on the underside of sedimentary layers protrude; those on upper bedding surfaces form indentations.

At mile 6.1 you cross the head of Salt Creek's companion stream. A short westward jog in the trail soon brings you to the brink of the stunning Tapeats gorge cut by Salt Creek. As you traverse above it, you slowly descend through layers of very coarse-grained sandstone. At mile 6.7 a right-hand switchback marks the beginning of a short, steep drop into the gorge, followed by a crossing of Salt Creek. A short walk up the wash leads to a series of switchbacks out the western side. You reach Salt Creek Camp at mile 6.8 (GPS 36°05.09'N, 112°09.79'W). The camp and toilets lie 50 yards upstream along a marked path. The Tonto Trail veers right here, beginning a long, northward traverse through the Bright Angel Shale back toward the Colorado River.

At mile 6.9 the trail crosses a small tributary wash with enormous boulders of Redwall Limestone scattered around it. Ribbons of red chert wind across these boulders, sticking out in bold relief because chert is more resistant to the elements than the surrounding limestone. You cross a small, east-trending wash at mile 7.3. Looking downcanyon, you get another good view of the Great Unconformity on the east flank of Salt Creek. The weathered horizon is especially obvious here, where it is so soft that it forms a hollow undercutting the Tapeats. For the next 0.7 mile the trail parallels Salt Creek's ever-deepening gorge. Although the crystalline rocks on the gorge floor appear light in color, a close look reveals alternating light and dark bands, a characteristic of the metamorphic rock gneiss (Figure 43). Until recently geologists believed this rock, named the Trinity Gneiss, was older than 1800 million years, which would make it one of the oldest rocks in the Canyon. However, recent radiometric dating has revealed that this gneiss is "merely" 1733 million years old, making it one of the earliest Zoroaster Granite plutons to intrude the Vishnu Schist. This was before the peak of metamorphism, so the Trinity Granite was metamorphosed, becoming the Trinity Gneiss.

After tiptoeing along the very brink of the Inner Gorge for a stretch, the trail rounds a point at mile 8, where it begins heading south, bound for Cedar Spring Camp. A gradual descent through the Bright Angel brings you to the Tapeats contact by mile 8.4. The trail soon clambers over a low ridge, then descends gently to Cedar Spring Creek and its campsites at mile 8.8. Cedar Spring only provides water seasonally.

From Cedar Spring Camp the trail leads westward before rounding a minor point at mile 8.9, where the path turns southwest and quickly crests a small

*Photo 60. The Monument. This impressive monolith consists of Tapeats Sandstone except for its narrow base, which is made of Trinity Gneiss, a 1733 million-year-old pluton in the Zoroaster Granite.*

hill. Here you get your first look at the gorge of Monument Creek, which you will spend the next 2 miles traversing. The trail drops off the hill into a small valley before turning left (south) to traverse around the gorge. After rounding a 90-degree left-hand bend at mile 9.4, you get your first view of the tall rock monolith that gives the creek its name (Photo 60). The amphitheater at the head of Monument Creek is called The Abyss, and from here it is easy to see why. Very little scarp retreat has occurred along the Toroweap and Hermit Formations, the typical slope-formers, so the wall is one of the most precipitous in the park. At this viewpoint you again reach the Bright Angel-Tapeats contact, and at mile 9.8 you begin descending steeply through the Tapeats itself.

At 100 yards into this descent, you negotiate a right switchback through mustard-yellow Tapeats outcrops. This discoloration is the first indication that you are approaching a fault zone. The trail becomes rocky where the fault has shattered the sandstone. The path descends into Monument Creek through good Tapeats exposures consisting of very coarse-grained sand and a few pebbles. The pebbles are mostly rounded, yellow quartz grains, but a few consist of red granite that came from the weathered zone below the Great Unconformity.

At mile 10 you reach the floor of Monument Creek wash. No water flows here during dry periods, but a fault-controlled spring 100 yards downstream provides the camp with perennial water. The trail enters Monument Camp at mile 10.1.

This is the most pleasant camp on the trail, equipped with lots of shade trees, a magnificent side hike to the Colorado River (see below), and a toilet.

The camp lies within the fault zone you discovered while descending into the wash. Immediately downstream from camp, a large, blocky Tapeats tower is the most prominent feature. On its right side it is connected to the main cliff by a saddle. A small, tight stairstep fold (a *monocline*) underlies the saddle, and the sandstone all around it is bleached. This tiny monocline sits directly above the fault, and the bleaching is due to large volumes of water that have flowed through the porous fault zone over time.

The camp sprawls across the next 250 yards. The final sites are situated at the junction between the Tonto and Monument Trails, right at the Great Unconformity. Tent site 6 nestles in a hollow formed by erosion of the weathered horizon below the Tapeats. As you sit in your camp chair at this unique site, admiring the spectacular view of The Monument (Photo 60), your head rests against 545-million-year-old Tapeats Sandstone while your feet are planted on weathered, 1700-million-year-old crystalline rocks. Your body thus spans a gap in time equivalent to one quarter the age of the earth!

At the junction, the Monument Trail follows the right fork on its way to the Colorado River. The Tonto Trail continues straight ahead, immediately climbing out of Monument Wash along a steep side stream. Seasonal springs in this beautiful tributary nourish a luxuriant growth of tall grasses, and the view of The Monument behind you is inspiring, especially at sunrise.

## MONUMENTAL DEBRIS

The 1.5-mile-long Monument Trail is an outstanding side hike that you won't want to miss after coming this far! From the Tonto-Monument Trail junction, the Monument Trail quickly descends directly below The Monument, making its closest approach at the third switchback. The Monument's pedestal consists of gray Trinity Gneiss cut by a pink pegmatite, whose clear quartz, pink potassium feldspar, and black biotite crystals are easy to spot. These crystalline rocks exhibit a sulfur-yellow discoloration caused by fluids percolating through the fault zone that runs through camp. Similar fluids percolating through the Tapeats may have cemented the rock of The Monument extra well, thus contributing to the formation of this singular monolith.

More tight switchbacks lead to the floor of a tributary wash 0.2 mile from the junction. This tributary is lined with 10-foot-high walls of loosely packed *conglomerate,* the legacy of a debris flow that roared down the wash in the geologically recent past. Debris flows are swiftly moving mixtures of water, mud, boulders, trees, and anything else that happens to be in the way. They flow as swiftly as a river, but they have the power and heft of a glacier. They are extremely efficient at scouring the channels they flow down because the debris they carry is dragged across the ground at a high rate of speed. Where they come to a stop, they deposit everything they have carried with them, such as the 15-foot-tall boulders that tower above the junction with Monument Creek at mile 0.25.

Fifty yards downstream, the gorge's 40-foot-tall left wall is composed of gneiss, with granite and quartz veins running parallel to its foliation. The veins were injected under pressure and found the foliation to be the path of least resistance. The black rocks that are so common in this area are schist created by the metamorphism of ancient basalt flows.

About 1 mile from the trail junction, the dark schists give way to lighter schists created by metamorphism of sedimentary rocks and volcanic ash. These rocks have been intensely folded, but you wouldn't realize this if it weren't for the many pink pegmatite veins slicing through them. In places these veins have been crumpled like an accordion, revealing the great extent to which these rocks have been folded (Color Plate 2).

You hear the Colorado River long before you reach it. The deep-throated roar of Granite Rapid bounces off the walls of Vishnu Schist, announcing the river's location several bends before you reach it at mile 1.5. Granite is one of the biggest rapids on the river; if you're lucky, you may see a river party challenging its huge waves (Photo 61). It is a typical Grand Canyon rapid in that it was created by debris flows that spilled from Monument Wash into the Colorado, restricting its channel and filling it full of boulders. Climb the small dunes to Granite Camp for a good view of the triangular debris cone projecting from the wash. The Colorado pools up above this cone, becoming glassy-smooth before bursting into the maelstrom below. Over the millennia the river has removed the buildup from countless Monument Creek debris flows, but no sooner does it remove one flow than it is confronted with another! Glen Canyon Dam has made the Colorado's job much harder, as it is no longer able to flood the riverbed and move the larger rocks downstream. Consequently, the biggest rocks deposited by earlier debris flows are now joined by those from more recent flows, resulting in a jam-up

*Photo 61. A raft crashes through Granite Rapid at the mouth of Monument Creek.*

of boulders that are gradually making the Grand Canyon's biggest rapids even larger and nastier.

Although the dam prevents the river from removing the rapids' larger rocks, it is speeding up the removal of sand from the Canyon's camping beaches. In the past, huge floods carrying sand from far upstream deposited it high above the average water line to replenish the beaches. Now, however, Lake Powell traps all of the sediment that used to be delivered from the Upper Colorado, leaving only the Paria and Little Colorado tributaries as sources of sand. With their sand supply thus reduced by about 85 percent, the beaches inevitably began to erode. Dramatic daily fluctuations in the dam's water releases to fulfill peak power demands added to the problem by creating daily mini-floods just big enough to erode the beaches rather than replace them. The beaches, the creatures and plants that inhabit them, and the Puebloan (Anasazi) artifacts found on them all began to vanish at an alarming rate. Scientists and policymakers teamed up to try to save the beaches. Glen Canyon's water release schedule was altered, and a series of large experimental floods began in 1996. These actions have slowed but not stopped the erosion. Vigorous efforts continue, but it is by no means certain that the beaches can be saved.

The Tonto Trail finishes its climb out of the tributary wash at mile 10.6, just at the Tapeats–Bright Angel contact. From here it turns northwest to traverse Monument Creek's western edge. Although you can't see Granite Rapid during this stretch, you can hear its roar, even though it lies deep in the Inner Gorge, 1000 feet below you. At 10.8 miles from Indian Garden (and 0.7 mile from Monument Camp), the trail crosses a southwest-trending dry wash (GPS 36°05.19'N, 112°11.45'W). To your right the wash enters an unusually narrow and steep gorge through discolored Tapeats. Because Monument Camp's kink fold lines up perfectly with the walls of this gorge, you can tell that they both lie along the same fault. Fifty yards beyond the wash,

*Photo 62. Hermit Rapid (bottom) formed when a debris flow from Hermit Creek constricted the Colorado River's channel.*

the trail takes a 90-degree bend, and both The Monument and Granite Rapid come into view.

At mile 11.3 the trail turns westward to ascend a small pass north of Cope Butte. Many good worm burrows are present in the slabs of Bright Angel rubble leading up to the pass. Your efforts on the climb are rewarded when you reach the top, where you have an impressive view down the Colorado River, with Hermit Rapid frothing below. The debris fan that constricts the river to form the rapid is evident from here (Photo 62). The slopes west of the pass are lined with the most abundant Bright Angel outcrops on the trail. Float blocks that have fallen from these outcrops contain numerous burrows. These are much longer and narrower than the ones you have seen up to this point, indicating that they were created by a different species of worm.

As the trail descends from the pass, it contours around a shallow amphitheater at the head of a short side creek. The Tonto Platform is almost nonexistent along this stretch of trail, where the cliffs of Muav and Redwall loom almost directly above you. Even the crumbly Bright Angel Shale forms a 50-foot-tall cliff here, with the soft, green mudstones protected by a cap of chocolate-brown sandstone. Cope Butte resembles a cathedral because several branches of the Hermit Fault divide it into a series of buttresses. At mile 12 you crest another small pass at the back of the amphitheater and begin to drop into the Hermit Creek drainage. After a short descent, at mile 12.2 you reach the signed junction with the Hermit Trail (see Hike 9). The left fork heads up to the South Rim at Hermits Rest; the right fork descends 1 mile to Hermit Creek Camp, which is situated in a shady Tapeats gorge. Many Tonto hikers camp there for a night or two before journeying back from the brink to the "real world."

# HAVASU CANYON TRAIL

## CASCADES OF BLUE-GREEN WATER

*Admire the spectacular Havasu and Mooney waterfalls as you travel through the home of the Havasupai tribe, the people of the blue-green waters.*

LENGTH ▪ 8 miles to Supai; 10 miles to Mooney Falls

ELEVATION CHANGE ▪ 2500 feet

TIME ▪ 1 day each way

DIFFICULTY ▪ Difficult; rocky tread and potential flash flood danger

BACKCOUNTRY ZONING ▪ Havasupai Reservation; stay only in Havasu Campground or the lodge in Supai. Advanced reservations required for both

WATER AND TOILETS ■ Water available continuously below mile 6. Toilets at the trailhead, Supai, and the campground

EMERGENCY SERVICES ■ Phones and emergency personnel available in Supai

MULE TRIPS ■ Available to Supai

MAP LIST ■ 1, 10, 11

KEY REFERENCES ■ 1, 19, 21, 32

DAY HIKES ■ Supai to Havasu and Mooney Falls (4 miles round trip); Colorado River to Beaver Falls (7.4 miles round trip from river) or Mooney Falls (12 miles round trip from river)

SEASONS ■ Year-round. A good winter choice due to lower elevation. Beware of flash floods, especially during the July–September monsoon season

SPECIAL NOTE ■ For hiking, helicopter or mule rides, camping, and lodging in Supai, you must make advance reservations; see Havasupai Reservations in Chapter 5.

**About the Landscape:** Havasu Creek is one of the biggest and most beautiful tributary streams in the Grand Canyon. Its vivid blue-green water and isolated setting offer the feel of a secluded tropical paradise. During the hike, you see hundreds of beautiful blue-green pools spilling over the tops of small, natural rock dams, creating stairlike series of cascades (Color Plate 5). In several places, the water leaps over world-renowned waterfalls, crashing into sparkling emerald pools below (Color Plate 15All of this is made possible by the perennial water issuing from Havasu Spring and by the mountains of travertine precipitating out of this water.

*Travertine* is a form of limestone deposited in caves, springs, rivers, and lakes. When groundwater passes through extensive amounts of limestone, as it does in the Grand Canyon, it dissolves the limestone and becomes saturated with calcium and carbonate. The carbonate forms carbon dioxide when it is dissolved in water. Where the groundwater emerges onto the earth's surface, it loses pressure, causing the carbon dioxide to bubble away just like it does when you crack open a soda. This loss of carbon dioxide causes travertine to precipitate out of the water. In Havasu Creek, three additional processes are also at work. First, some bacteria species secrete crystallized travertine, creating small dams. Second, the water cascading over the dam becomes agitated. Just like emerging groundwater, agitated water is prone to losing carbon dioxide, so travertine is continuously added to the dam. Finally, evaporating water concentrates the calcium and carbonate, leading to their precipitation on the pools' edges.

Many of the bacteria that crystallize travertine grow on twigs and leaves that line the stream's banks or collect in blockages, for instance, where a log has dammed the creek. Because of this, travertine often encrusts these twigs and leaves. As you explore, look for such encrusted twigs in some of the fresh

*Photo 63. Lower Havasu Creek meanders between colorful walls of thinly bedded Muav Limestone en route to the Colorado River.*

*Photo 64. Mooney Falls plunges behind a large stalactite of travertine.*

travertine deposits and for the hollow tubes present in older travertine where the original twig has decomposed.

Havasu Creek (Photo 63) arises in Havasu Spring, just upstream from where the trail enters Havasu Canyon. The groundwater reaching the surface there is saturated with calcium and carbonate it has dissolved during its passage through the Kaibab and Toroweap Limestones. It is this tremendous load of dissolved calcium and carbonate that gives the stream its distinctive blue-green color.

Below Supai village, the creek passes several former springs that are now dry but previously produced enormous quantities of travertine. Havasu Creek has eroded through most of these deposits, but where it has not yet carved through the larger travertine plugs, spectacular waterfalls plunge over them. Breathtaking and geologically unique, Havasu (Color Plate 15) and Mooney Falls (Photo 64) are not to be missed!

Havasu Canyon's human story is unique as well. Supai is the only place below the rim of the Grand Canyon where people permanently reside. The village lies beneath towering walls of crimson Supai Group rocks; in fact, the rocks inherited their name from this community. Supai is the main settlement of the Havasupai tribe, whose ancestors have occupied this valley for centuries. They call themselves "people of the blue-green water," acknowledging the creek's central role in their lives. It nourishes the crops they grow here on the abnormally wide, flat canyon floor. This flat floor owes its existence to silt and mud deposited at the bottom of a lake that covered this valley in the geologically recent past.

There is some debate among geologists as to how the lake formed. It is possible that travertine from one of the springs blocked Havasu Creek, creating a local lake. Another idea is that these sediments were deposited in a much larger lake that formed 680,000 years ago, when cascades of lava poured into the Inner Gorge of the Colorado, damming the river and creating a lake 300 miles long (Hike 18). The sediments on which the town of Supai is built may have accumulated in an arm of that lake. When the Colorado eventually breached the lava dam, the lake quickly drained, and most of the soft, loose sediments deposited in it were swept away. However, precipitation of travertine in Havasu Canyon would have cemented the lake deposits together in this area, preserving them and the flat canyon floor they created. When the Havasupai arrived, they found a flat valley with rich, fine-grained soils and all the water they could use.

**Trail Guide:** From Interstate 40 in Seligman, AZ, head north on Route 66 for 28 miles, then turn right on Indian Highway 18. After 61 miles this road ends at Hualapai Hilltop, which consists of a large parking area, a helipad, and pit toilets. No water or services are available here.

At Hualapai Hilltop you'll find a dusty parking lot bustling with activity. Mule trains regularly ply the trail, hauling both supplies and tourists down to Supai. Several days a week, a buzzing helicopter makes numerous trips between the village and the Hilltop.

The trail begins in the Toroweap Formation because the road to the Hilltop cuts through the Kaibab Limestone in its last few miles. Hikers familiar with trails in the eastern Grand Canyon would therefore expect to enjoy an initially gradual descent through the slope-forming Toroweap, but such is not the case.

The trail immediately drops down a steep series of switchbacks winding between small cliffs of limestone. The differences in the Toroweap become easy to explain once you recall the area's geography 265 million years ago. At the time, a shallow sea was encroaching from the west upon the supercontinent Pangea. The eastern Grand Canyon region marked the shoreline of this arid supercontinent (Chapter 2), where mud mixed with evaporite minerals accumulated. The soft mudstones and evaporites now form the Toroweap's gentle, easily eroded slopes in the eastern Canyon. In contrast, here in the western Canyon lay the deeper waters of the open ocean, where limestone accumulated instead. Therefore, the Toroweap in the western Canyon contains much more of this harder rock, forming cliffs and thus creating this steep initial descent.

After 0.25 mile you reach a metal culvert protected by a stone wall. The limestone here has a pinkish hue, and immediately below it lies tan sandstone. This is the contact between the Toroweap and the Coconino Sandstone (GPS 36°09.70'N, 112°42.50'W). Note the Coconino's well-exposed, sweeping crossbeds up to 20 feet tall; these reveal its origin as a stack of huge desert sand dunes (Photo 35).

Immediately below the contact, the trail makes a 180-degree left-hand switchback. More turns follow until mile 0.6, where you reach the end of the switchbacks at the Coconino-Hermit contact (GPS 36°09.67'N, 112°42.61'W). Although the brick-red Hermit is clearly visible below the Coconino on the cliffs north of you, rubble obscures the point where these two rock units meet on the trail.

From the bottom of the switchbacks, the path turns northward and descends more gradually into Hualapai Wash below. The Hermit is a soft layer that erodes very easily, gradually undercutting the cliffs of stronger Coconino Sandstone rising above it in a process known as *scarp retreat* (Color Plate 18). The Hermit's great thickness (600–1000 feet in the western Grand Canyon) has accentuated the scarp-retreat process, creating a broad, flat platform known as the Esplanade (Figure 36). The wide, flat floor of Hualapai Canyon below you is an example of a portion of the Esplanade under construction.

At mile 0.8 the path turns to the west and soon passes a hump of red soil (next to a stone shelter) that was produced by weathering of the underlying Hermit layer. From here the trail descends a low ridge. At mile 1.3 it drops into a small slot below the ridge. A cave left of the trail offers welcome shade on hot days. Two pink sandstone ledges to the right of the trail mark your passage onto the Esplanade Sandstone, the uppermost formation in the Supai Group.

At mile 1.5 you reach the wide floor of Hualapai Wash, where a sign warns of flash flood danger. Because you will be traveling down the wash for the next 6.5 miles, flash floods are a serious threat, particularly during the monsoon season (usually July through September). If storms are active anywhere in the

*Photo 65. A hiker descends the serene gorge of Hualapai Canyon, cut through the Esplanade Sandstone.*

area, use extreme caution, and remember that a flash flood can roar down your canyon even if it isn't raining on you; all it takes is a localized storm situated over part of the wash's catchment area. Several people have been swept away by flash floods in this wash. Because monsoon storms usually begin around midday, your safest bet is to start hiking early in the morning. In the case of a flash flood, run to high ground.

For the rest of the hike to the village, your path takes you ever deeper into the Supai Group as the canyon walls rise higher and higher above you (Photo 65). The uppermost formation in the Supai Group is the Esplanade Sandstone. Like the Coconino Sandstone, the Esplanade has high-angle cross-beds indicating its sand dune origin. The cross-beds aren't as tall here, though, because these were low coastal dunes rather than the massive, Sahara-sized dunes that formed the Coconino. In this area, many caves and potholes have been eroded in the Esplanade.

By mile 1.9 the sandstone cliffs have risen to a respectable height of 30 feet. Float blocks from all of the higher layers litter the wash. Keep your eye out for some good fossils of brachiopods, crinoids, and other Permian invertebrates on some of the gray Kaibab and Toroweap boulders (Figure 29). Telephone lines destined for Supai are attached to an especially big block of Esplanade Sandstone to the left of the trail. Opposite the boulder, a terrace of loose gravel and sand rises 5 feet above the wash. The first of many such deposits you will see between here and Supai, these layers were deposited by flash floods. They act as a constant reminder to be vigilant if the weather is at all unsettled.

A patch of oak trees occupies the wash at mile 2.7. Where the telephone wires cross the wash again, you pass a sign reporting that you are 3 miles from the trailhead. An increase in mudstone in the Supai Group rocks here indicates your passage below the Esplanade Sandstone into the underlying Wescogame Formation. This layer was named for Wescogame Point, a promontory on the Canyon rim directly above you. The underlying Manakacha and basal Watahomigi, named for other points overlooking Supai village, complete the tongue-twisting package of Supai Group formations.

Another sign situated next to a rusty ore cart marks your progress to the 4-mile mark. On the left, 300 yards beyond the sign, a lens of thinly bedded mudstone occupies an old channel carved into the surrounding sandstones. A switchback down a ramp at mile 5.5 deposits you on the floor of the wash just above a limestone pourover filled with discontinuous bands of red chert. The trail crosses to the wash's right side to circumvent the pourover. Downstream of this ledge, the canyon widens noticeably as you near its end.

You reach the confluence with Havasu Canyon at the trail's 6-mile mark in a cluster of cottonwood trees that signals Havasu Creek's perennial flow.

Another 100 yards downstream you reach a trail junction. The left fork directs you to Supai village; the right fork leads to Havasu Spring. The Havasupai tribe asks that visitors not travel up the canyon beyond this point without an invitation, so please respect their wishes.

Below the confluence, the character of the hike changes dramatically. Havasu Canyon is much wider and is filled with lush growth, a marked contrast to the nearly barren floor of Hualapai Canyon above. At 200 yards below the junction, you reach the banks of Havasu Creek and view its beautiful blue-green water for the first time.

You cross the creek on a metal I-beam bridge 0.5 mile below the junction, just upstream of the first tributary canyon entering from the left (west). Fences divide the pastureland here, and it is common to hear frogs croaking any time of day. Less than 0.5 mile later you crest a small rise and see the houses of Supai below you. To the left of the trail is a limestone outcrop with red and black chert belonging to the Watahomigi Formation, the lowest in the Supai Group. This limestone is capped by a lumpy brown patch of travertine, the first you have encountered along the trail.

On the short descent into the village you get excellent views of Wigleeva, the distinctive twin spires composed of Supai Group rocks. You soon reach Sinyella House, located across from the rodeo ground, which is the first of several stores where you can purchase cold drinks, snacks, film, and toiletries. From here the trail wanders through the streets along the eastern side of town until, 8 miles from the trailhead, it reaches the helipad and tourist office in the village center. Stop in at the tourist office to pay the remaining 50 percent of your camping and entry fees.

The post office and café are a short stroll beyond the airstrip. Just beyond the café, the clearly signed trail turns left at the church. After this left turn, the trail bears right at every major junction as it passes through town. It leaves the village as a wide, sandy path next to a small canal. A couple of narrow paths branch left, but the wide, main trail stays to the right. Throughout this stretch, the creek is hidden from view by thick riparian vegetation. From the main trail, you can hear but can't see Supai Falls, the first and smallest of Havasu Creek's five waterfalls.

About a mile below Supai village, the trail becomes a bit muddy where several springs exit from the base of the cliff on your right. A short distance below this, fences line the edge of a 50-foot-cliff where the creek, now visible, has carved into very fine-grained, soft, and unstable sediments. These are some of the fertile lake deposits that underlie the village and its surrounding fields. Navajo Falls comes into view here, tumbling down a travertine-coated escarpment carved into the lake sediments. A sign directs hikers headed to Havasu Campground to the left.

Although it will pale in your memory as soon as you see the next waterfall, Navajo Falls is an impressive site. Its overlook is situated on travertine, and this is a great place to study the travertine's weird shapes and fine laminations that are created as each succeeding generation layers on top of the preceding one. Thirty feet below this spot, small limestone cliffs rise up on either side of the creek. These cliffs are composed of Redwall Limestone, and Navajo Falls is positioned at the Redwall-Supai contact. The Redwall gorge deepens progressively downstream.

At 200 yards below Navajo Falls, the trail crosses to the left (west) side of the creek on a wooden bridge; 0.25 mile later, you reach an open area of travertine outcrop at the brink of stunning Havasu Falls. The trail hugs the cliff of Redwall Limestone as it descends a steep pitch beside the falls. The majestic twin jets are in full view during this inspiring descent (Color Plate 15). Where the trail flattens out, several spurs lead to the tranquil, turquoise-blue pool at their base. When the weather is hot, the sparkling pool beckons swimmers, and it also provides another great angle for viewing this natural wonder. The appearance of the falls has been altered by several historic flash floods and debris flows, but through all the changes, they have retained their spectacular beauty.

You enter Havasu Campground 300 yards below the falls (Color Plate 19). The large facility is strung along the creek all the way to Mooney Falls, nearly 0.75 mile downstream. The creek dances its way through the campground in a series of pools and small cascades created by sinuous travertine dams. Most campsites are equipped with picnic tables, and all have trees or metal poles on which to isolate your food from the bold rodents frequenting the area. Water is available from Fern Spring, which issues directly from the Redwall cliff near the center of the grounds. Two sets of toilets serve the campground, one at each end.

Once you've set up camp, it's only a short distance downstream to Mooney Falls. Be sure to heed the sign at the top, warning of the dangers of the unfenced area. Plunging 257 feet, Mooney is the tallest of Havasu Creek's waterfalls. Like Havasu and Navajo, it too plunges over the edge of a massive pile of travertine. The views of the falls are magnificent from the travertine terrace that the trail picks its way down. Of note are the huge travertine stalactites hanging from the lip (Photo 64). They are just like the stalactites you find in caves, formed by the slow crystallization of travertine from millions of water droplets that dripped from the roof of the overhanging cliff.

Fifty yards beyond a "10-mile" sign, the gradient gets much steeper. Another sign advises you to use extreme caution and to downclimb at your own risk. Just beyond this warning, a tunnel in the travertine provides access to the base of Mooney Falls, but this is the end of the line for casual hikers. Continue only if you are an experienced scrambler and are not afraid of heights. The path to the base of the falls is equipped with ladders and chain handrails, but the descent is extremely steep, and the travertine surface has become polished and slippery from repeated use. If you do want to explore lower Havasu Canyon, see below. If not, linger in the canyon a day or two to soak up the magic of this oasis and its incredible blue-green water.

## TAKE ME TO THE RIVER

The Havasu Canyon Trail ends at the top of Mooney Falls, but a well-trodden route leads from there to the Colorado River, a beautiful 6-mile walk. River runners frequently hike upstream to Beaver Falls, but those that go all the way to Mooney Falls are treated to a particularly scenic stretch of Havasu Canyon.

Just as the sign above Mooney Falls warns, the descent to its base requires extreme caution. From the sign, walk through the short tunnel. In the narrow gap between its end and the beginning of the next tunnel, you are treated to a particularly inspiring view of the waterfall, with huge travertine stalactites hanging above your head (Photo 64). You emerge from the second tunnel to find the falls thundering a short distance upstream and its spray making the already-slick travertine even more slippery. The path is easy to follow here because it has iron spikes for use as hand and footholds, as well as thick chains that provide some assistance down the steepest sections. A couple of wooden ladders guide you down the final cliff (Photo 66).

Many people pass a few hours picnicking at the base of the falls and then return to camp. If you have more time and energy, it is worthwhile to walk downstream, as the gorge here is beautiful and serene (Photo 63). Immediately below the falls, the path picks its way through grasses, mesquite trees, and thickets of prickly pear growing on the flat valley floor. You reach the first of many fords 200 yards below the falls. It is handy to wear your favorite wading shoes for this walk. Fifty yards downstream, the remains of a picnic table are wrapped around a tree, a sober reminder of a recent flash flood.

In 300 yards downstream from the first major left-hand tributary, the cliffs of Redwall Limestone that had previously reached the canyon floor now end about 50 feet above it. The slopes below are mostly covered with debris fallen from the cliffs above, but in places outcrops of thinly bedded, purplish limestone peek through. This is the Temple Butte Limestone, a shallow marine deposit dating from the

*Photo 66. Metal chains and wooden ladders assist intrepid scramblers down a cliff of travertine, dripping with stalactites, to the base of Mooney Falls.*

Devonian Period. In the eastern Grand Canyon it is only exposed as isolated lenses, which are preserved tidal channels. Havasu lies much farther west, in the open ocean of Devonian times, so the Temple Butte forms a continuous layer here.

The path now traverses travertine benches and open meadows, crossing the creek several times en route. It is generally easy to follow, and cairns usually mark the fords' entry and exit points. About 2 miles below Mooney Falls, you encounter a tricky section. Now on the right side of the creek, the path scales a cliff of Temple Butte Limestone. A few old, tattered ropes dangle over the rock face. Although you should first test the ropes before you rely on them, they provide a helpful boost up the first few feet. Ten feet above the creek, the gradient eases. A series of wooden steps then lead to a ledge, which consists of flash flood deposits later cemented in place by travertine.

The view into this particularly beautiful section reveals more travertine-controlled pools and drops in the vivid turquoise water. About 0.3 mile farther, the path draws even with the confluence between Havasu and Beaver Creeks. The last of Havasu's five waterfalls, Beaver Falls, is visible below, a short distance above the confluence. The path stays high until it is about 100 yards below the confluence, where it picks its way down a steep slope to the creek, which it immediately fords. From here a path leads up the river-left bank to the pleasant swimming hole below the falls. Rafters who are heading upstream from here to Mooney Falls will be coming up the river's left side. To avoid missing the path, you will need to watch for the rockwork revealing the trail on the river-right bank where it ascends to the ledge about 50 feet above the creek.

The Beaver Creek confluence marks the boundary between the Havasupai Reservation and Grand Canyon National Park as well as the contact between the Temple Butte and the underlying Muav Limestone, in which you will remain the rest of the way to the Colorado.

About 3.75 miles downstream of Mooney Falls you pass below a 50-yard-long overhang on river right. The underside of the overhang is speckled with 2- to 3-inch-long cylindrical worm burrows (Photo 86), evidence of the bustling animal community that lived here 520 million years ago. The vegetation surrounding the creek consists of mesquite trees and a variety of riparian species. In contrast, the dry shelves above the creek are covered with ocotillo, which herald your entry into the Mojave life zone. At 5.2 miles below Mooney Falls, an outcrop of travertine on the right bank blocks your way. The trail clambers up and over this outcrop, then descends the other side via a notched log and a short, natural tunnel.

At 5.5 miles below the falls, you ford the creek one last time, crossing to its left bank. You then scramble up a stepped outcrop of Muav Limestone to reach a shelf sitting 40 feet above the creek. You reach the river in another 0.5 mile. A big eddy at the mouth of Havasu Creek provides a raft anchorage for river parties wanting to explore upstream. This eddy of warm Havasu Creek water provides refuge for a few endangered Humpback Chub, a native fish that used to be abundant in the Grand Canyon. Only a few thousand of them remain (mainly in the Little Colorado River of the eastern Grand Canyon), largely due to changes brought about by Glen Canyon Dam. They have difficulty tolerating the much colder river water released from the reservoir's frigid depths, and they have been severely preyed upon by trout, which thrive in the colder water.

*Fading light on the Inner Gorge. Clear Creek Trail.*

# Part 4
# HIKES FROM THE NORTH RIM

# NANKOWEAP TRAIL

## JOURNEY TO THE CENTER OF A SUPERCONTINENT

*At the center of the Rodinian supercontinent you can examine fossils of ancient bacteria encased in 750 million-year-old rocks that have been crumbled by the Grand Canyon's mightiest fault.*

LENGTH ■ 14 miles

ELEVATION CHANGE ■ 5900 feet

TIME ■ 2 days each way

DIFFICULTY ■ Very difficult; very remote, uneven and unmarked trail. Narrow sections with steep drop-offs potentially hazardous when muddy

BACKCOUNTRY ZONING ■ Primitive; at-large camping (AE9)

WATER AND TOILETS ■ Perennial water at Nankoweap Creek and Colorado River; ephemeral seep near Marion Point. No toilets available

EMERGENCY SERVICES ■ Nearest ranger station is 1.4 miles north of Grand Canyon Lodge on the North Rim

MAP LIST ■ 1, 12, 13

KEY REFERENCES ■ 1, 6, 9, 22, 33–35

DAY HIKES ■ Saddle Mountain saddle (6 miles round trip); Colorado River to Butte Fault (6 miles round trip from river)

SEASONS ■ Year-round, but extremely hot in summer. Trailhead is accessible in winter but impassable when wet

**About the Landscape:** In 1882, John Wesley Powell, as director of the United States Geological Survey, supervised construction of the Nankoweap Trail, which follows an ancient Native American route into Marble Canyon. Powell was leading a major scientific expedition, and he used this trail to access some of the Canyon's most intriguing geology. Long and arduous, the trail is often considered the most difficult in the Canyon, but for experienced hikers, it provides an uncrowded opportunity to view geologic gems not found along any other trail. Nankoweap is one of our personal favorites!

The Butte Fault, the biggest in the eastern Grand Canyon, has orchestrated dramatic landscape changes throughout its 800-million-year life, with the eastern Canyon's other faults playing merely a supporting role. When the fault was born, the Grand Canyon region was covered by a shallow body of water that flooded the center of the supercontinent called Rodinia (Figure 7). The sediments of the Chuar Group (Figure 20), which are not accessible from any other trail, were deposited in this body of water. They provide a unique record of conditions in the center of this supercontinent and of the organisms that lived there at this critical time in the evolution of life. However,

*Photo 67. Seam of a Supercontinent. Nankoweap Butte (right skyline) is capped by a small cliff of ragged Sixtymile Formation. The Chuar Group rocks below were folded into a bowl-shaped syncline (revealed especially clearly by the bend of the dark, resistant layers in the middle). Both were deposited in the center of Rodinia just as it started to rip apart.*

even as the Chuar sediments were being laid down, tectonic forces began to tear Rodinia apart. Grand Canyon's western neighbors, Australia and Antarctica (Figure 8), pulled away, opening the ancestral Pacific Ocean in the growing gap.

As the region was pulled apart, the Butte Fault did the lion's share of the stretching, in the process dropping the Grand Canyon area down an astounding 10,000 feet relative to the Navajo reservation immediately to the east. The Chuar Group sediments continued to fill the growing sag, causing the layers to be folded into a bowl-shaped *syncline* (Figure 21a, Photo 67). Finally, about 742 million years ago, movement along the fault became so rapid that the orderly accumulation of Chuar Group sediments ceased. They were covered by rubble composed of angular boulders that tumbled off the cliff made by movement of the Butte Fault. This rubble is preserved as the Sixtymile Formation (Figure 21a, Photo 67), which is exposed at only two locations in the entire Grand Canyon, including Nankoweap Butte, visible from the lower Nankoweap Trail.

With the final breakup of Rodinia, the Butte Fault entered a 650-million-year period of hibernation. Throughout the Paleozoic and Mesozoic Eras, 10,000 feet of sediment slowly accumulated above this sleeping giant (Figure 21b). Its slumber was disturbed about 65 million years ago, when the Laramide Orogeny (Chapter 3) caused the fault to reverse its direction of motion. As its

*Photo 68. Distant rock layers arch down to the right along the East Kaibab Monocline.*

western edge slowly rose, the overlying sedimentary rocks rose with it, moving so slowly that they did not fracture, but instead flexed over the rising step like carpet tumbling over a staircase (Figure 21c, Photo 68), creating the East Kaibab Monocline.

Many monoclines (Figure 50) formed across the Colorado Plateau during the Laramide Orogeny, but the East Kaibab is the most important of them all. It is an especially long fold, stretching from Flagstaff in the south nearly to Bryce Canyon, Utah, to the north. Most important, its uplift formed the Kaibab Plateau, a broad dome sitting atop the larger Colorado Plateau (Figure 17). The spectacle of the Grand Canyon would not be possible without the presence of the Kaibab Plateau because the world's most famous gorge is carved right through it. Visitors approaching the Grand Canyon from the east marvel at the Kaibab Plateau's dramatic eastern wall (Photo 68), where the Kaibab Limestone sweeps 3000 feet upward in a graceful arch from the parched, blackbrush-covered plain of the Marble Platform to the cool spruce, fir, and aspen forests of the North Rim.

Along most of its length, this mighty fold reveals only its top rock layers, offering stunning views but providing few clues about the forces that raised this great blister in the crust. However, along the Nankoweap Trail, Nankoweap Creek has, through the millennia, carved deep into the body of the monocline, revealing the Butte Fault at its core.

More recently, extension of the Basin and Range province during the last 30 million years has caused the fault to stir yet again, turning it back into the normal fault that it began its life as, and causing it to downdrop rock layers on its western flank (Figure 21d).

**Trail Guide:** From Marble Canyon, Arizona, drive west on US 89A. Proceed 13 miles west of Cliff Dwellers and just before mile marker 560, turn left onto Route 8910 (House Rock Valley Road). Follow this dirt road 27.6 miles to the trailhead. All junctions are clearly marked for Saddle Mountain.

The trail can be accessed from either the North Rim or from House Rock Valley. The distance and the vertical drop are comparable for both approaches. Because the House Rock Valley trailhead is accessible year-round, we have described the trail from there. If you use the North Rim trailhead, simply hike down Forest Service Trail 57 for 3 miles to the beginning of the Park Service's Nankoweap Trail, joining this description at the Saddle Mountain saddle.

From the House Rock Valley trailhead, the trail leads south on a closed dirt road. The trailhead sits at the base of the East Kaibab Monocline, and the path immediately begins to climb up it. As you gain elevation, look behind you for impressive views of the monocline where it is cut by North and South Canyons (Photo 68). The cuts offer good views of the prominent white Coconino Sandstone cliff where it arches over the fold.

At mile 0.6 the trail veers left off the road at a sign that reads "Mankoweap [sic]." In 100 yards beyond the sign, the trail begins a gradual descent into Saddle Canyon. The descent steepens at mile 0.8. You have been walking on the Kaibab Limestone since the trailhead, but the first outcrop doesn't show up until mile 1 (GPS 36°20.11'N, 111°57.28'W) at a left-hand switchback. The rock's lumpy texture here is caused by hard chert nodules that resist weathering more than the surrounding limestone. Many of the chert lumps surround fossils such as brachiopods, crinoids, and bryozoans (Figure 29), most of which are poorly preserved.

The next outcrop lies at the base of a series of short switchbacks 0.1 mile farther down the trail. It consists of a dark, red-brown sandstone interbedded with mudstone and white evaporites, all crisscrossed with white calcite veins. This hodgepodge of different rock types is characteristic of the Toroweap Formation, which was deposited near the shore of an evaporating sea. No more outcrop appears along the rest of the descent to Saddle Creek, but somewhere along the way, you drop below the Toroweap and into the Coconino Sandstone.

You reach the creek and the signed junction with Forest Service Trail 31 about 1.2 miles from the trailhead. At the junction take the right fork (Trail 57), which ambles up the creek for the next 0.3 mile through beautiful stands of Gambel's oak, providing an ambiance more reminiscent of New England than the Grand Canyon. Many outcrops of white, cross-bedded Coconino

Sandstone peek out from behind the oaks to remind you where you are. The trail climbs out of the wash at mile 1.5, leaving the oaks and entering a ponderosa pine forest. The Coconino outcrop to your left and the red dirt on the trail (derived from the underlying Hermit Formation) indicate that you have reached the Coconino-Hermit contact (GPS 36°19.78'N, 111°57.32'W).

From this contact, the trail climbs up the East Kaibab Monocline for the next 1.6 miles to the Saddle Mountain saddle. Few rocks poke their heads above the duff on the forest floor. A wildfire ravaged the area in the summer of 2000. The trail skirts the edge of the burn, but the devastation on Saddle Mountain is easy to see. Several signs through this section indicate that you are still on Trail 57. At 3.1 miles from the start, you reach the saddle at the National Park boundary. A 15-yard detour from the junction takes you to a slickrock overlook that provides your first, breathtaking view into the Canyon. This spot also marks the contact between the Hermit Formation and the Supai Group. The slickrock edge you are sitting on belongs to the uppermost Supai layer, the Esplanade Sandstone.

The saddle is the official start of the Park Service's Nankoweap Trail, which is marked by a sign. The trail first heads east along the ridge for 100 yards, then bends to the south and plunges into the Canyon down a series of steep, rocky switchbacks through Esplanade Sandstone.

The trail reaches the bottom of the Esplanade and the switchbacks 0.2 mile from the saddle. From here it settles into a 4-mile-long traverse of the Supai Group. Grand Canyon hikers are accustomed to lengthy Supai traverses, but this one takes the prize for being the Canyon's longest. Hikers on this traverse are exposed to the full intensity of the sun, not only from the sky but also from radiant heat emanating from the surrounding red rocks. From late spring through fall, this section of trail can be brutally hot. There are no reliable water sources until you reach Nankoweap Creek, so make sure that you bring enough water to make it there. Small pinyon pines dot the landscape, offering dappled shade, and the Esplanade cliff blocks the sun during the early-morning hours.

Along the first 3 miles of the traverse, the trail never moves far from the base of the impressive Esplanade Sandstone cliff. Although fairly easy to follow, the trail is not maintained, so the going can be rough, with short scrambles to avoid boulders that have tumbled into the path. About a mile into the traverse, the trail passes beneath a section of cliff marked by three prominent vertical cracks. The base of the cliff here is undercut due to rapid erosion of the soft mudstone beneath. In places, the bottom of the overhang is covered

*Photo 69. Monocline. Kwagunt Butte forms the nearly flat skyline on the left of the photo. Beds of Supai Group and Redwall Limestone arch steeply up along the East Kaibab Monocline to the right of the butte.*

with worm burrows and ripplemarks. A thin sandstone bed sandwiched between mudstones has weathered into a series of bulbous knobs, resembling a string of worry beads. Each bead on the string is separated by joints. The soft nature of this sandstone leads to accelerated erosion along each joint, causing the distinctive spheroidal weathering displayed here.

Be sure to take breaks from your labors to enjoy the magnificent panoramas that continuously unfold around you. Mount Hayden is the impressive spire of Coconino Sandstone rising from a base of Hermit Formation to your right (southwest). Marble Canyon is the shadowy slot to the southeast, guarded by the massive, flat-topped, twin sentinels of Nankoweap Mesa to the left and Kwagunt Butte to the right. If you look closely at the right flank of both mesas, you can see layers of Redwall Limestone and Supai Group arching sharply toward the sky where they have been bent along the East Kaibab Monocline (Photo 69). These layers form a craggy hogback that is easy to see on topographic maps.

Directly in front of the twin sentinels, Nankoweap Butte (Photo 67) is easily identified by its ragged cap of Sixtymile Formation. To the right of Nankoweap Butte lies a tangle of spires ringing Kwagunt Canyon, the next major tributary to the south. Below these spires, a cliff of horizontal Tapeats Sandstone is evident, and below the Tapeats lie the tilted rocks of the Chuar Group. You can trace the Group's tilted, resistant sandstone and limestone beds down to Nankoweap Butte, where the layers bottom out before rising again to the east. This bowl-shaped fold is the Chuar Syncline (Photo 67), created by extension on the Butte Fault during the breakup of Rodinia. Based on the horizontal nature of the Tapeats, you can deduce that fault movement had ceased by the time it was deposited, 545 million years ago (Figure 21b).

At mile 5.1 (2 miles from Saddle Mountain saddle), you reach the ridge leading to Marion Point (GPS 36°18.20'N, 111°56.46'W). Two decent tent platforms here offer the first camping since the saddle. In wet years, a small seep exists about 400 yards down the path, but you should not count on its presence. From here, a false trail continues southeast, leading down the ridge toward Marion Point. The actual trail turns sharply left at the highest tent platform, trending north into the back of a shallow amphitheater beneath an overhanging cliff of Supai sandstone. In two spots, rockfall from the overhang has littered the trail with boulders that you must pick your way through.

You reach the back of the amphitheater, and the northernmost point on the Supai traverse, at mile 5.4. When it is flowing, the seep oozes down a moss-covered joint about 50 yards before. Trending southeast, the trail continues beneath the Esplanade cliff, still following the amphitheater around.

The views of Nankoweap Butte and the Chuar Syncline continue to get better along this section of trail. As you round a prominent point at mile 5.8, you can, for the first time, see down to the blackbrush-covered river terraces in the Nankoweap valley.

The trail quality, poor throughout the Supai traverse, degrades even more at mile 6.3. Two especially narrow sections located above steep drop-offs are noteworthy. Hiking these 10-yard trail segments requires no more than heightened concentration during dry weather, but if you happen to arrive after a rainstorm, use extreme caution; wet Supai mudstone can be very slippery. Soon after passing these obstacles, the trail leaves the base of the Esplanade cliff and travels down through the lower Supai formations on its way to Tilted Mesa, whose eastward-angling beds of Redwall Limestone form a prominent landmark.

After 4 fatiguing miles, the Supai traverse finally ends on a slickrock platform of white Supai sandstone (GPS 36°18.24'N, 111°55.01'W), where several flat spots would make decent dry camps. At this platform you are straddling the axis of the East Kaibab Monocline. Notice the obvious eastward tilt of both the Redwall Limestone on Tilted Mesa and the Supai Group rocks on the flank of Saddle Mountain. On the western flank of Nankoweap Mesa, the contorted Redwall and Supai layers mark the continuation of the monocline in that direction (Photo 69).

As the trail continues down the ridge toward Tilted Mesa, you must cross several low ledges of resistant Supai sandstone. The first is formed by the white sandstone bed on which you are standing. Cairns on the west side of the ridge mark a slot offering an easy passage. Almost immediately below, you encounter a taller ledge of red sandstone. Joints here have formed another slot, this one occupied by a juniper snag, which aids in the descent. The trail then forks, with separate branches leading to different crossing points of two more small ledges. These branches soon rejoin to continue down the ridge.

The Supai sandstones and mudstones here are joined by a few resistant beds of gray limestone studded with wisps of red chert. These limestone beds are a feature of the lowermost Supai, and they herald your approach to the Redwall-Supai contact, which you reach at the first of two narrow necks on the ridge at mile 7.5 (GPS 36°18.14'N, 111°54.83'W).

Another 0.3 mile brings you to the second neck, the low point on the ridge (GPS 36°18.03'N, 111°54.58'W). Here the trail leaves the ridge via its southern (right) flank, winding down a large cone of landslide debris leaning against the steep Redwall cliff.

You step off the landslide at mile 8.7 (GPS 36°17.73'N, 111°54.35'W) at the first of many outcrops of drab, olive-tinted Muav Limestone, which is composed of thin, nodular beds. At this point the trail becomes more treacherous because a thin veneer of pebbles covers the outcrop, providing ball bearings capable of taking you for a fast and unintended ride down the steep slope!

The trail passes a prominent, 5-foot-tall spire of Muav Limestone at mile 8.9, then 150 yards farther makes a 90-degree left bend, where it meets the edge of the landslide again. The outcrops you pass just before reaching the landslide are composed of thin, brown sandstone layers sandwiched between bright green mudstone, indicating that you have passed below the Muav into the Bright Angel Shale (GPS 36°17.69'N, 111°54.33'W).

From the left bend the trail hugs the boundary between the landslide debris and the Bright Angel Shale for 200 yards before veering left (south) again. Here the trail begins a long, gradual descent through the Bright Angel, with excellent views of Nankoweap Butte en route. You cross the Bright Angel–Tapeats contact at mile 9.9 (GPS 36°17.42'N, 111°53.90'W). Blocks of brown Tapeats Sandstone litter the slope below the contact, and the crest of the low ridge to your right is crowned by Tapeats outcrop.

A right bend 150 yards beyond the contact heralds the beginning of a steeper descent through the Tapeats, which ends at mile 10.3 (GPS 36°17.32'N, 111°53.78'W) when you reach the Galeros Formation. The Galeros, along with the Kwagunt Formation, forms the Chuar Group (Figure 20, Photo 5). The Galeros here consists of mudstone in a rainbow of colors: gray, maroon, yellow, and black. Very little vegetation grows on it because its clay minerals absorb water and swell when it rains, only to dry out and shrink in the desert heat, as seen by the modern mudcracks covering the outcrop. Like the back-and-forth motion you use to extract a splinter lodged in your finger, plant roots are pushed out by this shrinking-and-swelling process. Due to evaporation, salt also builds up on the clay surfaces, making it an even harsher environment for plants.

One clear sign of this salt buildup can be seen at the base of the Tapeats boulders littering the Galeros slope. Their bases have been corroded into weirdly shaped overhangs by salt weathering, which occurs where salty water evaporates. Salt crystallizes in the rock's pore spaces, prying the grains apart as they grow. Up the slope, similar boulders resting on Tapeats outcrop exhibit much less salt weathering, probably due to the porous nature of the Tapeats Sandstone, which wicks the salty water away. The inability of the Galeros mudstone to transmit water prevents wicking, causing the water and its salts to accumulate at the ground surface and corrode the overlying rocks.

About 0.2 mile below the Tapeats-Galeros contact, the trail enters the head of a shallow gully and begins to traverse down its right side. The trail then descends a resistant fin of brown Galeros sandstone forming a small ridge next to the gully. The ridge ends at a low, flat terrace of recently deposited river gravels on the valley floor at mile 10.7.

The lower reaches of the ridge and the alluvial terrace below it offer an excellent view of Nankoweap Butte, with its Sixtymile Formation cap and its

*Photo 70. Growth fault. The lower slopes of Nankoweap Butte expose the thinly bedded layers of the Galeros Formation that are offset along a small normal fault (lower center). Notice that the layers' offset decreases progressively higher up the butte. This is a characteristic feature of a growth fault.*

layers folded in the bowl-shaped Chuar Syncline (Photo 67). A tall outcrop of gray and maroon Galeros mudstone forms the base of Nankoweap Butte. A few resistant limestone and sandstone beds protrude from this outcrop, and they are offset by several small normal faults, each offsetting the layers only a few feet. An interesting aspect of these faults is that the amount of layer offset decreases toward the top of the outcrop (Photo 70). This variable offset is the distinguishing characteristic of a *growth fault,* a type of slowly slipping fault that remains active during a prolonged period of sediment deposition. Because the lower sediment layers are older, they are offset more than the higher, younger layers, which were deposited after part of the fault movement had already occurred.

The presence of growth faults is, along with the Chuar Syncline, one of the main clues that convinces geologists that the Butte Fault was active while the Chuar Group sediments were being laid down.

As the trail trends southeast across the valley floor, it points directly toward a small cliff of jet-black basalt belonging to the Cardenas Lava and lying adjacent to the Galeros Formation. The Cardenas ordinarily lies well below the Galeros (Figure 20), but this outcrop lies along the Butte Fault, which dropped the Galeros rocks down to the same level as the Cardenas during its first life as a normal fault (Figure 21a).

At mile 10.9 you reach the lip of the alluvial terrace, where the trail descends a short slope to perennial Nankoweap Creek and a nice campsite under a cottonwood tree (11 miles from the trailhead). From here, the trail simply follows the creek bed all the way to the Colorado River. From this spot, a short excursion up Nankoweap Creek offers you a unique glimpse of ancient life forms that thrived in the center of the Rodinian supercontinent.

## LIFE IN THE FAULT ZONE

The Chuar Group rocks contain abundant fossils of several organisms that lived here 750 to 800 million years ago while the supercontinent of Rodinia was breaking up. From the campsite where the trail first meets Nankoweap Creek, walk upstream along the creek's south bank. Outcrop of black basalt (the Cardenas Lava) gives way, as you cross the Butte Fault, to thinly bedded, gray mudstones, sprinkled with a few resistant limestone beds, belonging to the Galeros Formation (GPS 36°16.73'N, 111°53.47'W; 0.15 mile from the camp). This is the outcrop cut by growth faults mentioned earlier (Photo 70). You can follow the Chuar Syncline by tracing a 1-foot-thick limestone bed near the base of the outcrop as it tilts down to the west until it disappears below the stream gravel. It reemerges a few yards upstream, but now it is tilting eastward on the other side of the fold.

Keep an eye out here for seven cylindrical, quarter-sized holes in the limestone bed. These holes were drilled by paleomagnetists, geologists who study the earth's past magnetic field. The samples they remove allow them to determine the latitude, and often the age, at which rocks were deposited. These particular samples helped paleomagnetists determine that the Galeros Formation was deposited at a tropical latitude 750 to 800 million years ago.

Both this bed and the next higher limestone layer possess distinct, wavy laminations. These are *stromatolites,* the remains of ancient colonies of bacteria that coated the bottoms of lakes and shallow seas throughout Precambrian time. Since no multicellular animals existed

*Photo 71. Stromatolite fossils. A boulder of Kwagunt Formation displays stromatolites, which give the rock a cabbage-like texture. Each "cabbage head" was formed by a separate colony of bacteria that coated the seafloor about 750 million years ago.*

then, no predators inhibited the luxuriant growth of these bacterial mats. Pond scum ruled the kingdom of Rodinia!

Continue upstream, hugging the rock outcrop on the creek's south side. About 0.3 mile from the camp you reach the mouth of a small tributary wash. Walk up this tributary 120 yards, all the while examining the really large (bigger than 5-foot) limestone blocks littering the creek bed. Many of these have a very odd cabbagelike texture, ranging from the size of an onion to a basketball or larger (Photo 71). These limestone blocks have tumbled down the slope from the overlying Kwagunt Formation, the layer of the Chuar Group that you haven't yet seen, and the spheres are more stromatolites. Each sphere marks a separate colony of bacteria. The best examples in this creek are at GPS 36°16.64'N, 111°53.59'W.

The Kwagunt Formation also contains a variety of microscopic fossils, as well as the oldest macroscopic fossils of individual organisms in the Grand Canyon, *Chuaria* circularis. The *Chuaria* are carbonized disks 1 to 2 millimeters in diameter found on the bedding surfaces of Kwagunt black shale layers. Look for *Chuaria* fossils on the palm-sized blocks of black shale scattered throughout the wash. Paleontologists believe that *Chuaria* represent the cyst stage of an algae's growth. The black color of these shales is due to huge concentrations of organic material from *Chuaria* and other tiny organisms preserved in the rocks. Between 3 and 10 percent of these rocks is composed of organic carbon, making them potential sources of oil and gas in southern Utah, where equivalent rocks are buried deep enough to generate hydrocarbons.

One of the most interesting microfossil species found in the Kwagunt is a vase-shaped fossil that researchers have concluded is a testate amoeba. Similar amoebae alive today are heterotrophic, meaning they eat other organisms. These are the oldest fossils ever discovered of an organism that feeds on others, leading scientists to believe that even though the late Precambrian world of Rodinia had no complex, multicellular organisms, significant ecological complexity had developed by this time, laying the groundwork for the explosion of complex life that would sweep the world a short 100 million years later.

You reach Nankoweap Creek amidst the chaos of the Butte Fault zone. The block of Cardenas Lava you observed earlier occupies the creek's right bank, and a matching block lies on the left side 0.2 mile downstream, overlain by beds of brown Nankoweap Formation. This outcrop is particularly interesting, as it provides an exceptionally clear view of the fault's first two lives. An angling ramp separates the black basalt to the left (west) from red and gray mudstone belonging to the Dox Formation on the right (Photo 72). The ramp is a strand of the Butte Fault, and the younger Cardenas Lava has slid down its western side, demonstrating that this is a normal fault (Figure 50). This "normal" extension is a remnant of the fault's activity during the Precambrian Era, when Rodinia was stretching at the seams. In contrast, the Paleozoic rock layers that lie above the outcrop have all been uplifted along the ramp's west side to form the East Kaibab Monocline, a clear indication of the fault's second life as a reverse fault during the compression of the Laramide Orogeny (Figure 21c).

As you walk downstream from here you can see these uplifted layers of Tapeats, Bright Angel, and Muav tilt gently down to the east until mile 11.7 (GPS 36°17.31'N, 111°53.23'W), where they become so tightly folded in the monocline that they go from an eastward tilt of about 20 degrees to nearly vertical in the space of less than 100 yards, just like a carpet tumbling over a step.

Where the monocline ends, the narrow gorge of Nankoweap Canyon begins. From here to the Colorado River, still 2.4 miles away, the Muav Limestone forms

*Photo 72. Life of a fault. The Butte Fault, which appears as an angling ramp, lies between dark Cardenas Lava to the left and older, light-colored Dox Formation to the right. The fact that younger rocks lie above the fault's ramp means the Butte Fault was once a normal fault.*

the gorge's polished lower walls (Photo 10). Much more massive cliffs of Redwall Limestone tower above the Muav. Looking downstream, the gorge abruptly ends at the even higher wall of Marble Canyon. Here the entire sequence of strata, from the Muav to the Kaibab, is exposed in an unbroken cliff soaring 2600 feet. The walking is flat and easy, affording you plenty of time to soak up the aura of this amazing spot.

As you exit the gorge, you find yourself on a huge delta built by numerous debris flows and flash floods that have washed down Nankoweap Creek and pushed the Colorado River hard against Marble Canyon's eastern wall. The delta is a popular camping spot for rafting parties, so numerous trails weave their way across it. Follow any of these down to the river at Nankoweap Rapid.

Be sure to make the short excursion to a row of Puebloan granaries perched above the river just 0.2 mile downstream of Nankoweap Creek. As you enter Marble Canyon, veer to the right (south) on any established trail, carefully avoiding the cryptobiotic soil that abounds here. These trails climb steeply from the delta to the overlying bluffs, where you are treated to one of the finest views of the Colorado River in the entire park (Color Plate 1). The

*Photo 73. Ancestral Puebloan granaries built under a limestone overhang in Marble Canyon.*

granaries are a short but steep slog up the slope to the right (Photo 73). Please admire but don't disturb these amazing artifacts from our shared heritage. As you stand in this magnificent spot, try to envision the many life forms that have existed here over the eons, from bacteria thriving in the seam of a supercontinent 800 million years ago to cliff dwellers subsisting in the center of a monocline just 800 years ago.

# UNCLE JIM TRAIL

### Hike 14

## FORESTS OF SINKHOLES

*Ramble along the gently undulating surface of the Kaibab Plateau, pockmarked with sinkholes formed by dissolution of the fossil-rich Kaibab Limestone.*

LENGTH ▪ 4 miles round trip

ELEVATION CHANGE ▪ 200 feet

TIME ▪ 3 hours round trip

DIFFICULTY ▪ Easy; a pleasant stroll

BACKCOUNTRY ZONING ▪ Uncle Jim Point day-use area (UNJ) and Ken Patrick primitive area (NC9); at-large camping only in NC9

WATER AND TOILETS ▪ Neither available; closest services are North Rim general store

EMERGENCY SERVICES ▪ Nearest ranger station is 1.4 miles north of Grand Canyon Lodge on the North Rim

MULE TRIPS ▪ Available

MAP LIST ▪ 1–3, 14

KEY REFERENCES ▪ 1, 8, 18

SEASONS ▪ Spring through fall. The road to the North Rim is closed from mid-October through May

**About the Landscape:** The Uncle Jim Trail meanders over a nearly flat plateau landscape that is thickly forested. The trees that thrive at this 8000-foot elevation include ponderosa pine in the drier areas and a mixture of spruce, fir, and aspen where it is cooler and wetter (Photo 74). Slight differences in slope angle and in aspect govern the temperature and soil moisture of each local microclimate, helping to control which trees are present. These local conditions are determined in part by erosion patterns in the Kaibab Limestone, which underlies the soil here. Like any rock layer, the Kaibab is cut by gullies and stream valleys, but being a limestone, it also dissolves in water, creating a less common type of topography known as *karst*. Over time, acidic

*Photo 74. Aspen trees peeking behind tall ponderosa pines. Subtle erosion patterns in the Kaibab Limestone help form microclimates that govern which tree species will thrive in a given location.*

groundwater dissolves caves in the limestone, and eventually the roofs of shallower caves collapse, forming circular sinkholes. On a plateau as flat as the Kaibab, these sinkholes are important contributors to the subtle changes that allow an aspen grove to flourish in one location while ponderosa pines grow just a short distance away. The sinkholes' circular shapes are not immediately obvious in the forested terrain along this trail, but they are quite evident in the grassy meadows just outside the park entrance. When you leave the park, look for the many circular depressions, some holding small lakes, that dot the meadows on either side of Highway 67 (Photo 75).

**Trail Guide:** From the North Rim entrance station, follow AZ Highway 67 south 10.5 miles to the clearly marked North Kaibab trailhead parking lot on the left.

Start by following signs for the Ken Patrick Trail, which shares this path for the first 0.5 mile. Initially, the trail traces the north rim of Roaring Springs Canyon, providing impressive vistas into its depths. All the Paleozoic rock layers from the Kaibab to the Bright Angel are visible. Toward the top of this beautiful scene are the prominent white cliffs of the Coconino Sandstone. Look for the inclined layers *(cross-bedding)* in the Coconino, evidence of its origin as piles of desert sand dunes blown across this region 270 million years ago (Figure 27). The prominent lower cliff band is the Redwall Limestone, deposited in an ocean that occupied this same area 80 million years earlier.

In the far distance, across the South Rim, you can see San Francisco Mountain, over 60 miles away. The peaks that you see are the jagged remnants of a stratovolcano, a large, explosive volcano similar to Washington's Mount Saint Helens. San Francisco Mountain was active between about 2 million and 400,000 years ago.

After 0.2 mile, the trail bends away from the rim to meander through the forest, which alternates between groves of ponderosa pines and mixed zones of spruce, fir, and aspen (Photo 74). Slight changes in slope and in aspect, some caused by the underlying Kaibab Limestone as it dissolves, help to create the microclimates in which these different species thrive. As you walk, look for differences in the surface topography indicating the karst in this area.

At mile 0.5 you reach the signed Ken Patrick Trail junction. The Uncle Jim Trail takes the right-hand fork. After descending a gentle slope, you

*Photo 75. Sinkhole. The circular depression formed by collapse of a shallow cave in the underlying Kaibab Limestone bedrock.*

encounter the trail's first outcrop, a block of Kaibab Limestone. Just 200 yards farther, the trail descends into a gully, the headwaters of Roaring Springs Canyon. This section is lined with Kaibab blocks. Look closely at these and you will see many intersecting, tubular burrows (about 0.5 inch wide and 2 to 3 inches long, Photo 86) that were shaped 260 million years ago by invertebrate animals feasting on the muddy bottom of the shallow Kaibab Sea.

After crossing the gully, the trail begins a moderate climb up the other side, soon encountering a second, unsigned trail junction at mile 0.9. Both forks are part of the Uncle Jim Trail, which makes a lollipop loop here. To follow this trail description, take the left fork to navigate the loop in a clockwise fashion. At 0.3 mile past this junction, the cliffs rimming Bright Angel Canyon appear. Hidden from your view, the lower portion of the North Kaibab Trail follows this valley all the way to its junction with the Colorado River.

The Uncle Jim Trail soon leaves the rim again, returning to it 1 mile from the start of the loop, at another trail junction. The right fork completes the loop, but continue straight along the 100-yard spur that leads to the vista at Uncle Jim Point. Ponderosa pines tower above a hitching post here. The point's southern exposure makes it too hot and dry for pine trees, so it is covered instead with Gambel's oaks.

From the point, you get an expansive view of the Grand Canyon and, in the distance beyond it, several peaks in the San Francisco volcanic field. On the near side of the Canyon, the large, flat area to the left is the Walhalla Plateau, with, from left to right, Deva, Brahma, and Zoroaster Temples to its right. Walhalla Plateau is a portion of the Kaibab Plateau that has been nearly cut off from the rest of the North Rim through erosion by Bright Angel and Nankoweap Creeks. Deva, Brahma, and Zoroaster Temples are resistant remnants of Coconino Sandstone that still bravely stand despite the erosion that successfully cut off and whittled away at the Plateau's outlying portions (Figure 34, Color Plate 3). The temples are examples of the future fate of Cape Royal, Bright Angel Point (where the North Rim visitor facilities lie), and Uncle Jim Point, where you now stand.

On your right, the jagged path descending into Roaring Springs Canyon (Photo 76) is the North Kaibab Trail, which pierces the cliffs of Coconino Sandstone by following a gully formed along the Roaring Springs Fault. The motion crushed the sandstone, weakening the rock and increasing its susceptibility to weathering and erosion. Because of this effect, it is very common for valleys, canyons, and gullies to form along faults. Notice that the block of Coconino just left of the trail is dropped down relative to the block to its right. The block of Coconino even farther left (left of a second gully) is again raised. This difference in elevation is due to the fault's splitting into two branches here. The middle block of Coconino occupies a trough dropped down between the two fault

*Photo 76. The North Kaibab Trail snakes its way between sheer cliffs of Coconino Sandstone. The Coconino is offset along two branches of a normal fault, which dropped the center block down and provided a weakness along which to build this trail.*

branches, which are marked by the gullies. The North Kaibab Trail sneaks its way down through the cliff band along the right-hand branch.

Uncle Jim Point is formed from Kaibab Limestone outcrops, and this limestone is loaded with fossils. The limestone has a lumpy texture, and virtually every lump contains a trace of ancient life. Some of the most distinctive fossils are *brachiopods,* **D**-shaped shells with ridges radiating outward from the hinged center (Figure 29, Photo 50). The narrower, cornucopia-shaped fossils with parallel ridges are *horn corals,* and the gray-white, translucent nodules with a "wormy" texture are *sponges.* The presence of all these fossils shows that 260 million years ago, the rocks of Uncle Jim Point were covered by a shallow, open sea. Outcrops of Kaibab Limestone in the extreme eastern Grand Canyon contain very few of these fossils and instead have more salt-tolerant species, including mollusks. This change in fossil species toward the east, along with

231

greater concentrations of salts *(evaporites)*, indicates that restricted coastal estuaries with abnormally high salt content lay in that direction, just a short distance from here (Figure 30).

After enjoying the spectacular views, backtrack to the hitching post. Veer left here and walk 1 mile back to the loop junction. Turn left again to return to the trailhead, enjoying your peaceful stroll through the forests of sinkholes.

# NORTH KAIBAB TRAIL

## WATER MAKES THE RIM GROW DISTANT

*Splash in the abundant creeks, waterfalls, and springs that continue to extend the longest rim-to-river trail in the park.*

LENGTH ■ 14.2 miles

ELEVATION CHANGE ■ 5840 feet

TIME ■ 2 days each way

DIFFICULTY ■ Difficult to very difficult; smooth tread but very long

BACKCOUNTRY ZONING ■ Corridor; camp only at Cottonwood Camp (CCG) and Bright Angel Camp (CBG). Cabins and meals available at Phantom Ranch with advance reservations

WATER AND TOILETS ■ Toilets and treated water at Supai Tunnel and both campgrounds; toilets also available at Roaring Springs. Perennial water available below Roaring Springs

EMERGENCY SERVICES ■ Emergency phone 5.6 miles below North Rim; ranger stations at Cottonwood Camp and Phantom Ranch

MULE TRIPS ■ Available to Supai Tunnel (half day) or Roaring Springs (full day)

MAP LIST ■ 1–3, 7, 14

KEY REFERENCE ■ 1

DAY HIKES ■ Supai Tunnel (5.4 miles round trip); Roaring Springs (9.4 miles round trip); Phantom Ranch to Ribbon Falls (11.2 miles round trip from river)

SEASONS ■ Spring through fall. The road to the North Rim is closed from mid-October through May

**About the Landscape:** Along the North Kaibab Trail, water is unusually abundant, creating lush oases in an otherwise stark desert landscape. At Roaring Springs, sufficient water pours from a cliff of Muav Limestone to supply all of the South Rim facilities, with enough left over to form a perennial stream. Just below Roaring Springs, the trail meets Bright Angel Creek, one of the Grand Canyon's largest tributaries and a habitat for beavers. Several smaller tributaries add their water to Bright Angel Creek as it surges toward its rendezvous with the muddy Colorado River. One of these streams tumbles over Ribbon Falls, creating a 30-foot-high mound of travertine and a scenic spectacular in the process.

If you are from Minnesota, the amount of water you see along this trail may not seem like much, but for the desert, it is a deluge. Veterans of the bone-dry South Kaibab Trail, just across the river, can verify this fact. In addition, the North Kaibab Trail is much longer than the South Kaibab, or any other South Rim trail. A quick map survey reveals that many long tributaries, such as Bright Angel Creek, descend from the North Rim, as opposed to the relatively short tributaries that enter from the south. In fact, in Grand Canyon National Park, nearly two-thirds of the area below the rim lies north of the Colorado River.

Why are the northern tributary canyons so much longer than their southern counterparts?

The answer is water. This distinctive geography is the result of the relative abundance of water north of the Colorado River, for which there are three reasons. The first is simply a matter of elevation. The North Rim sits at 8000 to 9000 feet. By contrast, most of the South Rim lies near 7000 feet. The North Rim's extra elevation allows it to wring additional moisture from passing storms, resulting in more water flowing in streams and percolating into the ground.

The second reason relates to the direction that streams and runoff from precipitation flow. Because the Kaibab Plateau here has a general southward slope, it forces most of the precipitation that falls on the North Rim to flow toward the Canyon. In contrast, most of the water falling on the South Rim streams away from it.

The third reason is the path of groundwater flow. Although the Grand Canyon's Paleozoic rock layers appear horizontal, they actually dip southward at an angle of 1 to 3 degrees. This tilt, slight as it is, explains the surprising fact that although the North and the South Rim visitor centers both stand on Kaibab Limestone, the South Rim center sits 1400 feet lower! The tilt plays a crucial role in directing the Canyon's groundwater. Under the force of gravity, groundwater percolates downward through *permeable* rocks (ones that allow water to easily pass through) until it reaches an *impermeable* layer (a rock layer that doesn't allow water to pass through it) such as mudstone. At that point, the water continues its journey by flowing downhill along the base of the permeable layer until it exits as a spring (Figure 37). Therefore, the slight southerly dip in the Canyon's Paleozoic rocks directs groundwater north of the Colorado River toward the Canyon while guiding most groundwater south of the river away from it.

How does more water make the North Rim grow distant? Water is the desert's primary agent of erosion. It has carved the Grand Canyon's tributaries through two processes: stream erosion and spring sapping. The greater moisture of the North Rim provides more water to Bright Angel Creek and other northern tributaries, so they are more efficient at scouring their bedrock channels and "eating" their way headward (Figure 22), extending their length in the process. More powerful streams thus form longer tributaries.

Where springs emerge, the water plucks individual grains from the rock face in a process called *spring sapping* (Figure 33). This grain-by-grain plucking occurs very slowly, but over time it undercuts the cliffs above. Eventually, the undercut cliff intersects one of the many joints, or cracks, riddling the Grand Canyon's walls, and a large slab of rock collapses in a landslide (Color Plate 18). This process, called *scarp retreat*, has created the amphitheater shape of all the Canyon's tributaries. Because of the greater number and volume of northern springs, this process also contributes to more rapid lengthening of the northern tributaries compared to their southern counterparts.

The North Kaibab Trail descends the western side of Roaring Springs Canyon, abruptly dropping through most of the Paleozoic rock layers before joining Bright Angel Canyon. Like most of the Grand Canyon's tributaries, both canyons have formed along faults, and along this entire hike you will never be far from their trace. Shortly after reaching Bright Angel Canyon, you pass through remnants of the Grand Canyon Supergroup before reaching the ancient, crystalline rocks of Bright Angel Creek's spectacular lower gorge.

**Trail Guide:** From the North Rim entrance station, follow AZ Highway 67 south 10.5 miles to the clearly marked North Kaibab trailhead parking lot on the left.

From the parking lot, the well-maintained trail quickly passes through the Kaibab Limestone, reaching the Toroweap Formation at mile 0.6. Although the place where these rocks meet is obscured by soil, vegetation, and tumbled blocks, the Park Service has come to the aid of trailside geologists by marking this contact with a metal interpretive sign. The trail descends through the 265-million-year-old Toroweap in a series of sweeping traverses through stands of pine, spruce, aspen, and Gambel's oak. Arizona's highest mountains, the San Francisco Peaks, are framed by the Canyon walls and provide an especially dramatic backdrop when they are capped with snow.

Atop the Coconino Sandstone (mile 0.8; GPS 36°12.89'N, 112°03.17'W), the trail abruptly spills onto a bedrock clearing known as the Coconino Overlook. The sheer sandstone cliff plunges down to your left, demonstrating how difficult passage through the Coconino would be if not for the Roaring Springs Fault. At this location the fault consists of two branches, or splays, and the trail advances along a block that dropped down between them (Photo 76). Notice how the top of the Coconino cliff is higher to both sides than at the vantage point where you are standing.

The North Kaibab Trail continues through the beautiful white sandstone in a tight series of switchbacks, reaching the soft, brick-red Hermit Shale on the right side of the trail at mile 1.7. The next contact, between the Hermit Shale and the Supai Group, is harder to see, owing to the units' similar color. Once again, the Park Service has obligingly placed a sign at this location. If you want to find the contact for yourself, look at the cliffs to the east (left) of the trail. The top of the Supai is generally marked by the highest red cliff of substantial size: the Esplanade Sandstone. Above this, the Hermit contains some thin, resistant sandstone beds, but nothing approaching the scale of a cliff.

At 2.7 miles from the rim you reach Supai Tunnel, blasted through the Esplanade Sandstone in the 1930s when the Roaring Springs section of this trail was constructed. Here you will find drinking water and a toilet, making this an ideal day-hike destination. At the tunnel, you are in a pinyon pine and Utah juniper forest. Below Supai Tunnel there is no longer enough vegetation to provide reliable shade, and treated water is not available again until Cottonwood Campground.

After the tunnel, the trail crosses the rest of the Supai Group in another series of short, tight switchbacks. At mile 3.3 (GPS 36°12.60'N, 112°02.83'W), you reach the contact with the impressive Redwall Limestone.

## TROPICAL BRECCIA

Some 320 million years ago, the ocean that had deposited the Redwall Limestone receded, exposing it to the elements. At the time, the Grand Canyon region was located at tropical latitudes. Because limestones dissolve very easily, those exposed to tropical weathering typically develop extensive systems of caves and sinkholes, and the Redwall was no exception. Five million years later, swampy muds and sands covered the remaining Redwall. These bright red deposits, called the Surprise Canyon Formation, filled in many of the old sinkholes and caves, surrounding blocks of the light gray limestone that had tumbled into the holes. One such chaotic jumble, called a *breccia,* is present to the east (left) of the trail just below the top of the Redwall.

From the contact, the trail descends steeply through the Redwall. Near its base, the trail negotiates a right-hand switchback beneath a large overhang. Sixty yards farther, the trail descends a series of wooden steps onto the Temple Butte Limestone.

*Photo 77. Tubular worm burrows cover this rock.*

The Temple Butte is a rock unit from the Devonian Period that, in the eastern Grand Canyon, was almost completely eroded away before the Redwall Limestone was deposited. The Temple Butte is preserved only where channels were cut by tides into the underlying Muav Limestone, allowing the sediments to settle into these relatively protected "foxholes." As a result, the Temple Butte is exposed in a discontinuous series of lenses (Figure 46). Luckily, one such lens is visible where the trail descends the wooden steps. The Temple Butte has a distinctive purple cast that contrasts with the gray (or red-stained) Redwall above and the yellowish Muav Limestone below. You can also tell that you have left the Redwall by noting the transition from its thick, massive layers to the thin (1 to 5 inch) beds in the Temple Butte.

Near the stairs, notice that many of these thin beds look wavy. This pattern was created by ripplemarks left by ancient tidal currents. The Temple Butte here also contains numerous trace fossils, mainly small, tubular worm burrows (Photo 77). One hundred yards farther, a sign marks the transition from the lens of Temple Butte to the more extensive Muav Limestone below (mile 4.3). If you look back up the trail from this point, you can see the large roof in the lower Redwall under which the trail passed. Below this roof, trace the Temple Butte's thin, purple beds to the right until they pinch out against a massive Redwall cliff. The pinchout is the eastern limit of this "foxhole" of Temple Butte Limestone.

In a long traverse, the trail slowly descends through the Muav Limestone. You are still in the Muav when you reach the Roaring Springs Trail junction at mile 4.7, but the contact with the Bright Angel Shale, marked by another sign, lies only 40 yards down the trail. Roaring Springs is an impressive cascade of water issuing from a cliff of Muav Limestone. The springs form where groundwater reaches an impermeable layer near the Muav–Bright Angel contact. Groundwater is conducted along a joint from the base of the bold cliff of permeable Redwall Limestone almost completely through the Muav. Where that joint intersects an impermeable layer (one that doesn't transmit water) near the Bright Angel contact, water comes gushing out (Figure 37).

At the junction with the spur trail, consider dropping your pack and taking the 5-minute stroll down to the Roaring Springs oasis. The riparian area in the canyon bottom is a wonderful place to eat lunch, and a toilet is located there. The spur passes beneath a good exposure of Bright Angel Shale before all bedrock is covered by loose slope deposits that contain boulders the size of refrigerators.

Back on the main trail, the route descends through green Bright Angel Shale and, beyond mile 5.1, through brown Tapeats Sandstone outcrops all the way to the floor of Bright Angel Canyon and beyond, to the mouth of Manzanita Creek. Where a bridge crosses Bright Angel Creek, look downstream to the creek's left bank. Where the creek begins a right-hand meander, notice the wall of Tapeats Sandstone above. The left side of this cliff ends abruptly in a rubbly slope below a saddle. The saddle and the broken slope mark the trace of the Bright Angel Fault, which runs down this canyon to Phantom Ranch and beyond.

As the trail follows the right-hand meander, it crosses onto the fault's western side and enters the Grand Canyon Supergroup (Figure 20), crossing onto the Dox Formation at mile 5.3 (GPS 36°11.06'N, 112°01.93'W). The trail follows a succession of Dox mudstones and one tan sandstone bed all the way to Cottonwood Camp at mile 6.8. A 4- to 6- hour hike from the North Rim, Cottonwood Camp is a great place to break up the journey to Phantom Ranch, offering cottonwood-shaded campsites, running water, toilets, a ranger station, and an emergency telephone.

As you leave Cottonwood Camp, you traverse rubble-covered slopes and occasional outcrops of the Dox Formation. At 0.3 mile beyond (GPS 36°10.06'N, 112°02.66'W), the Dox is intruded by a series of diabase dikes (Photo 22), which fed the flows of Cardenas Lava during their eruption 1100 million years ago. Along this trail, these flows were eroded before the Tapeats Sandstone was deposited. The dikes are black to dark green in color, and if you examine a fresh surface, you will be able to spot small crystals, a sign that these magmas cooled just a short distance below the surface.

Shortly before the tributary of Wall Creek enters from the left, the trail crosses into bold, pink outcrops of the Shinumo Quartzite (mile 7.6). The Shinumo is cut by diabase dikes and sills (Figure 23) in the area just upstream

*Photo 78. Ribbon Falls tumbles over a cliff of Shinumo Quartzite onto a pedestal of travertine.*

of the Ribbon Falls Trail junction, which you reach about 8 miles from the Rim. At the junction, the trail's drainage berm is composed of several blocks of green-black diabase.

The 10- to 15-minute detour to scenic Ribbon Falls is well worth the effort. The Ribbon Falls Trail descends toward Bright Angel Creek past good Shinumo Quartzite outcrops. It crosses the creek on a bridge, heads downstream past a sign marking the Shinumo, then bends right into the Ribbon Falls tributary. Thirty yards from the Shinumo sign is a "Day Use Only" sign. A diabase dike slashes across the Shinumo behind this sign. Compared to the resistant Shinumo, the diabase is soft and easily eroded, as shown by the gully and saddle it forms to your left. The quartzite's resistant nature is even more obvious 200 yards upstream as you enter the Ribbon Falls amphitheater, where sheer walls of Shinumo tower 300 feet above you. From a slot in the back of the amphitheater, Ribbon Falls plunges 120 feet. At first the water falls free, but 30 feet above the floor it lands on a cone of *travertine* (a limestone crystallized from fresh water). In this wet microclimate, mosses, maidenhair fern, yellow columbine, and monkey flower thrive (Photo 78).

How did the travertine pedestal form? Before its dramatic leap, the water of Ribbon Falls Creek flows through several limestone layers, dissolving calcium carbonate along the way. The calcium and carbonate ions remain in the water until it plunges over the falls, releasing carbon dioxide. The effect is similar to the escape of carbon dioxide when you open a can of soda. The corresponding change in water chemistry causes the calcium and carbonate to recombine and crystallize as solid travertine.

While relaxing in this cool oasis, explore the grotto to the right of the falls. A short trail leads up to this alcove, which is decorated with travertine stalagtites and a pillar stretching from floor to ceiling. These were precipitated in the same way as Ribbon Falls' pedestal. The alcove was formed by spring sapping (Color Plate 16, Figure 33). Look closely at the beds just below the overhang, and you'll see that they are composed of thin mudstones interbedded with thicker quartzite. The impermeable nature of the mudstone has focused a series of springs along this layer. These springs, in turn, have undercut the Shinumo cliff as they carry sand particles away. The spring is still seeping, dampening the alcove.

After you finally tear yourself away from the coolness and splendor of the falls, either retrace your steps back to the main trail or, if the water is low, take the shortcut that fords Bright Angel Creek. If you return to the main trail junction, you will immediately begin to climb over a knob of Shinumo Quartzite. As you descend the other side, you step for the first time onto the orange Hakatai Shale (mile 8.6; GPS 36°09.46'N, 112°03.13'W), the layer below the Shinumo (Figure 20). To your left you can see the distinctive orange Hakatai far above you on the slope. This is because you are once again standing near the Bright Angel Fault, which has uplifted and tilted the layers on the left flank of the canyon. The Hakatai here has been intruded by a large diabase sill, which you reach at mile 8.8. The trail continues through the diabase nearly to some beaver ponds (marked by a sign at mile 10). At the far end of the ponds, behind a sign directing the way to Ribbon Falls, is an interesting exposure of Bass Limestone, the lowermost unit of the Grand Canyon Supergroup.

These layers are noteworthy for a couple of reasons. First, like the Hakatai outcrops upstream, they are tilting at a dizzying 70-degree angle because these layers lie in the kink of a monocline (Figure 50) located just east of the Bright Angel Fault. This monocline has lifted the rocks east of Bright Angel Creek 600 feet relative to those west of it. These trailside rocks have been tilted almost vertically between the two levels. The monocline is also evident looking downstream, where nearly vertical Bass layers become less steep to the right, near the toe of the fold.

The second point of interest at this stop is the thin, wrinkled layering visible in the Bass Limestone (particularly on the right side of the outcrop). These wrinkled layers are ancient stromatolite fossils, to which we owe our existence.

## THE ORGANISMS THAT CHANGED THE WORLD

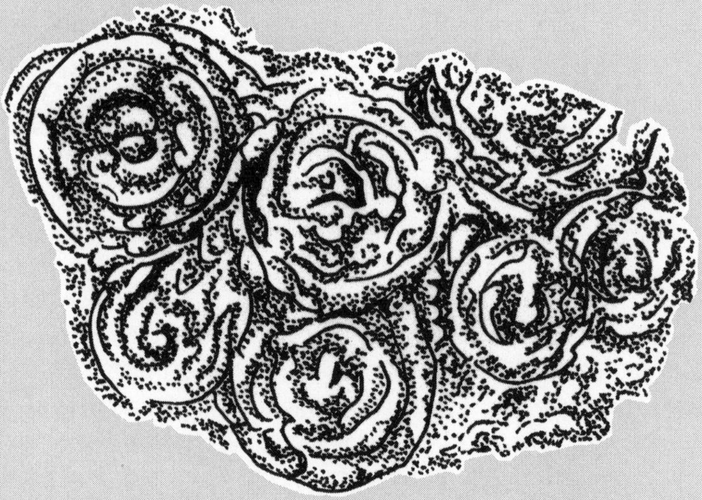

*Figure 35. Some of the longest-lived creatures on earth, stromatolites are the oldest macroscopic fossils found in the Grand Canyon (©2004 by Dona Abbott).*

When the Bass Limestone was deposited 1200 million years ago, the world's shallow seas teemed with mats of cyanobacteria (photosynthesizing bacteria). As sediment settled through the sea covering the Grand Canyon area, it coated these mats. The next generation of bacteria grew up through the thin sediment blanket, binding the particles together with gelatinous organic secretions. In this way, thin layer after thin layer was stacked, one on top of another, and were later cemented into rock, forming stromatolites (Figure 35, Photo 79). Although most of the organic matter decayed long ago, the wavy sediment laminations that mimic the bacterial mats' structure reveal the abundance of life on earth so many years ago.

Cyanobacteria such as these were responsible for converting the earth's poisonous primordial atmosphere into the oxygen-rich mixture we enjoy today. In a very real sense, we owe our lives to these tiny creatures. Cyanobacterial mats thrived throughout the Precambrian Era because mollusks and other bacteria-eating or-

*Photo 79. Oldest fossils. The wavy layers were formed by sediment that draped over generations of bacterial mats. Stromatolites like these constitute the world's oldest fossils visible to the naked eye.*

ganisms had not yet evolved. In an ironic twist, the oxygen these bacteria released allowed such predators to evolve in the Cambrian Period, beginning the stromatolites' gradual decline. They still exist today, making them one of the longest-lived organisms on earth, but stromatolites are now found only where unusually harsh conditions (such as excessive salinity) exclude grazing predators.

Downstream of the Bass outcrop, Bright Angel Creek bends to the right, leaving the fault zone. At mile 10.3 (GPS 36°08.30'N, 112°04.10'W), the Bass Limestone butts up against the trail's first crystalline rocks: the Vishnu Schist. Notice the vertical foliation, along which pink veins of Zoroaster Granite have intruded. Where it meets the Vishnu, the base of the Bass is a conglomerate called the Hotauta Conglomerate Member. The Hotauta is a mixture of partially rounded quartz and granite pebbles in a sandstone matrix, and its presence attests to an episode of vigorous erosion here 1200 million years ago.

The Hotauta's nearly horizontal layers contrast sharply with the vertical foliation in the Vishnu, making it easy to trace their contact. This thin line is an *unconformity* representing 500 million years missing from the Grand Canyon's history in stone (Photo 1). Although this is less than half the gap at the Great Unconformity, it is still an immense blank spot.

For the remainder of the hike, the only rocks exposed are the imposing Vishnu Schist and lighter Zoroaster Granite. Upstream, Bright Angel Creek occupies a fairly wide valley, but as it cuts into these resistant crystalline rocks, it carves a narrow gorge that gets progressively deeper and more spectacular. Many outcrops display the dark-and-light banding typical of gneiss. The intruding pink granite and pegmatites stand in thin, vertical ribbons because they were injected parallel to the now-vertical foliation. Stretching of the crust has caused these granite ribbons to pinch and swell, to the point where, to a hungry geologist, they look like strings of link sausages on display at a butcher shop. This texture is thus named *boudinage,* the French word for sausage. One good example lies on a left bend of the creek at mile 11.1, 200 yards past the second of a pair of bridges crossing Bright Angel Creek.

In a particularly narrow section of the gorge known as "The Box," the Vishnu walls tower 1000 feet above you. Here (mile 12.7) an even narrower slit meets Bright Angel Creek. This slot was carved by Phantom Creek, another of the North Rim's perennial streams. At this point, you are only 1.5 miles from Phantom Ranch, so you can easily explore this creek and its welcoming box elder trees on a day hike from there. At mile 13.4 you pass the junction with the Clear Creek Trail, and shortly thereafter you gratefully arrive at Phantom Ranch, 14.2 miles from the trailhead.

As you heave off your pack and plunge your tired feet into the cool waters of Bright Angel Creek, it is ironic to think that these very waters have contributed to your fatigue, because it is the abundant water that makes the rim grow distant!

# BILL HALL TRAIL TO THUNDER RIVER TRAIL

## THE WALLS CAME TUMBLING DOWN

*Hike across an enormous landslide that changed the course of the Colorado River, and witness one of the Canyon's largest springs disgorging from a parched, vertical cliff to create spectacular Thunder River.*

LENGTH ▪ 12.7 miles

ELEVATION CHANGE ▪ 5250 feet

TIME ▪ 1–2 days each way

DIFFICULTY ▪ Very difficult; remote, long, and steep

BACKCOUNTRY ZONING ▪ Primitive and threshold; at-large camping in Esplanade (AY9) and Surprise Valley (AM9) but designated sites at Upper Tapeats (AW7) and Lower Tapeats (AW8) camps

WATER AND TOILETS ▪ Perennial water at and below Thunder River. Toilets at Upper Tapeats Camp

EMERGENCY SERVICES ▪ Nearest ranger station at North Rim, 1.4 miles north of Grand Canyon Lodge

MAP LIST ▪ 1, 15, 16

KEY REFERENCES ▪ 1, 8, 36

DAY HIKES ▪ Monument Point to the Esplanade (5–8 miles round trip); Colorado River to Thunder River (7 miles round trip from river); Colorado River to Thunder River and down Deer Creek (8.5 miles round trip; requires raft shuttle; see Hike 17)

SEASONS ▪ Spring through fall. The road to Monument Point is closed during winter

**About the Landscape:** The Bill Hall Trail quickly drops through the Grand Canyon's Permian rock layers, eventually joining the Thunder River Trail on the flat Esplanade terrace (Photo 80). In comparison to the same layers in the eastern Grand Canyon, these strata have some noticeable differences. For example, in the west, the Toroweap Formation is more resistant and contains more cliffs, the Coconino Sandstone is thinner, and the Hermit Shale is much thicker. Factors such as a layer's thickness or resistance strongly influence the Canyon's shape, creating such distinctive features as the western Grand Canyon's Esplanade.

The Esplanade owes its existence to the substantial thickness (up to 1000 feet) of the Hermit Shale. As the Colorado River was carving the western Grand Canyon, it first sliced a narrow, steep-walled gorge through the resistant limestones

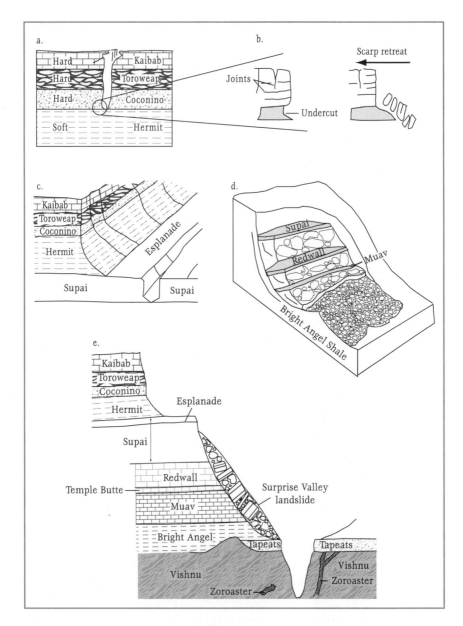

*Figure 36. Scarp retreat in the Grand Canyon. a. The river cuts a narrow gorge through hard rock layers. b. The river meanders more as it erodes softer layers like the Hermit Shale. This undermines the cliffs above, which collapse in landslides when joints are undercut. c. Repeated landslides cause the upper cliffs to retreat far from the river, creating the Esplanade. An Inner Gorge is cut as the river slices through the resistant Supai Group. d. Scarp retreat occurs largely through land-slides. Note that large blocks of rock are rotated so that they tilt into the cliffs from*

and sandstones of the Kaibab, Toroweap, and Coconino Formations (Figure 36a). When the river reached the softer Hermit Shale, it began to swing lazily through a series of broad bends called *meanders*. These meanders repeatedly undercut the cliffs above, causing them to collapse in a series of landslides (Figure 36b). This process, called *scarp retreat* (Color Plate 18), eventually caused the upper cliffs to retreat several miles away from the river, creating the Esplanade (Figure 36c). Because scarp retreat slows dramatically once the river begins cutting through resistant layers below, the Esplanade would be much narrower if the Hermit Shale were thinner, because there would be much less time for undercutting and scarp retreat to occur.

Geologists ascribe the differences between the eastern and western Permian rock layers to one simple geographic fact: the western Grand Canyon region lay in the direction of the encroaching Permian sea. At first, in the early Permian, about 286 million years ago, the entire Grand Canyon region was a floodplain traversed by meandering rivers that deposited the Hermit Shale. Later in the Permian, the climate dried, creating desert sand dunes, which formed first in the eastern Grand Canyon area, then spread to the west. Because the dunes that formed the Coconino accumulated over a longer period of time in the east, the Coconino there is thicker. Likewise, the shorter duration of dune deposition in the west resulted in much thicker Hermit Shale deposits there. Still later in the Permian, a sea flooded the area, depositing the Toroweap Formation. Because the sea approached from the west, the water was deeper there, and consequently Toroweap outcrops in the western Canyon contain more cliff-forming lime-stones, which are constructed from the shells of shallow marine organisms. In contrast, to the east, the Toroweap is composed of much softer shale and evapor-ite deposits that accumulated in arid, nearshore mudflats.

After crossing the Esplanade, the Thunder River Trail drops abruptly into Surprise Valley, which was created by a tremendous landslide that blocked the course of the Colorado River and dammed it up. The river was forced to carve a new gorge to the south, creating such a young stretch that it is still the nar-rowest point on the river in the entire Grand Canyon.

The Surprise Valley landslide is the most recent example of the same pro-cess of scarp retreat that formed the Esplanade (Figure 36c). After carving a narrow, inner gorge through the resistant Supai Group, Redwall, Temple Butte, and Muav Limestones below the Hermit, the river reached the soft Bright Angel Shale, meandered across it, and through landsliding whittled away at the cliffs above. Because the Bright Angel Shale is not as thick as the Hermit, the second episode of scarp retreat did not last as long. Therefore, the Supai

*which they came. The Surprise Valley landslide was triggered by undercutting of the cliff when the river reached the soft Bright Angel Shale. e. The current stairstep configuration of the Thunder River area is the result of scarp retreat.*

and Redwall cliffs have retreated much less than the Permian cliffs did across the Esplanade (Figure 36e).

**Trail Guide:** From the North Rim entrance station, drive 4.7 miles north on AZ Highway 67. Turn left on Forest Road 22 and drive 17.8 miles. Turn left onto Forest Road 425 for 10.3 miles, then turn right onto Forest Road 292. Follow this 1.3 miles to a four-way junction. Continue straight (on road 292A) for 1.6 miles to its end at the Monument Point trailhead. Signs mark the direction to Monument Point at each major intersection. These good gravel and dirt roads are easily navigable by two-wheel-drive vehicles in good weather. AZ Highway 67 is closed in winter, usually from November through May.

From the parking lot, the Bill Hall Trail descends to a saddle, then briefly climbs up to Monument Point. The trail then drops down the point's south ridge through outcrops of Kaibab Limestone. Shortly after you start down, 1 mile from the parking lot (GPS 36°25.75′N, 112°26.38′W), the trail passes through a particularly fossil-rich layer where good brachiopod and crinoid fossils are abundant. The crinoids are circular in cross section, and the brachiopods have a distinctive **D** shape (Figure 29, Photo 50).

Shortly after reaching the Toroweap Formation at mile 1.2, the trail bends to the right and begins to angle down the southwest flank of Monument Point. The Toroweap here is composed of resistant limestone bands alternating with

*Photo 80. The Esplanade is a flat bench floored by the resistant Esplanade Sandstone. The cliffs of the upper Permian layers, seen here near the top of the photo, have retreated several miles from the river to form this platform.*

mudstones that include white patches. The white areas are evaporite minerals formed by saltwater evaporation along the shore of the shallow Toroweap Sea. Looking southwest, you get inspiring views onto the Esplanade, the large tableland still 1000 feet below. In addition, look along both sides of the trail to view some impressive cryptobiotic soil (Photo 19). The traverse ends near the base of the Toroweap, where the trail negotiates a 12-foot step down a resistant limestone band. Veterans of eastern Grand Canyon hikes will be surprised by such an obstacle in the Toroweap, which is generally a soft, slope-forming layer. This step is a tangible illustration of the Toroweap's greater limestone abundance in the western Grand Canyon, which lay under deeper water when much of the Toroweap was deposited.

Below this step, 2 miles from the parking lot, the trail begins a steep descent down forty-nine switchbacks (count them!) through the cross-bedded Coconino Sandstone and the thick Hermit Shale. The Coconino-Hermit contact (mile 2.1; GPS 36°26.02'N, 112°26.75'W) is not exposed on the trail, which descends a steep cone of rubble, but it is easily recognized to either side as the transition from white sandstone cliffs to brick-red mudstone slopes below.

The Bill Hall Trail joins the Thunder River Trail at mile 3.4 (GPS 36°25.60'N, 112°27.31'W), at the same location where you cross from the Hermit Shale onto the Esplanade Sandstone, the uppermost formation of the Supai Group. Turn left (south) here and follow this trail across the expansive Esplanade (Photo 80) for 3 nearly flat miles. Most of the route traverses a beautiful slickrock bench where the trail is marked by cairns. In areas of more abundant soil, small pinyon and juniper trees dot the landscape. At mile 4.4 the trail passes through a gap in a resistant sandstone band. Several excellent tent platforms are located here, and this is an ideal location to stash a water cache for the hot return hike. The low ridge cut by this notch is capped by a resistant, 10-foot-thick sandstone layer with high-angle cross-beds. The narrower pedestal below is fashioned from softer, less-resistant mudstone. The characteristics of the rocks here provide clues to the setting in which the Esplanade Sandstone was deposited: an arid, low-relief floodplain crossed both by meandering rivers, which deposited the mudstone, and by small sand dunes, which left the cross-bedded sandstone.

The trail completes its traverse of the Esplanade at mile 6.4 and abruptly begins its descent into Surprise Valley. The first few switchbacks traverse outcrops of Supai sandstone and mudstone, but the trail soon crosses onto a large debris cone from the great Surprise Valley landslide. As you descend, you cross rubble of all sizes, weaving your way between blocks of Supai sandstone the size of large rooms. You pass the rubble-covered Supai-Redwall contact at mile 6.9 (GPS 36°24.34'N, 112°28.35'W); then, at mile 7.5, far below the contact, you encounter a series of red Supai sandstone and mudstone layers that appear to be in place. Because these layers lie well *below* the Supai-Redwall contact exposed in the background cliffs and because these layers have a steep,

247

*Photo 81. Tumbling walls. The three low hills (bottom center) are blocks of Redwall Limestone that slid far down the slope with the Surprise Valley landslide. Their layers tilted back towards the cliffs they came from, showing they moved in a rotational landslide.*

northward tilt in an area where the cliff faces are obviously horizontally bedded, you know that these layers moved a long distance in the landslide. As they moved, the strata rotated back toward the cliffs from which they came (Figure 36d). The most graphic display of this tilt is provided by three Redwall Limestone mountains that are prominent landmarks on the northeast side of Surprise Valley (Photo 81). The trail passes just west (right) of the western one at mile 7.6. Their steep northward tilt affirms that they rotated with the landslide as they slid hundreds of vertical feet below their original positions.

At mile 7.7 (GPS 36°24.05'N, 112°28.53'W) you reach an unsigned trail junction. The right branch is the start of the Deer Creek Trail. To reach Thunder River, take the left fork and continue along the valley through more landslide debris for another 1.2 miles. At mile 8.9 the trail crosses a low pass and arrives at the brink of another steep descent. Visible for the first time, Thunder Spring ejects water from two *joints* (linear fractures) near the base of the Muav Limestone. The exiting water crashes down the steep slope below in a series of waterfalls linked by noisy, tumbling cascades, forming the sensational Thunder River (Color Plate 20). The outstanding views continue as the trail switchbacks 0.5 mile down through more landslide rubble. At mile 9.5 you reach a fork between the main trail, which veers right, and a short spur trail that leads to Thunder River just below the spring.

## THUNDER FROM THE MOUNTAIN

One of the largest springs to pour out of the Grand Canyon's sheer cliffs, Thunder Spring is a scenic spectacular. What causes such a huge volume of water to disgorge from the flank of a parched, vertical wall? Much of the rain that falls on the North and South Rims percolates into the earth to become groundwater. Pulled by gravity, this groundwater rambles down through the sedimentary layers. It travels most easily through *porous* sandstone and limestone layers, but gets blocked at mudstones, which have a shingle-like arrangement of platy clay minerals that stops the passage of water. When groundwater reaches one of these mudstone obstructions, like the Bright Angel Shale, it turns parallel to the boundary between the porous and the platy *(impermeable)* strata and starts running down their tilt. When this water emerges from the ground, usually near the base of a cliff of permeable rock, it exits as a spring (Figure 37). Joints, which cut through all the Canyon's rock layers, become conduits for groundwater, providing the only efficient means for water to pass through otherwise impermeable layers.

*Figure 37. Thunder Springs exits from joints in the permeable Muav Limestone near the contact with the impermeable Bright Angel Shale.*

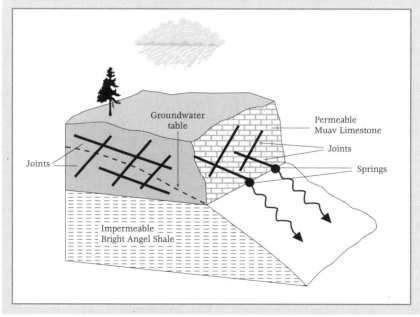

Because so much water is focused along joints, the biggest springs in the Canyon are formed where joints in porous rocks intersect impermeable layers, forcing the water to emerge from the ground. Such is the case at Thunder Spring, which exits the Muav Limestone through two joints just above the contact between the porous Muav and the impermeable Bright Angel Shale below (Color Plate 20). Looking up and right of the modern springs, you can see other vertical joints in the Muav with narrow, elongated caves formed along their length. These caves were the exit points for prehistoric springs that have since dried up as the main flow of groundwater shifted to the modern Thunder Spring.

Continuing to the right along the main trail, you cross from chaotic landslide debris onto outcrop of Bright Angel Shale at mile 9.6. Here the Bright Angel contains the orderly, brown sandstone and green mudstone beds typical of the formation. Look for worm burrows (Photo 86), and ripplemarks (Photo 20) along the bedding surfaces. To your left, Thunder River tumbles over a particularly thick, resistant sandstone layer in the Bright Angel, forming a beautiful four-stranded waterfall. The cliff to the right of this waterfall is caked with a small travertine deposit.

As the trail continues to descend the right bank of Thunder River, you pass directly from the Bright Angel Shale to the Shinumo Quartzite (Figure 20), part of the Grand Canyon Supergroup (mile 9.7; GPS 36°23.58'N, 112°27.33'W). Although you don't cross the Tapeats Sandstone here, if you look east at the far wall of Tapeats Creek, you can distinguish the chocolate-brown Tapeats from the greenish Bright Angel Shale above. Why is the Tapeats Sandstone absent along the Thunder River Trail? During the Cambrian Period, as the Tapeats was deposited along the shores of a shallow sea, knobs in the very hard, resistant Shinumo Quartzite jutted out of the sea as small, rocky islands (Figure 28). The Tapeats was deposited around the shores of these islands, such as the Tapeats you see to the east, but the islands were not completely buried by sediment until the Bright Angel Shale was deposited in deeper water several million years later.

Along this section of trail, the Shinumo Quartzite contains evidence of soft-sediment deformation, which is the contortion of sediment before it solidifies into rock. A good example of this is found at mile 9.7 on a Shinumo block where someone carved "1939." Just above this graffiti, thin beds in the quartzite have been folded back on themselves. Other blocks in this area display similar features, as do many of the outcrops around Upper Tapeats Camp. This contorted *marblecake bedding* was caused by earthquakes that rocked the area 1100 million years ago, turning parts of the water-saturated sediment into quicksand

and contorting the bedding in some places while leaving other areas undisturbed (Photo 42).

After 10.4 miles you reach the shady Upper Tapeats Camp, home to a toilet and perennial Tapeats Creek. The trail then continues down the creek, crossing the contact between the Shinumo Quartzite and the brick-red Hakatai Shale at mile 10.7 (GPS 36°23.34'N, 112°27.24'W). From here, paths exist on both sides of the creek. Because the creek is sometimes treacherous to ford, we describe the trail that sticks to the right bank. A short distance farther, the trail squeezes between the creek and a small cliff of Hakatai Shale, where it ascends a rising ledge of soft shale lying between more resistant sandstone layers. While treading carefully across the narrow, rubbly ledge, be sure to search for the outstanding ancient ripplemarks and mudcracks (Photos 2, 20) displayed in the rubble and on the undersides of overhangs. Mudcracks and ripplemarks are common in many of the Canyon's rock layers, but the Hakatai and other units in the Supergroup provide the best and most abundant examples because when these layers were deposited, there were no plants or animals around to disrupt the surface and obscure the sedimentary features.

The trail alternates between flat, sandy stretches next to the creek and short climbs over Hakatai outcrops. At mile 11.3 your hands are useful to negotiate a 5-foot step formed by a resistant sandstone bed. Looking downstream from here,

*Photo 82. Stromatolites. The cabbage-like lumps in this Bass Limestone are the remains of ancient bacterial colonies.*

high above the east bank, is a 300-foot cliff of Tapeats Sandstone rising above the Hakatai Shale. This boundary forms the Great Unconformity here, and its undulating surface provides a graphic illustration of the relief that existed on the seafloor during Cambrian times.

After one more climb in the Hakatai Shale, the trail turns sharply left and descends a steep, east-facing slope to rejoin Tapeats Creek. On this descent, the trail crosses the contact between the Hakatai Shale and the Bass Limestone (mile 12; GPS 36°22.62'N, 112°27.90'W). After cutting across a creek-side sandbar, the trail squeezes through a narrow gap between a Bass outcrop and Tapeats Creek (mile 12.1). This is an outstanding location to observe *stromatolite* fossils in the Bass. Look for wavy, undulating laminations, which were formed by mats of bacteria that flourished on the seafloor 1200 million years ago. Because multicellular life didn't evolve until about 650 million years ago, the stromatolites are the only macroscopic fossils in the Unkar Group (Figure 20), and they are the oldest fossils in the Canyon. Even better stromatolites are located on the bed of Bass that gradually rises above the creek immediately beyond the narrow gap. The trail ascends the surface of this bed, which is dotted with round lumps, many with concentric bands (Photo 82). These cabbage-like lumps are what stromatolites look like from above.

As the trail climbs higher above the creek, you get great views into the deepening gorge, which is carved through black diabase. This diabase forms a *sill* that intruded between two weak layers of Bass Limestone. The limestone adjacent to the sill was bleached by the extreme heat (the sill was over 2200°F when it intruded), so it forms a conspicuous white band between the black diabase and the grayish color of the unbleached Bass Limestone (Photo 24).

At mile 12.4, you are treated to an impressive view of the Colorado River and Tapeats Rapid, a large one at 7 (out of 10) on the Grand Canyon river-rating scale. This is a great place to observe how a typical Grand Canyon rapid formed (Photo 83). Tapeats Creek enters the river directly below you, and trailing downstream from the confluence you can see the debris fan the creek has dumped into the Colorado River. Upstream, the Colorado is wide and flat, but immediately below the confluence with Tapeats Creek, the channel is pinched by the debris fan. Narrowing the channel accelerates the river's current, which rushes over the fan's boulders. The resulting turbulence creates the rapid's exciting waves and holes. A short distance downstream of the confluence, the channel restriction ends, the current slows, and the whitewater is over.

About 100 yards beyond the view of Tapeats Rapid, the trail arrives at the head of a steep gully that slashes through the diabase cliff below. The entrance to this gully is marked by several cairns. Although the gully may look intimidating, the descent is not as precarious as it appears from above. The first part

*Photo 83. Tapeats Rapid was formed when a debris flow or flash flood racing down Tapeats Creek dumped sediment in the Colorado River, constricting its channel. The fan of debris is visible in the lower right.*

passes outcrops of white Bass Limestone, decorated with more good stromatolites. In 0.1 mile, you reach the contact with the black diabase. Green, fibrous minerals at this contact are asbestos, formed during contact metamorphism (Photo 24) of the Bass by the intruding sill (Photo 23).

Observe the tiny crystals present in the diabase outcrops next to the Bass. Lower in this gully, as you approach the heart of this unusually thick sill, the crystal size increases. This is because the diabase that touched the cold "host rock" cooled rapidly, but the magma in the sill's interior was insulated, providing more time for larger crystals to grow.

At 12.7 miles from Monument Point, you happily arrive at Lower Tapeats Camp and the Colorado River. Here you are still surrounded by the diabase sill, which forms the cliffs above the river for several miles upstream. While here, be sure to take the time to explore the Colorado River's new course.

## THE RIVER'S NEW COURSE

The Surprise Valley landslide was a massive earth movement that occurred sometime during the last few million years, practically yesterday in geologic time. A 4-mile length of the Canyon rim gave way and tumbled 2000 vertical feet down to the Colorado River. Millions of tons of rock clogged the river, forcing it to divert to the south, where it carved a new channel. This new course forms the narrowest section of river in the entire Grand Canyon. Two vantage points along the Thunder River Trail offer exceptional views of this narrow gorge and the Colorado's ancient, boulder-clogged channel.

From Lower Tapeats Camp, take a short stroll downstream of Tapeats Rapid, where you can look west into the 75-foot-wide slot created by the Colorado's recent realignment. To the right of this slot and adjacent to a dark brown cliff of Tapeats Sandstone lies a yellow cliff studded with boulders (Photo 84). This is the Colorado River's previous channel, completely clogged with landslide debris. Up and to the right is Point 4060, a block of Redwall Limestone that tilted to the north

*Photo 84. A raft enters the narrowest part of the Grand Canyon, carved after the river's original course was blocked by debris from the enormous Surprise Valley landslide. The river's old course is visible to the upper right, where its lens-shaped channel is filled with light-colored rock (to the right of the darker Tapeats Sandstone cliff on the skyline).*

as it rotated downward during the same landslide (Figure 36d).

You can obtain an even more impressive view of the ancient channel via a short detour from the Thunder River Trail. Follow the path back to where it finishes the climb out of the steep gully leading through the diabase. From here, turn left (south) and follow a faint path 100 yards along a limestone ledge. This route takes you around the corner to the right, where you get an outstanding view of the Colorado. Easily visible downstream are the ancient yellow channel and its flanking brown Tapeats outcrop, which formed the Canyon wall at the time this course was active. From this viewpoint, you are at the same elevation as the ancient channel, and the height of your perch gives you a more panoramic view of the narrow gorge the Colorado River now occupies.

Hiking the Bill Hall Trail to Thunder River Trail beautifully illustrates some of the most distinctive geologic and scenic characteristics of the western Grand Canyon, including the thunder of water in the desert and roaring echoes from a distant time when the walls came tumbling down.

Hike 17

# DEER CREEK TRAIL

BURROWING THROUGH TIME

*Cross a gigantic landslide to explore a beautiful slickrock gorge with walls covered by worm burrows, then swim in a refreshing pool just below the Great Unconformity at the base of magnificent Deer Creek Falls.*

LENGTH ■ 3.5 miles from the Thunder River Trail junction; 11.2 miles from Monument Point trailhead

ELEVATION CHANGE ■ 5250 feet from the rim

TIME ■ 1–2 days each way from the rim

DIFFICULTY ■ Difficult to very difficult; rocky tread, remote, and difficult access

BACKCOUNTRY ZONING ■ Primitive and threshold; at-large camping in Esplanade (AY9) and Surprise Valley (AM9), but designated sites at Deer Creek Camp (AX7)

WATER AND TOILETS ■ Perennial water at and below Deer Spring. Toilet at Deer Creek Camp

EMERGENCY SERVICES ■ Nearest ranger station at North Rim, 1.4 miles north of Grand Canyon Lodge

MAP LIST ▪ 1, 16, 17

KEY REFERENCES ▪ 1, 8, 21, 36

DAY HIKES ▪ None from the rim. Colorado River to Deer Spring (3 miles round trip from river); Colorado River to Thunder River and down Deer Creek (8.5 miles round trip; requires raft shuttle; see Hike 16)

SEASONS ▪ Spring through fall. The road to Monument Point is closed during winter

**About the Landscape:** The upper Deer Creek Trail traverses debris from the enormous Surprise Valley landslide almost to Deer Spring, which pours from a joint in the Muav Limestone near its contact with the Bright Angel Shale. Not far below the spring, the trail meets Deer Creek, with its spectacular Tapeats Sandstone gorge that twists and turns like a polished snake. In the gorge, small overhangs are covered by tubular blobs, which are the burrows of worms and other invertebrates that were the primary inhabitants of this region during the Cambrian Period, about 545 million years ago.

Although multicellular animals first evolved about 650 million years ago, it was not until the Cambrian that their population exploded and diversified. For the first time, these animals developed a stiffened body, an innovation that allowed them to burrow into the mud. Burrowing was an advantage both for filter feeding and for protection from predators, and Cambrian sediments around the world abound with fossilized burrows (Photo 86).

Preservation of burrows is aided by the jumbling of the sediment caused by the animal's passage. This jumbling increases the sediment's porosity, allowing more water to percolate through the burrows than through the surrounding sediments. The additional water precipitates extra cementing minerals in the old burrow, making it more resistant to erosion than the surrounding rock. Organic materials secreted by the organisms also change the local sediment chemistry, often enhancing the cementation. Later erosion removes the surrounding, softer sediment, and the more resistant burrows stand out in bold relief. Paleontologists call these burrows *trace fossils,* because while not parts of the organism itself, they provide evidence of the organism's existence.

**Trail Guide:** Access is via the Bill Hall Trail to Thunder River Trail (Hike 16).

From mile 7.7 of the Thunder River Trail, the Deer Creek Trail branches to the right (GPS 36°24.05'N, 112°28.53'W) and begins its traverse across Surprise Valley. After 0.5 mile, the trail meets a lower cutoff from Thunder River (GPS 36°23.87'N, 112°28.92'W) and turns to the right. Shortly after this unsigned junction, the trail crosses beds of red Supai sandstone that are tilted down to the north (GPS 36°23.88'N, 112°29.00'W). These rocks appear to be in place, but their northward tilt in a region where all the cliffs have horizontal bedding, and the fact that these Supai beds lie 700 feet lower than corresponding

Supai outcrop on the cliffs above, indicate that they are part of a large block in the Surprise Valley landslide (Figure 36d). It is incredible to think of the awesome power that was unleashed the day this 4-mile long, 600- to 800-foot-tall chunk of Canyon wall gave way and tumbled down, with some of it even reaching and blocking the Colorado River (Photo 84).

The trail exits Surprise Valley at a low pass and continues west as it drops down a dry wash. The trail is generally easy to follow, but in places it runs down the wash for short (20 to 80 yard) stretches. The main trail is marked by cairns, but it is common to briefly lose it in these washes, where a maze of alternative paths exist.

At mile 1.7 the trail drops more steeply, crossing below a cliff of bouldery rubble (GPS 36°23.98'N, 112°29.98'W) on the wash's left bank. This is an excellent place to examine the chaotic jumble of materials in the landslide debris, with sizes ranging from dust to boulders. At mile 2 you encounter the first outcrop on the trail: thinly bedded, gray to purple limestone and dolomite layers of the Temple Butte Formation. In the eastern Grand Canyon, this rock unit from the Devonian Period occurs as isolated lenses, but here in the Canyon's western reaches it forms a continuous layer between the Redwall and Muav Limestones. The Temple Butte was deposited in a series of tidal channels at the margin of a large sea that opened to the west and south of the present Grand Canyon. Because the eastern region was close to the Devonian coast, later erosion removed nearly all of the Temple Butte there. Here, to the west, the sea was a bit deeper, so a greater thickness of Temple Butte was deposited, and more of it was spared from erosion. The following rise in sea level deposited the Redwall Limestone above it, protecting what was left.

The trail soon crosses out of the slope-forming Temple Butte onto outcrops of the Muav Limestone, which forms bold, yellow-gray cliffs. As you pass from the Temple Butte to the Muav, you cross a major disconformity (Figure 46) that transports you from the Devonian to the Cambrian Period. After descending several switchbacks, you reach Deer Spring, the first running water on the trail. The spring pours out of a joint in the Muav Limestone a short distance above its contact with the underlying Bright Angel Shale. The spring is located here because of the focusing of groundwater flow along joints and the impermeable boundary presented by the Bright Angel Shale (Figure 37). Below Deer Spring, the trail winds down more Surprise Valley landslide debris. The view west, across the Deer Creek Valley, takes in a jumble of boulders comprising the western portion of this same landslide. The present valley of Deer Creek used to be covered by similar debris, but the creek has since reestablished its course by eroding into it.

After 2.5 miles, the trail reaches Deer Creek, immediately fording it to reach the right (western) bank. Here the trail traverses gravel and sand terraces,

Photo 85. Deer Creek's narrow slot canyon winding through the resistant Tapeats Sandstone.

*Photo 86. The Tapeats overhang (left) is covered with tubular worm burrows. An Ancestral Puebloan handprint is visible on the right side of the photo.*

crossing through Deer Creek Camp, complete with shady tent sites, perennial water, and a toilet. Shortly thereafter, the trail enters the gorge of lower Deer Creek (Photo 85). The gorge is a narrow, winding slot of polished Tapeats Sandstone. The trail stays high, following a soft mudstone layer, while the creek drops ever farther into the slot below. In this gorge, the Tapeats is adorned with trace fossils. One good place to view them is 150 yards into the gorge. About 15 feet up the right-hand wall is an ancient Puebloan handprint that was stenciled onto the rock with red dye at least 800 years ago. Immediately to the left of this handprint is a small overhang. The underside of this overhang is a riot of cylindrical tubes 1 to 2 inches long and 0.25 to 0.5 inch wide (Photo 86). Each of these is the burrow of a worm or other invertebrate animal. After you have trained your eyes, you will see these burrows everywhere, including the overhang 5 feet below and left of the handprint, as well as the one only 6 inches above the trail.

Besides its beauty and the amazing array of trace fossils, another notable feature of the lower Deer Creek gorge is the brilliant green color of some of its rocks. The green color is caused by the presence of the mineral *glauconite*. Glauconite grows in place on the seafloor by replacement of other minerals.

259

Studies have shown that glauconite almost always forms in shallow (less than 500 feet deep) seas where the rate of sediment accumulation is low, and there is a reasonable amount of organic material present (the bodies of the invertebrate organisms that made the burrows). The presence of glauconite in the Tapeats thus tells us that those conditions existed here 545 million years ago.

At mile 3.3, the trail exits the gorge, opening onto magnificent views of the Colorado River. Just upstream you can see the narrowest point along the entire river gorge. Here the Canyon was cut more recently than adjacent portions after the Surprise Valley landslide blocked the previous channel (Photo 84) and forced the Colorado to start anew. The trail bends right and soon begins to descend a series of switchbacks through Tapeats outcrops. To the right lies chaotic rubble of the Surprise Valley landslide. Stay on the tightly zigzagging trail whose tread is the same brown color as the Tapeats; don't be fooled by trails leading off to the right, onto the yellowish soil that developed on the landslide debris. At the base of the switchbacks, the trail finally crosses onto the yellow debris. However, it soon crosses back onto the Tapeats and worms its way down a slot lying along a joint cutting a 10-foot-thick, resistant sandstone band. An easy scramble down the slot lands you on a softer mudstone layer. Turn left here and follow the obvious trail along this ledge, past a few water seeps.

After the seeps, the trail descends again through switchbacks as it reaches the Great Unconformity near the end of the trail. The unconformity itself is not well exposed, but soon you will notice Precambrian-age granite beneath your feet. Here, too, the trail splits into a maze of smaller paths, but they all lead down to the beach at the mouth of Deer Creek. Once on the beach, you are treated to a spectacular view of Deer Creek Falls, which pours out of a narrow slot cut through a resistant Tapeats Sandstone bed. The falls plunge about 120 feet into a deep green pool of water that is a popular swimming hole for rafters and hikers alike (Photo 87). The falls is a wonderful place to view the Great Unconformity, the 1200-million-year-gap in the history of the Grand Canyon. Look for the dramatic change in character of the rock about 30 feet below the top of the falls (Color Plate 8). Above lie horizontal beds of brown Tapeats, but below the tan granite lacks bedding and has an imperfect vertical fabric to it. Another good example of the unconformity lies across the river. Here, the horizontal beds of the Tapeats are underlain by Vishnu Schist. The schist's strong vertical foliation is readily apparent, highlighting the unconformity where this vertical grain is met by the horizontal Tapeats.

The gorge and the waterfall on the lower Deer Creek Trail are among the most beautiful sights in the Grand Canyon. When you can pry your eyes from the spectacle, more subtle features in the gorge give you tantalizing glimpses into the muddy activities of the Canyon's first engineers 545 million years ago.

*Photo 87. A swimmer cools off in the pool below scenic Deer Creek Falls.*

# LAVA FALLS ROUTE

### A Clash of Fire and Water

*Descend a frozen stream of lava to Lava Falls, the Colorado's most thunderous rapid, then stand at the spot where lava repeatedly dammed the river, impounding huge reservoirs that later drained catastrophically.*

LENGTH ■ 1.5 miles

ELEVATION CHANGE ■ 2540 feet

TIME ■ 2–4 hours down; 2–6 hours up

DIFFICULTY ■ Very difficult; very remote and rocky; some exposed scrambling required. This is a route, not a trail, and is appropriate only for very experienced desert hikers

BACKCOUNTRY ZONING ■ Threshold; camping only at the Colorado River (NN9). There is a drive-in campground near Toroweap Overlook

WATER AND TOILETS ■ No water available at Tuweap, the campground, or along the route. Available only at Colorado River. Take an ample supply and consider leaving a cache for the return hike. Toilets available at the campground

EMERGENCY SERVICES ■ Nearest ranger station at Tuweap, but the ranger is not always present

MAP LIST ■ 18

KEY REFERENCES ■ 1, 19, 37, 38

SEASONS ■ Fall through spring. Summer hikes not recommended due to intense heat

**About the Landscape:** The Lava Falls Route has a character unlike that of any other Grand Canyon hike. Its 2500-foot plunge in a mere 1.5 miles makes it by far the shortest and steepest rim-to-river route in the park. This memorable hike is made possible only by the area's unique geological features, which create a narrow entry corridor in otherwise inaccessible terrain.

The Lava Falls Route descends to the river along the still-active Toroweap normal fault (Figure 9). Because normal faults stretch the earth's crust, they allow hot, partially molten material from the underlying mantle to well up to shallow depths. Commonly, some of this material squeezes all the way through the weakened rocks and erupts onto the surface, creating a chain of volcanoes aligned along the fault. Such has been the case in the Toroweap area, where during the last million years, over 150 separate basalt *lava flows* have erupted along or near the Toroweap Fault. Many of these flows have poured over the sheer cliffs of the Supai Group and Redwall Limestone into the Canyon's Inner Gorge (Photo 88, Figure 38). The Lava Falls Route follows the youngest of these

*Photo 88. Less than one million years ago, black lava spilled over the Canyon rim, forming a steep ramp and challenging route to the Colorado River.*

lava cascades, erupted a mere 10,000 to 20,000 years ago. On at least thirteen occasions, lava flows filled the narrow Inner Gorge from wall to wall, releasing enormous plumes of steam in what John Wesley Powell termed "a conflict of water and fire."

These lava flows formed dams that impounded huge lakes behind them. The oldest was the Prospect Dam (named for Prospect Canyon, which lies directly across the river from this hike). Prospect Dam formed 680,000 years ago from a series of flows that, within a matter of weeks, plugged the Inner Gorge to a height of over 2300 feet above the river, more than three times the height of Hoover or Glen Canyon Dam! The impounded waters formed a lake over 300 miles long that backed up beyond Moab, Utah. It is estimated that the lake took 23 years to fill, and at its peak, if you gazed down from the viewpoints near Grand Canyon Village, its shores would have reached nearly to the base of the Redwall Limestone.

Over time, the huge quantities of silt and sand carried by the Colorado River were deposited in Prospect Lake and eventually replaced the reservoir of water with a reservoir of mud (as is happening today in Lake Powell). Geologists estimate that it took over 3000 years for the lake to "silt in," but when it did, a titanic, 2000-foot waterfall (20 times higher than Niagara Falls!) likely spilled over the dam near Lava Falls. What a sight that must have been! The water carried boulders and other debris over the falls, and their impact on the streambed caused intense erosion. Thus the river chipped away at Prospect Dam, weakening it to the point that it failed catastrophically, sending an enormous wall of water down the lower Grand Canyon.

*Figure 38. The Lava Falls area looking northeast. Note the dark lava flows spilling into the Canyon from Vulcans Throne, the black cinder cone perched on the rim (© 2004 by Dona Abbott).*

Not long after Prospect Dam was swept away, a new series of flows created the Ponderosa and Lava Butte Dams. This was followed 560,000 years ago by the Toroweap Dam. The resulting Toroweap Lake took two and a half years to fill and stretched to Lees Ferry, 180 miles upriver. Over time, the lava flows and the ensuing dams became smaller. The most recent dam blocked the river just 140,000 years ago, and its lake reached 45 miles upstream, to the junction with Tapeats Creek.

**Trail Guide:** Drive 7 miles west of Fredonia, Arizona, on AZ Highway 389 and turn left on BLM road 109 (signed to Toroweap). Drive 54 miles on dirt road to Tuweap. In good weather this road presents no problems for a two-wheel-drive vehicle; however, it can quickly become impassable when wet. Tuweap consists only of a ranger station; no water, gasoline, food, or lodging is available. Be sure to stop at the ranger station for trail updates and to pick up the Park Service's useful Lava Falls Route description.

From Tuweap, continue 3.5 miles to a fork. The main (left) fork takes you to the drive-in campground (2 miles) and the spectacular Toroweap Overlook (2.8 miles). To reach the trailhead, take the unmarked four-wheel-drive road to the right, which bypasses the obvious cinder cone of Vulcans Throne on the right and dead-ends at the trailhead 2.4 miles from the fork. Vulcans Throne Road is usually passable in two-wheel drive for about 0.5 mile to the dry Toroweap "Lake."

The trailhead lies in a small hollow under the southern flank of Vulcans Throne (Photo 89), a cinder cone that erupted about 74,000 years ago. *Cinder cones* are small, conical basalt volcanoes built of solidified lava fragments spewed from an erupting volcanic vent. Like popcorn around the base of a corn popper, these cinders collect around the vent to form the cone.

From the trailhead, the route immediately begins to descend black cinders to the right (west) of a small gully. To the left (east) of this gully lies a distinctive pile of red cinders that forms a small, dissected cone. Following a ridge of basalt, the path has a clearly visible tread, and small cairns are frequently stacked beside it. About 0.2 mile from the trailhead, the path reaches the gully between these black and red cinders.

From most vantage points along the route's upper section, you can observe several features of special geologic interest. Due south, across the Colorado

*Photo 89. Vulcans Throne. This basaltic cinder cone erupted on the flat Esplanade platform a mere 74,000 years ago.*

River, lies the tributary of Prospect Canyon. Perched on its western rim is a small cinder cone (Photo 16) that erupted about 38,000 years ago. The cone sits atop the Esplanade, the flat platform marking the top of the Supai Group (Figure 36). Below the Esplanade, the cliffs of the Inner Gorge are composed of, from top to bottom, the Supai Group, the Redwall Limestone, the Temple Butte Limestone, and the Muav Limestone. Comparison of the elevation of the Esplanade platform on the left (east) and right (west) sides of Prospect Canyon (Photo 90) reveals that the Esplanade is several hundred feet higher to the east. This is because the Toroweap Fault runs beneath Vulcans Throne, under your feet, across the river, and up Prospect Canyon. The Toroweap is a normal fault along which the block of rock to the west has dropped relative to the block on the east, resulting in 800 feet of vertical movement, which continues to this day. The Toroweap Fault is part of a family of normal faults that are stretching the earth's crust to form the distinctive ranges and valleys of the Basin and Range province west of the Colorado Plateau and the Grand

*Photo 90. Toroweap Fault. The right (sunlit relative to the left, shadowed portion) side of the flat Esplanade platform has been dropped down 800 feet due to movement on the Toroweap Fault, which runs up Prospect Canyon, along the sun/shade boundary. A small cinder cone is perched on the Canyon rim (middle right).*

*Photo 91. Evidence of lava dams. Just above Lava Falls Rapid, an outcrop of light-colored, bedded Bright Angel Shale is covered with a thin layer of Colorado River gravel. Above, black basalt is broken into columns by numerous vertical cooling joints. At the very top, a second lava flow lacks these joints. Both lava flows are part of the Toroweap Lava Dam, which blocked the Colorado River 560,000 years ago.*

Canyon. The Toroweap Fault is one of the youngest and largest of the Basin and Range faults that have begun to encroach on the Colorado Plateau, gradually pulling it apart (Figure 9). If we were to return to this spot in a few million years, the Toroweap area would likely have a topography more similar to that of Las Vegas than to the narrow gorge cut through the Colorado Plateau that we see today.

The Toroweap Fault was the conduit for the lava that surrounds you, including the series of lava flows plastered against the side of the wall just upstream from Prospect Canyon. These flows include partial remains of the Prospect, Ponderosa, Toroweap, and "D" dams that each temporarily blocked the Colorado River before the force of water and sediment overtopping the dams breached them and removed the obstruction.

After reaching the gully, the route begins to descend it, passing to the right of the red cinders. The gully quickly steepens, and the route crosses from the cinders it has been following to solid basalt from a lava flow. Because the route is now in solid rock, the tread is not as obvious, but many small cairns continue to mark the way. In this section, the route drops over several small ledges. You must clamber over these using your hands and feet, but all are in solid basalt with ample hand- and footholds, so experienced scramblers should not need a rope. At 0.3 mile from the trailhead, you reach the largest (6-foot) of these drop-offs, and another, more exposed, 4-foot drop lies 50 yards beyond.

Just after the 4-foot ledge, the cairned route bends to the left to begin a southeastward traverse across the slope. Looking west, you get good views of the lava cascades you are descending. To appreciate how these cascades make a hiking descent to the river possible, compare the relatively gradual slope of black basalt with the sheer cliffs of red Supai Group and white Redwall Limestone beyond (Photo 88).

The route continues its southeastward traverse as it passes right of a big basalt cliff at mile 0.4. From here, you can glimpse a small stretch of the Colorado, and the offset of layers across the Toroweap Fault is still quite evident on the South Rim (Photo 90). At 0.5 mile from the trailhead, the traverse ends, and the route directly descends the slope. Aim for a saddle composed of red cinders with black basalt pinnacles on its right flank. The tread of the path is visible from above as it crosses the red saddle, which you reach at 0.9 mile (GPS 36°12.19'N, 113°04.52'W).

From the saddle the route takes a sharp left and descends 50 yards down a northeast-trending gully. Many cairns mark the path, which soon exits the gully on the right and heads for a notch in the ridge below flanked by two more pinnacles. You reach this notch about 1 mile from the trailhead. From the notch the river looks much closer than it did when you last saw it. Numerous cairns below direct you toward the two-pronged gully that comprises the lower third of the route.

About 50 yards beyond the notch, the path bends to the right (west) and traverses across the head of this gully. This is a good place to look back and get a mental picture of the notch so that it is easy to locate on the return journey. Cairns lead you into the west fork of the gully at mile 1.2. Once you reach its floor, climb immediately over a small, subsidiary ridge into the east prong. Distinctive cooling columns (Photo 91) cut the basalt on the gully walls. Most of the basalt you have passed so far has been massive and lumpy, the result of uneven cooling. However, when molten basalt cools fairly uniformly, the contraction causes long cooling joints to form, breaking the rock into prismatic columns like these.

The route now descends the gully's eastern prong, which was eroded directly along the Toroweap Fault. Fault motion crushed and weakened these rocks, increasing their susceptibility to the elements. For most of the gully's length, the footing is surprisingly good, but a few spots are littered with scree, and caution is necessary to avoid launching rocks onto people below. A large boulder shown lodged in the gully in the Park Service's route description has now been washed away, making for easier progress. At mile 1.3 a 100-foot cliff of columnar basalt comes into view on the right (west). About 50 yards farther you emerge from the narrow gully between two tall cliffs that fanciful hikers have likened to the gates of Hades. From here the view once again opens onto the river, now just a short distance below you. The path begins to angle right, traversing onto the gully's western flank.

After another 100 yards you reach a double downclimb. The first of these is 6 to 7 feet tall, but the handholds here are good, and the exposure is minimal. The second downclimb is shorter, but the rock is a bit looser. The second downclimb begins in black basalt, but finishes in an undercut area composed of tan sandstone and pebble conglomerate. The basalt that you just downclimbed is a remnant of the Toroweap Dam that blocked the river 560,000 years ago. The dam was built by a series of lava flows that entered the gorge over a period of months or years. Enough time passed between flows that the upstream lake overflowed the dam and deposited river sand and gravel on top of it. The next lava flow covered these river gravels and added to the dam's height, temporarily stopping the overflow. The sandstone and conglomerate at the base of the second downclimb are remnants of one such river deposit laid down during a temporary overflow of the Toroweap Dam.

*Photo 92. Lava Falls Rapid, the biggest in the Grand Canyon, was created by multiple debris flows that roared down Prospect Canyon (just off the photo on the left).*

At the bottom of the second downclimb, the path crosses southwestward over open slopes as it winds its way between large basalt boulders that have fallen off the cliffs above. Many of these boulders display excellent examples of columnar jointing. At mile 1.4 you finally encounter the first extensive outcrop that isn't basalt. The rock is Bright Angel Shale, and it is composed of dark brown, desert-varnished sandstone interbedded with green mudstone and tan sandstones. Just downstream lies a large, polished boulder that affords a close-up view of more basalt columns. About 70 yards past the boulder, the route bends right and parallels the river, reaching it 1.5 miles from the start.

The route continues along the river, alternately walking along sandy beaches and clambering over outcrops of yellow limestone. At 250 yards downstream from where the route first met the river, you reach Lava Falls Rapid (Photo 92). The top of a large basalt block offers an excellent view of the foaming whitewater. This is the most notorious rapid in the Grand Canyon (although the Lava Cliff Rapid, 67 miles downstream, was even bigger until it was drowned by Lake Mead). If you are lucky, you will get the chance to watch a few boats take the wild ride. Despite what its name suggests, Lava Falls was not created by lava; it was formed by multiple debris flows that roared down Prospect Canyon beginning in 1939.

The wall north of the rapid is composed of Bright Angel Shale overlain by river gravels, above which lie columnar and then more massive basalt (Photo 91). Both basalt types comprise portions of the ancient Toroweap Lava Dam. Examine the Bright Angel Shale up close to see abundant ripplemarks and burrows. A short descent from the scouting boulder (possible only during lower river flows) brings you to the edge of the rapid. As you clamber down, notice some white cobbles scattered within the basalt. These are chunks of limestone picked up by the lava as it flowed into the Canyon.

Unless you are catching a ride with a passing raft, the only way out is back the way you came. Consider spending a night at the river to enhance your chances of seeing a party run Lava Falls and to get an early-morning start on the hike out. A night along the river will also give you more time to soak up the ambiance of this unique spot filled with the echoes of ancient waterfalls, floods, and repeated clashes of fire and water.

# *Appendix A*
# THE CAST OF CHARACTERS

To hike the geology of the Grand Canyon is to walk through the deep history of our planet. The story that unfolds is more amazing than the most outlandish science-fiction movie plot. But, like any movie, you can't follow the plot until you become familiar with the cast of characters, in this case the rocks of the Grand Canyon.

Rocks are composed of minerals. There are thousands of different minerals in nature, but most rocks consist of only a handful of these (Figure 39). Although it is not necessary for rock identification, if you can recognize the minerals, it will help you classify the rock. Geologists divide rocks into three major categories: *sedimentary, igneous,* and *metamorphic.* The first goal of a trailside geologist is to assign the rock you are examining to one of these three categories, which helps you take the first step in understanding its history.

## SEDIMENTARY ROCKS

As you gaze into the Canyon from the rim, nearly all the rocks you see are sedimentary. Sedimentary rocks form on the earth's surface. They are distinguished by their individual, rounded sediment grains (Figure 40b) and the way they form distinctive, parallel layers (Photo 7). There are two major ways that rocks form on the surface, and this difference divides sedimentary rocks into two categories, clastic and biochemical (Figure 41).

*Clastic* rocks are formed through the cementation of sediments that came from the breakdown of other rocks. Where sand-sized particles have accumulated and been cemented together, a *sandstone,* such as the Coconino (Photo 14)

---

**FIGURE 39: COMMON ROCK-FORMING MINERALS**

| MINERAL | APPEARANCE |
| --- | --- |
| Calcite | White, gray, or tan sugary crystals |
| Quartz | Colorless to light-colored, glassy crystals |
| Feldspar | Light-colored with distinct crystal faces |
| Muscovite (mica) | Light-colored, soft and flaky |
| Biotite (mica) | Dark-colored, soft and flaky |
| Hornblende | Dark green to black, elongate crystals |
| Pyroxene | Dark green to black, rectangular crystals |
| Olivine | Green, small crystals |

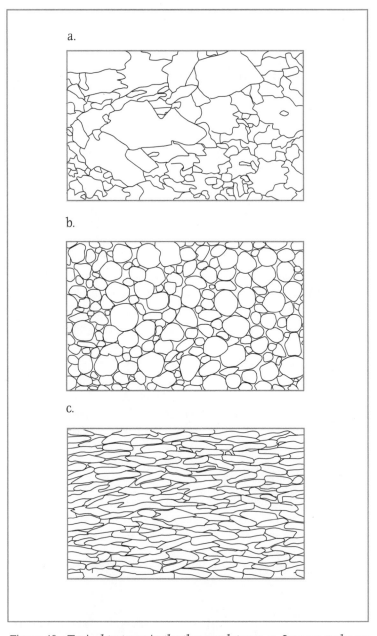

a.

b.

c.

*Figure 40. Typical textures in the three rock types. a. Igneous rocks are characterized by interlocking crystals similar to the pieces of a completed puzzle. b. Sedimentary rocks are composed of rounded sediment grains cemented together. c. Metamorphic rocks often have aligned, elongated crystals, forming a foliation.*

**FIGURE 41: CLASSIFICATION OF SEDIMENTARY ROCKS**

Clastic

| SEDIMENT | PARTICLE SIZE (MM) | ROCK |
|---|---|---|
| Gravel | Boulder ( > 256) | Conglomerate |
| | Cobble (64–256) | |
| | Pebble (2–64) | |
| Sand | Sand (.062–2) | Sandstone |
| Mud | Silt (.0039–.062) | Siltstone |
| | Clay ( < .0039) | Mudstone |
| | | Shale (breaks along bedding) |

Biochemical

| ROCK | SEDIMENT |
|---|---|
| Limestone | Mainly bioclastic debris such as shells |
| Chert | Silica-rich sediments |
| Evaporites | Salts left from evaporation |

or the Tapeats (Photo 8), is formed. The rest of the clastic rocks have equally sensible names, derived from the size of sediment particles of which they are composed (Figure 41). Another name for mudstone is *shale,* such as the Bright Angel Shale (Photo 9).

As their name suggests, *biochemical* rocks are formed by biological and chemical processes. *Limestone,* the most common biochemical sedimentary rock, is composed of calcium carbonate, either crystallized directly out of seawater or formed from fragmented seashells (Photos 12, 15). Another common biochemical sedimentary rock is *chert,* which is simply microscopically small crystals of quartz. The final class of biochemical sedimentary rocks commonly found in the Grand Canyon are *evaporites* (Photo 30), which are rocks formed from the evaporation of sea or lake water. Halite (rock salt) is composed of sodium chloride, simple table salt. Another abundant evaporite is gypsum, which is used to make sheetrock.

## THE TAXONOMY OF SEDIMENTARY ROCKS

Many people are familiar with the taxonomic groupings biologists use to classify organisms. Geologists employ a similar approach of nested groupings to name sedimentary rocks. The fundamental unit is called a *formation,* which is a grouping of rock layers in a specific region that were deposited at approximately the same time and by similar depositional processes. Once a geologist defines a formation, he or she names it after a geographical feature in the area of its best exposure. Distinctive layers (or groups of layers) within a formation are called *members*.

In the other taxonomic direction, clusters of related formations are bundled together into groups. For example, the Tapeats Sandstone, Bright Angel Shale, and Muav Limestone together are called the Tonto Group. Finally, related groups of formations can also be bundled together to form supergroups. The Grand Canyon Supergroup is just such a cluster of groups and formations (Figure 20), consisting of the Chuar and Unkar Groups, along with the Nankoweap and Sixtymile Formations.

## IGNEOUS ROCKS

Most of the Canyon's igneous rocks lurk deep in the bowels of the Inner Gorge, the "canyon within a canyon" that confines the Colorado River. A rock is classified as igneous if it has solidified from an originally molten state (called *magma*). Most rock materials don't melt until the temperature exceeds about 1500°F, so, right off the bat, if you can identify a rock as igneous, it speaks to you of a fiery period in the land's history. Igneous rocks are subdivided into two categories: *volcanic* and *plutonic* (Figure 42). Volcanic rocks (Photo 91) are, not surprisingly, those igneous rocks erupted from a volcano. Volcanic rocks form from lava, which is magma that reached the earth's surface. Plutonic rocks (Color Plate 9) are igneous rocks formed from magma that cooled and solidified below the earth's surface.

When magma cools, its minerals freeze into a series of interlocking crystals. This interlocking pattern is the hallmark of igneous rocks (Figure 40a). Volcanic rocks are composed of very tiny crystals, owing to the fact that the

**FIGURE 42: CLASSIFICATION OF IGNEOUS ROCKS**

| **Volcanic** Fine-grained | Rhyolite | Dacite | Andesite | Basalt | |
|---|---|---|---|---|---|
| **Plutonic** Med. to coarse-grained | Granite | Granodiorite | Diorite | Gabbro | Ultramafics (peridotite) |
| **Silica %** | >70% silica | 63–70% | 53–63% | 45–53% | <45% silica |
| | Light-colored | | | Dark-colored | |
| | | **Minerals commonly found in each rock** | | | |
| | Quartz | Quartz | | | |
| | Muscovite | Muscovite | | | |
| | Feldspar (potassium) | Feldspar (sodium) | Feldspar (sodium, calcium) | Feldspar (calcium) | |
| | Biotite | Biotite | Biotite | | |
| | Hornblende | Hornblende | Hornblende | | |
| | | | Pyroxene | Pyroxene | |
| | | | | Olivine | Olivine |

**FIGURE 43: COMMON METAMORPHIC ROCKS**

| ROCK | PARENT ROCK | TEXTURE | APPEARANCE |
|---|---|---|---|
| Quartzite | Quartz-rich sandstone | Non-foliated | Sugary with interlocking crystals |
| Marble | Limestone | Non-foliated | Granular with interlocking crystals |
| | | | |
| Slate | Shale, siltstone | Foliated | Splits into thin sheets |
| Schist | Shale, siltstone, volcanic ash | Foliated | Sparkly due to alignment of micas |
| Gneiss | Granite, shale, siltstone, sandstone | Foliated | Dark and light banding, often contorted |

1500°F lava is unceremoniously dumped on the 60° to 70°F surface of the earth, causing it to solidify quickly. The individual crystals in volcanic rocks are usually too small to see with your naked eye.

Plutonic rocks, on the other hand, solidify deep in the earth's interior (typically 3 to 18 miles deep), where the insulating effect of the overlying rock keeps the temperature very warm, even by a magma's standards. In contrast to lava, which solidifies into a volcanic rock in a matter of minutes or years, plutonic rocks take tens of thousands of years to cool. The resulting large crystals are easily visible with your naked eye. *Pegmatites* are a special class of plutonic rocks, common in the Grand Canyon, that have exceptionally large crystals (Photo 55).

Geologists go one step further in subclassifying volcanic and plutonic rocks based on the amount of silica that the rock contains (Figure 42). The more silica an igneous rock has, the lighter its color, offering a handy field method for identification. *Granite* is light gray, but *gabbro* is jet black. The same is true for the volcanic rocks. *Basalt,* the volcanic cousin of gabbro, is black or very dark gray, but *rhyolite*, the volcanic equivalent of granite, is usually white, pink, or light gray. A few other common igneous rocks have intermediate silica contents, so they come in intermediate or "salt-and-pepper" hues.

## METAMORPHIC ROCKS

The dark metamorphic rocks of the Vishnu Schist (Color Plate 9) contribute greatly to the powerful, foreboding presence of the Inner Gorge. A metamorphic rock is one whose physical or chemical properties have been changed without melting in the process. This solid-state transformation occurs due to increases in heat and/or pressure, so most metamorphism occurs after a rock has been buried deep in the earth. Sedimentary, igneous, and other metamorphic rocks can all be metamorphosed into a new rock type. By definition, a rock becomes metamorphic if it is altered in a solid state at a temperature greater than 300°F. Metamorphism is a continuous process whose effects become more pronounced the deeper and the longer the rock is buried. Mildly metamorphosed rocks will look nearly identical to their parent rock; however, intensely metamorphosed rocks are distinctively altered.

The specific name of a metamorphic rock depends not only on the degree and type of metamorphism but also on the identity of its parent rock (Figure 43). Like igneous and sedimentary rocks, metamorphic rocks are subdivided into two main classes: foliated and nonfoliated. Whether or not a metamorphic rock is foliated can be an important clue to deciphering the rock's history. *Foliation* is the alignment of mineral grains in one preferred direction (Figure 40c). As a rock becomes metamorphosed, its original mineral grains grow larger, fuse together, and form new grains. If the rock is subjected to a more intense pressure from one direction than from the others, any elongated minerals will align themselves, resulting in a preferred fabric called foliation.

If a rock is buried more and more deeply by the accumulation of overlying layers, the pressure will increase, but it will remain equal in all directions. The situation changes, however, where two tectonic plates are converging (Appendix C), and extra pressure is exerted in the direction of plate convergence. It is in these settings that large bodies of foliated metamorphic rocks, such as the Vishnu Schist, are formed. The presence of foliation in metamorphic rocks is thus a powerful clue to past convergent tectonic events.

# *Appendix B*
# ROCKS OF AGES: GEOLOGIC TIME

Geologists tell time in two ways: relative and numerical. Relative time places events and rocks in a sequence from oldest to youngest; numerical time attaches an actual age to each one.

## RELATIVE TIME

Determining relative ages for the Canyon's sedimentary rock layers is "relatively" straightforward. In a stack of sedimentary rocks, the layer on the bottom is the oldest, while the layer on top is the youngest. Geologists call this rule the *Law of Superposition.* Determining the relative sequence for igneous and metamorphic rocks requires a little more sleuthing. Volcanic rocks, such as the Grand Canyon Supergroup's Cardenas Lava, were erupted on the earth's surface, so they also follow the Law of Superposition. Plutonic rocks, which were injected from below, don't follow this law, but we can use their relationships with surrounding rocks to determine when, relatively, they formed. For example, we know that the pegmatites of the Inner Gorge (Photo 55) were intruded into the metamorphic rocks of the Vishnu Schist *after* the Vishnu rocks were metamorphosed. Had the pegmatites been intruded prior to the metamorphic event, they would be metamorphosed as well. Using similar reasoning, the Supergroup's intrusive diabase dikes must be younger than every sedimentary formation they cut across (Photo 22), because logic dictates that a rock layer must be present before it can be cut by another.

Determining the relative sequence of rock layers and geologic events in the Grand Canyon (or anywhere else) requires no sophisticated equipment or specialized knowledge, just a bit of detective work as you walk down the trail. This sleuthing is fun and rewards you with a better understanding of the Canyon's geologic history.

## NUMERICAL TIME

Using deductive reasoning, a keen field observer can determine the relative ages of geologic events, but in order to attach specific dates to these events, laboratory analysis is required.

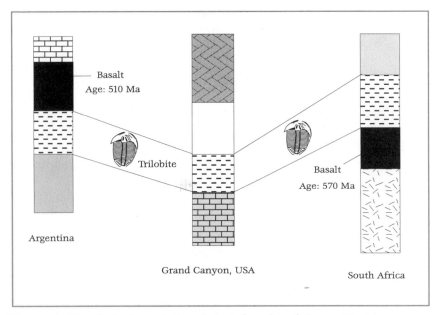

*Figure 44. Hypothetical correlation of strata based on their constituent fossils. The trilobites at all three locations are the same and therefore lived at the same time. Using the Law of Superposition and radiometric dates from the basalts, we know the trilobite-containing layers were all deposited between 510 and 570 million years ago.*

Radiometric dating is the cornerstone of all numerical age calculations. The radiometric "clock" begins ticking when a rock is heated either to the point of melting, for an igneous rock, or to the point of metamorphism, for a metamorphic rock. Because sedimentary rocks have not been heated to this extent, it is rarely possible to radiometrically date them. Geologists have had more success dating the Canyon's sedimentary layers by combining relative and numerical dating techniques. For example, using the Law of Superposition, all of the Canyon's Paleozoic sedimentary rocks (and the fossils that they contain) lie above the Supergroup's Cardenas Lava (Figure 2), so they must be younger than the Lava's 1100-million-year-old radiometric age. The 680,000-year-old basalts of the Lava Falls area (Hike 18) lie above these same layers, so the sedimentary rocks must have been deposited between 1100 million and 680,000 years ago. By performing such correlations around the world (Figure 44), geologists have been able to assign numerical ages for the boundaries between time periods on the Geologic Time Scale (inside cover) and, as a result, they can date the layers of the Grand Canyon using just their constituent fossils.

# THE CANYON'S INVISIBLE STORY: UNCONFORMITIES

After dating the Grand Canyon's rocks, geologists have discovered several major time gaps in the rock record, called unconformities. Although most of the events that occurred during these gaps are lost forever, characteristics of the unconformities do allow us to piece together important parts of the missing story. Geologists identify three types of unconformities (Figure 45), classified in terms of the relationships between the rocks above and below the gap in time. The Grand Canyon provides "textbook" examples of each one.

## NONCONFORMITIES

*Nonconformities* are found where sedimentary layers overlie older crystalline rocks. The boundary between the crystalline Zoroaster Granite and Vishnu Schist with the overlying Tapeats Sandstone marks an amazing 1200-million-year-gap in the Canyon's rock record, which John Wesley Powell dubbed the Great Unconformity (Photo 6, Color Plate 8).

Like all nonconformities, the Great Unconformity tells us that a large mountain range existed in the Grand Canyon region during this gap in time (Chapter 1). Granite and schist are formed miles beneath the earth's surface. The only way to bring them to the surface is by raising a mountain range through intense folding and faulting. Because of its elevation, the mountain range is then subjected to more numerous and intense storms than the surrounding lowlands and thus is the scene of more extensive erosion. Over the course of tens to hundreds of millions of years, mountain ranges are dissected down to

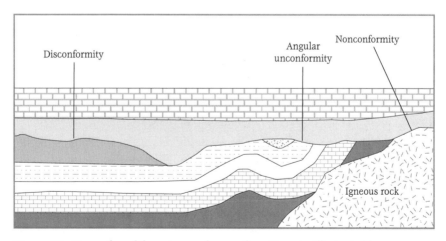

*Figure 45. Examples of three types of unconformities. As illustrated here, an unconformity of regional extent may change from one type to another along its length.*

their crystalline roots and planed flat. Once the mountains are gone, sedimentary deposition can resume, marking the end of the nonconformity.

## ANGULAR UNCONFORMITIES

Although the Tapeats Sandstone lies in direct contact with the Zoroaster Granite and Vishnu Schist throughout much of the Grand Canyon, at several locations a thick sequence of tilted sedimentary rocks, the Grand Canyon Supergroup, separates these units. Where the Supergroup is exposed, its tilted beds meet the horizontal beds of the Tapeats in an *angular unconformity* (Photos 3, 25, 34). Like nonconformities, angular unconformities represent a period of mountain-building followed by erosion. Because sedimentary layers are originally deposited horizontally, an episode of faulting was required to tilt the Supergroup layers. By the time the still-horizontal Tapeats Sandstone was deposited on top of the Supergroup 545 million years ago, these mountains had also been eroded to a nearly flat plain (Chapter 1).

## DISCONFORMITIES

*Disconformities* are more subtle than their cousins. They are surfaces where two parallel sedimentary layers of different ages come into contact. Many disconformities interrupt the sequence of Paleozoic sedimentary rocks forming the upper Canyon walls. An example is the surface between the Cambrian Muav Limestone and the Mississippian Redwall Limestone. The entire Ordovician, Silurian, and Devonian Periods are missing from the rock record, but you can't tell that this gap exists by observing a change in rock

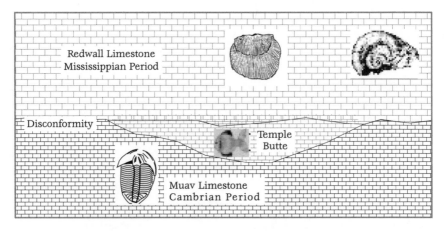

*Figure 46. Example of a disconformity between the Cambrian Muav Limestone and the Mississippian Redwall Limestone. In places the Temple Butte Formation fills part of this time gap.*

type or difference in the angles of strata. Instead, disconformities are recognized by gaps in the fossil record.

In contrast to angular unconformities and nonconformities, the characteristics of disconformities do not imply that a mountain-building episode occurred during the gap in time. Instead, disconformities represent periods of nondeposition, often accompanied by mild erosion. Because most sedimentary layers are deposited near sea level, a general retreat of the sea often creates a disconformity. The accompanying erosion is usually patchy, so it is often possible to trace the disconformity laterally and find remnants of the missing time, such as where the Canyon's Temple Butte Formation fills part of the gap between the top of the Muav Limestone and the overlying Redwall Limestone (Figure 46).

# Appendix C
# PLATE TECTONICS: THE RESTLESS EARTH

Rocks can be turned topsy-turvy by a process called *plate tectonics*, the dominant force shaping the configuration of our world. The earth's surface is composed of about a dozen huge slabs of crust, known as *tectonic plates*, that are condemned to endlessly roam across the globe (Figure 47). The plates are constantly being rearranged, with old plates being destroyed and new ones being created. The pressures exerted where these plates butt up against one another are sufficient to tilt, bend, and fracture rock. The fractures form *joints*, which are planar cracks. *Faults* are similar cracks along which one side has moved relative to the other. When rocks are deformed without breaking, they form *folds*.

Beneath the great tectonic plates on the earth's surface lies another layer, a portion of the mantle known as the *asthenosphere* (Figure 48). It lies about 100 miles below the surface and, while not molten, its material is hot enough to flow in a solid state, somewhat like silly putty. It flows very slowly in enormous cycles, rising in some places, then moving horizontally across the top of the asthenosphere before finally sinking back down (Figure 48), like water boiling in a pot. The rigid, overlying plates are carried along by the sideways-moving part of these cycles like boxes on a conveyor belt.

The plates move at different rates and in different directions across the earth's surface, so they necessarily must interact with one another. They can do so in one of three ways. First, where two asthenospheric cycles rise and diverge, the overlying plates move apart from one another, forming a *divergent plate boundary* (Figure 49). Second, where the asthenosphere sinks back down to deeper levels, it drags the overlying plate down with it, creating a *convergent plate boundary* called a *subduction zone* (Figure 3). Finally, in some locations two plates slide horizontally past one another, forming what is known as a *transform plate boundary*. Such boundaries are dominated by strike-slip faults (Figure 50c), the most familiar example of which is California's San Andreas Fault.

The boundaries between plates are the scenes of tremendous geologic activity, with earthquakes and volcanoes commonplace. Most great mountain ranges are built along plate boundaries. Plate interiors, by contrast, are relatively quiet, with erosion and sediment deposition making up the dominant geologic processes. Because the plate boundaries shift through time, places like the Grand Canyon that today lie far from a plate's edge once upon a time lay right in the middle of all the geologic action.

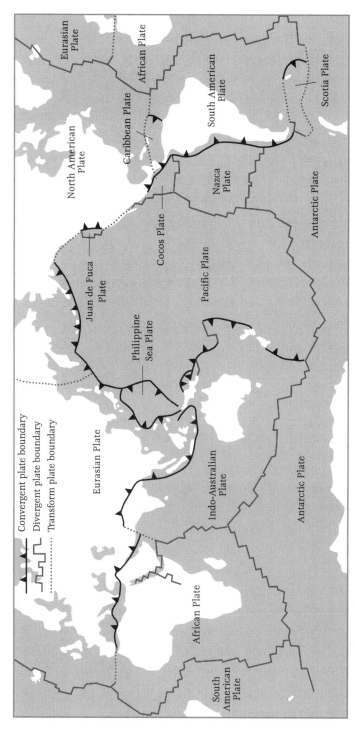

*Figure 47. The Earth's major tectonic plates.*

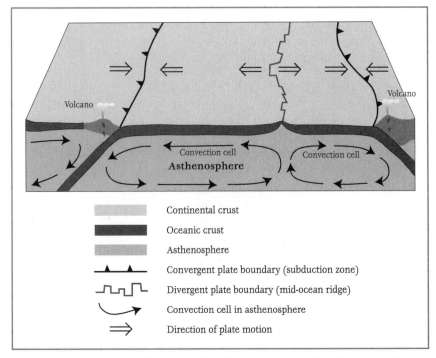

Continental crust
Oceanic crust
Asthenosphere
Convergent plate boundary (subduction zone)
Divergent plate boundary (mid-ocean ridge)
Convection cell in asthenosphere
Direction of plate motion

*Figure 48. Cross-section showing subsurface convection cells, the cause of plate motions.*

In order to fully appreciate how these plates interact with one another, it is important to realize that the earth's crust is composed of two distinct types of material, *oceanic crust* and *continental crust*. As the names imply, oceanic crust is the material that forms the seafloor for most of the world's oceans; the continents are composed of continental crust. Oceanic crust is constructed almost exclusively of *basalt* (Figure 42), a dense material that readily sinks deep into the earth when guided by convection cells moving downward. Continental crust, in contrast, is composed of much lighter material that is too buoyant to be pulled down into the underlying mantle. This difference in crustal density has profound implications for the evolution of the earth's surface.

Divergent plate boundaries progress through three stages. They often begin under a continent, stretching and lowering the earth's crust (Figure 49a, b). Because it is ripping the continent apart, it is called a *rift zone*. The most famous modern example is the Great Rift Valley of East Africa. As you can see along the South Kaibab Trail, the Grand Canyon area lay at the fringe of just such a rift 750 million years ago (Chapter 1).

Two telltale signs of a rift zone are the eruption of basalt volcanoes and the formation of normal faults (Figure 50a). Pools of magma rising from the

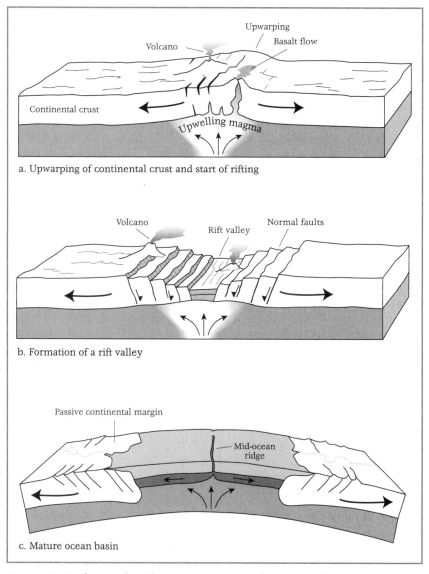

Figure 49. *Evolution of a rift zone into an ocean basin at a divergent plate boundary.*

asthenosphere erupt in a series of basalt flows that cover the floor of the rift and solidify to become newly manufactured oceanic crust. Normal faults accomplish the stretching of the earth's crust, slowly dropping the land down until eventually it sinks below sea level and is flooded by seawater to form a narrow ocean basin like the modern Red Sea or Gulf of California.

As the plates continue to pull apart, the continents drift farther from each other, and new oceanic crust is manufactured to fill in the gap. A larger ocean basin is thus formed, with a submarine "mid-ocean" ridge of basaltic volcanoes lying at its very center, along the rift (Figure 49c). The Atlantic Ocean is an example of such an ocean basin. Over time the edges of the continent move farther from the active plate boundary, forming what geologists call a *passive continental margin* (Figure 49c). Earthquakes and volcanic eruptions cease and the passive margins accumulate thick deposits of sediment. All of the Grand Canyon's horizontal rock layers were deposited in a passive margin setting during the Paleozoic Era.

The earth is not growing or shrinking, so the fact that new oceanic crust is formed at the mid-ocean ridges requires that old crust be destroyed elsewhere. This destruction of crust is accomplished at *subduction zones* (Figure 3), where old oceanic crust is recycled deep into the earth's interior. Dragged down by the sinking part of the asthenosphere's "conveyor" cells, a slab of oceanic crust descends 100 miles or more below the earth's surface, where it begins to melt due to the high temperatures of the earth's interior (Figure 48). The resulting magma is less dense than the surrounding rock, so it rises like a helium balloon. Eventually, pods of this magma collect in chambers at shallow levels of the crust, where they feed explosive volcanoes like Mount Saint Helens. Strings of volcanoes thus form along the plate boundary. These volcanoes are composed of low-density, buoyant continental crust, so subduction zones are areas where old oceanic crust is consumed and new continental crust is forged.

Most tectonic plates are composed partially of oceanic crust and partially of continental crust, so it is common for a continent to be attached to subducting oceanic crust. In such circumstances, the continent will eventually be dragged into the subduction zone. Because the strings of volcanoes that form on the overlying plate are composed of continental crust, a collision between two plates of continental crust occurs (Figure 5). Continental crust is too buoyant to be dragged down into the subduction zone, so instead of diving and melting, one crustal plate is heaved up and over the other, forming a large, nonvolcanic mountain range. This collision process forms many of the world's great mountain ranges, such as today's Himalaya and Alps. Chapter 1 describes just such a collision that occurred in the Grand Canyon area 1700 million years ago.

When two plates meet at a subduction or collision zone, there is less space available, so the rocks must somehow be shortened. This shortening is accomplished along *reverse*, or thrust, faults (Figure 50b), which stack slabs of rock up and over one another. This stacking is exactly how collision-zone mountain ranges are uplifted. Folding of rock layers also accomplishes the desired shortening (Color Plate 2), so subduction and collision zones have many rock layers that have been kinked into arched *anticline* and bowl-shaped *syncline*

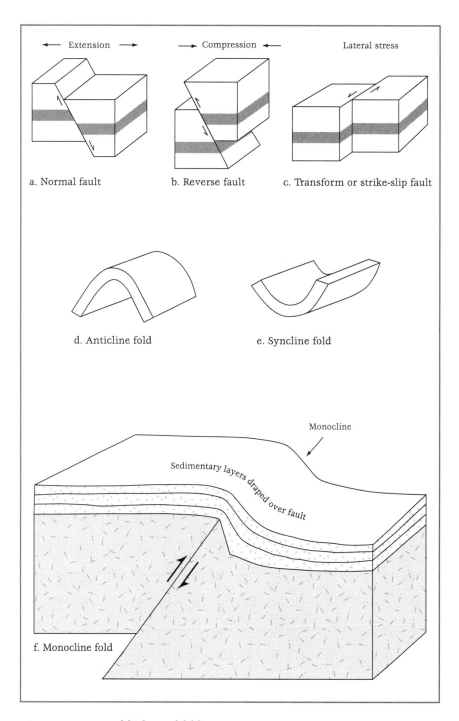

*Figure 50. Types of faults and folds.*

folds (Figure 50d, e). In places where the compression is relatively modest, a type of half fold, known as a *monocline,* is formed (Figure 50f). Several monoclines are present in the Grand Canyon (Photos 28, 68), left from a time of compression that gripped the region 65 million years ago.

Because oceanic crust is heavy enough to sink and be destroyed at subduction zones but continental crust is not, the oceanic crust that lies between continents is inevitably totally consumed, bringing the continents into a collision during which they are welded together. Eventually, all of the world's continents are joined in such a manner to form a supercontinent. At least two such supercontinents have existed during the earth's history. The earlier of the two is known as Rodinia (Figure 7), and the later one is called Pangea (Figure 15). The Pacific Ocean is presently being consumed, a situation that will eventually lead to the formation of another supercontinent in which people (if we're still here) will be able to take a short stroll from San Francisco to Tokyo without getting their feet wet.

The earth contains a tremendous amount of internal heat that must be released, much like the heat that builds up when you exercise with heavy clothes on. Supercontinents, like good down parkas, trap that internal heat, causing it to build up. This buildup leads to a reorganization of the "conveyor" cells deep in the asthenosphere, and ultimately to rift zones in the supercontinent. The destiny of all supercontinents is thus to break up, beginning the cycle anew (Figure 49a).

# *Appendix D*
# KEY REFERENCES

1. Beus, S., and M. Morales (eds.). *Grand Canyon Geology.* New York, New York: Oxford University Press, 2003.
2. This Old Continent: Constructing the Basement of North America. B. Ilg. *Boatmans Quarterly Review,* v.10, 1997, p. 20–22.
3. Brian, N. *Rim to River.* Flagstaff, Arizona: Earthquest Press, 1992.
4. Persistent Influence of Proterozoic Accretionary Boundaries in the Tectonic Evolution of Southwestern North America: Interaction of Cratonic Grain and Mantle Modification Events. K. Karlstrom and E. Humphreys. *Rocky Mountain Geology,* v. 33, 1998, p. 161–179.
5. Thermal, Structural, and Petrologic Evidence for 1400-Ma Metamorphism and Deformation in Central New Mexico. J. Marcoline et al. *Rocky Mountain Geology,* v. 34, 1999, p. 93–119.
6. Grand Canyon Supergroup: Six Unconformities Make One Great Unconformity. M. Timmons, K. Karlstrom, and C. Dehler. *Boatmans Quarterly Review,* v.12, 1998, p. 28–33. And, Grand Canyon Supergroup: Geologic Follow-up to Part One. C. Dehler, S. Porter, and K. Karlstrom. *Boatmans Quarterly Review,* v. 12, 1999, p. 31–36.
7. Middle and Late Proterozoic Grand Canyon Supergroup, Arizona. D. Elston. In: D. Elston et al. (eds.). *Geology of Grand Canyon, Northern Arizona.* Washington, D.C.: American Geophysical Union, 1989, Chap. 9, p. 94–105.
8. Geologic Map of the Eastern Part of the Grand Canyon National Park, Arizona. P. Huntoon et al. Grand Canyon, Arizona: Grand Canyon Association, 1996. 1:62,500.
9. Chuar Group of the Grand Canyon: Record of breakup of Rodinia, associated change in the global carbon cycle, and ecosystem expansion by 740 Ma. K. Karlstrom et al. *Geology,* v. 28, 2000, p. 619–622.
10. Refining Rodinia: Geologic Evidence for the Australia–Western U.S. Connection in the Proterozoic. K. Karlstrom et al. *GSA Today,* v. 9, 1999, p. 1–7.
11. Southwest U.S.–East Antarctic (SWEAT) Connection: A Hypothesis. E. Moores. *Geology,* v. 19, 1991, p. 425–428.
12. Billingsley, G., and S. Beus. *Geology of the Surprise Canyon Formation of the Grand Canyon, Arizona.* Flagstaff, Arizona: Museum of Northern Arizona, 1999.

13. Baars, D. *Navajo Country*. Albuquerque, New Mexico: University of New Mexico Press, 1995.

14. The Mouth of the Grand Canyon and Edge of the Colorado Plateau in the Upper Lake Mead Area, Arizona. I. Lucchitta. *GSA Centennial Field Guide—Rocky Mountain Section*. Boulder, Colorado, Geological Society of America, 1987, p. 365–370.

15. Young, R. *Proceedings of June, 2000 Grand Canyon Symposium*. Grand Canyon, Arizona: Grand Canyon Association, 2002 in press.

16. Evolution of the Colorado River in Arizona. E. McKee et al. *Museum of Northern Arizona Bulletin*, v. 44. Flagstaff, Arizona, 1967.

17. Differential Incision of the Grand Canyon Related to Quaternary Faulting—Constraints from U-Series and Ar/Ar Dating. J. Pederson et al. *Geology*, v. 30, 2002, p. 739–742.

18. Duffield, W. *Volcanoes of Northern Arizona*. Grand Canyon, Arizona: Grand Canyon Association, 1997.

19. Late Cenozoic Lava Dams in the Western Grand Canyon. W. Hamblin. *GSA Memoir 183*. Boulder, Colorado, Geological Society of America, 1994.

20. The Making of a Grand Canyon. S. Perkins. *Science News*, v. 158, 2000, p. 218–220.

21. Coder, C. *Grand Canyon Prehistory*. Grand Canyon, Arizona: Grand Canyon Association, 2000.

22. Hughes, J. *In the House of Stone and Light*. Grand Canyon, Arizona: Grand Canyon Association, 1978.

23. Billingsley, E., E. Spamer, and D. Menkes. *Quest for the Pillar of Gold*. Grand Canyon, Arizona: Grand Canyon Association, 1997.

24. Grand Canyon Caves, Breccia Pipes, and Mineral Deposits. K. Wenrich and H. Sutphin. *Geology Today*, May/June 1994, p. 97–104.

25. U-Pb Dating of Uranium Deposits in Collapsed Breccia Pipes of the Grand Canyon Region. K. Ludwig and K. Simmons. *Economic Geology*, v. 87, 1992, p. 1747–1765.

26. Geology Along the South Kaibab Trail, Eastern Grand Canyon, Arizona. S. Beus. *GSA Centennial Field Guide—Rocky Mountain Section*. Boulder, Colorado, Geological Society of America, 1987, p. 371–378.

27. Breed, J., V. Stefanic, and G. Billingsley. *Geologic Guide to the Bright Angel Trail*. Tulsa, Oklahoma: AAPG, 1986.

28. Chronic, H. *Pages of Stone: Grand Canyon and the Plateau Country*. Seattle, Washington: The Mountaineers, 1988.

29. Thybony, S. *Grand Canyon Trail Guide: Hermit*. Grand Canyon, Arizona: Grand Canyon Association, 1989.

30. Proterozoic Ultramafic Bodies in the Grand Canyon. S. Seaman et al., *Geological Society of America Abstracts with Programs*, v. 29, 1997, p. 89.

31. Relation of Inversely Graded Deposits to Suspended-Sediment Grain-Size Evolution During the 1996 Flood Experiment in Grand Canyon. D. Rubin, J. Nelson, and D. Topping. *Geology,* v. 26, 1998, p. 99–102.

32. When the Blue-Green Waters Turn Red. T. Melis et al. USGS *Water Resources Investigations Report 96-4059.* Washington, D.C., United States Geological Survey, 1996.

33. Preliminary Polar Path from Proterozoic and Paleozoic Rocks of the Grand Canyon Region, Arizona. D. Elston. In: D. Elston. et al. (eds.). *Geology of Grand Canyon, Northern Arizona.* Washington, D.C.: American Geophysical Union, 1989, Chap. 12, p. 119–121.

34. Source-Rock Potential of Precambrian Rocks in Selected Basins of the U.S. J. Palacas. *USGS Bulletin 2146-J.* Washington, D.C., United States Geological Survey, 1997.

35. Testate Amoebae in the Neoproterozoic Era; Evidence from Vase-Shaped Microfossils in the Chuar Group, Grand Canyon. S. Porter and A. Knoll. *Paleobiology,* v. 26, 2000, p. 360–385.

36. Gravity Tectonics, Grand Canyon, Arizona. P. Huntoon. In: D. Elston. et al. (eds.). *Geology of Grand Canyon, Northern Arizona.* Washington, D.C.: American Geophysical Union, 1989, Chap. 26, p. 219–223.

37. Cosmogenic 3-Helium Dating of Lava Dam Outburst Floods in the Western Grand Canyon, Arizona. C. Fenton. Unpublished Masters Thesis, University of Utah, Salt Lake City, Utah, 1998. And: Displacement Rates on the Toroweap and Hurricane Faults: Implications for Quaternary Downcutting in the Grand Canyon, Arizona. C. Fenton et al. *Geology,* v. 29, 2001, p.1035–1038.

38. Tectonic Geomorphology of the Toroweap Fault, Western Grand Canyon, Arizona: Implications for Transgression of Faulting on the Colorado Plateau. G. Jackson. *Arizona Geological Survey Open File Report 90-4.* Tucson, Arizona: Arizona Geological Survey, 1990.

39. Whitney, S. *A Field Guide to the Grand Canyon.* Seattle, Washington: The Mountaineers, 1996.

# *Appendix E*
# MAP LIST

1. Trails Illustrated™ Grand Canyon National Park. National Geographic Maps, 2000. 1:73,530.
2. Earthwalk Hiking Map & Guide, Grand Canyon National Park. H. Larson, Earthwalk Press, 1997. 1:48,000.
3. Grand Canyon National Park Trails. K. Schulte, Sky Terrain, 2001. 1:40,000.

The following topographic maps are all part of the United States Geological Survey 7.5-Minute Series at a scale of 1:24,000.
4. Desert View Quadrangle, Arizona
5. Grandview Point Quadrangle, Arizona
6. Cape Royal Quadrangle, Arizona
7. Phantom Ranch Quadrangle, Arizona
8. Grand Canyon Quadrangle, Arizona
9. Red Butte Quadrangle, Arizona
10. Havasu Falls Quadrangle, Arizona
11. Supai Quadrangle, Arizona
12. Point Imperial Quadrangle, Arizona
13. Nankoweap Mesa Quadrangle, Arizona
14. Bright Angel Point Quadrangle, Arizona
15. Powell Plateau Quadrangle, Arizona
16. Tapeats Amphitheater Quadrangle, Arizona
17. Fishtail Mesa Quadrangle, Arizona
18. Vulcans Throne Quadrangle, Arizona

# Glossary

**andesite**—fine-grained, gray volcanic rock with silica content between basalt and rhyolite

**angular unconformity**—gap in the rock record in which the layers above and below are not parallel

**anticline**—arch-shaped fold

**ash**—fine-grained material erupted by volcanoes

**basalt**—fine-grained, dark-colored volcanic rock rich in iron-bearing minerals

**Basin and Range**—physiographic region in western North America character-ized by parallel mountain ranges separated by valleys. Created by extension of the crust, with normal faults bounding the valleys

**bedding**—layering of sedimentary rocks

**bench**—horizontal rock surface formed on top of a resistant layer or by erosion

**biotite**—brown-to-black mica mineral that breaks off in paper-thin sheets

**brachiopod**—ancient double-shelled marine invertebrate commonly found as fossils in Paleozoic limestones

**breccia**—sedimentary rock composed of angular, pebble- to boulder-sized fragments in a matrix of finer-grained material

**breccia pipe**—tubular cavity filled with breccia. Formed from the collapse of caves or sinkholes

**bryozoans**—ancient marine invertebrates commonly found as fossils in Paleozoic limestones; one type looks like mosquito netting, the other like branched twigs

**calcite**—light-colored mineral composed of calcium carbonate ($CaCO_3$) that forms the sedimentary rock limestone

**carbonate**—compound of carbon and oxygen ($CO_3$)

**cement**—minerals crystallized from groundwater that bind sediment grains together to form a sedimentary rock

**Cenozoic**—the most recent geologic era, between 66 million years ago and the present, that is characterized by relatively modern fossils

**chemical weathering**—degradation of rocks by chemical processes such as dissolution

**chert**—exceptionally hard sedimentary rock composed of microscopic quartz crystals

**chilled margin**—edge of an igneous intrusion that cools more rapidly and therefore contains finer-grained crystals

**cinder cone**—conical hill formed by accumulation of basalt fragments

**clay (mineral)**—mineral formed by chemical weathering of preexisting rocks

293

**conglomerate**—sedimentary rock composed of rounded pebble- to boulder-sized particles in a finer-grained matrix

**contact metamorphism**—changes in the mineralogy and texture of a rock resulting from the heat of a nearby igneous intrusion

**continental crust**—buoyant crust composed of silica-rich rocks; forms the continents

**crinoid**—ancient stalked marine animal, commonly found as small, disk-shaped fossils in Paleozoic limestones

**cross-bed**—pattern of slanting, parallel lines common in sedimentary rocks that marks advancing crests of wind-blown dunes or water-transported sediment

**crust**—outermost shell of the earth, composed of low-density, silica-rich rocks

**cryptobiotic soil**—living soil crust composed of symbiotic cyanobacteria, lichens, and mosses

**crystalline (rocks)**—the granitic rocks, schists, and gneisses that crop out in the Grand Canyon's Inner Gorge

**desert varnish**—dark, iron and manganese oxide coating often found on desert rocks that is produced by bacteria

**diabase**—dark-colored, intrusive igneous rock that resembles basalt

**dike**—narrow igneous intrusion cut through surrounding rock

**dip**—angle between a bedding or fault plane and the horizontal

**disconformity**—unconformity between parallel sedimentary beds

**dolomite**—sedimentary rock composed mostly of the mineral dolomite $(CaMg[CO_3]_2)$

**eon**—largest division of geologic time, embracing several eras

**era**—division of geologic time, including several periods, but smaller than an eon

**erosion**—all processes by which soil and rock are loosened and moved downhill or downwind

**evaporite**—sedimentary rock left behind by the evaporation of sea or lake water

**extension**—pulling apart of the earth's crust, usually along normal faults

**fault**—break in rocks along which movement has occurred

**feldspar**—the most common rock-forming mineral, composed of aluminum, silicon, oxygen, and either potassium, sodium, or calcium

**floodplain**—level plain of layered, loose sediment on either side of a stream, submerged during floods

**fold**—bent or warped sequence of rock layers that was originally horizontal

**foliation**—set of flat or wavy planes in a metamorphic rock, defined by the parallel alignment of metamorphic minerals

**formation**—basic unit for the naming of local or regional rock layers

**fossil**—remains or traces of organisms preserved from the geologic past

**Geologic Time Scale**—the division of geologic history into eras, periods, and epochs accomplished through fossil correlation

**glauconite**—green mica mineral formed in place during slow sedimentation on the shallow seafloor

**gneiss**—metamorphic rock that displays distinct banding of dark and light mineral layers (pronounced "nice")

**graben**—downdropped block of rock bounded on both sides by normal faults

**granite**—light-colored, coarse-grained intrusive igneous rock with quartz, feldspar, and mica as dominant minerals

**granodiorite**—coarse-grained, intrusive igneous rock with less quartz and more feldspar than granite

**Great Unconformity**—the unconformity between the Precambrian and Paleozoic rocks in the Grand Canyon, first defined by John Wesley Powell in 1869

**groundwater table**—upper surface of water-saturated sediment beneath the ground

**hematite**—common iron mineral typically formed during weathering; the mineral that forms rust

**horn coral**—ancient marine invertebrates commonly found as cornucopia-like fossils in Paleozoic limestones

**hornblende**—black silicate mineral found in Grand Canyon pegmatites

**hornfels**—dense, fine-grained rock formed by contact metamorphism

**igneous (rock)**—rock formed by the solidification of magma

**impermeable**—rock formation or soil that does not transmit groundwater easily or rapidly

**intrusion**—emplacement of magma into other rocks below the earth's surface

**invertebrate**—animal without a backbone

**joint**—large, planar fracture in a rock

**karst**—type of topography characterized by sinkholes, caves, and underground drainage; usually forms on limestone

**Laramide Orogeny**—Mountain-building episode from 70 to 40 million years ago that raised the Colorado Plateau and southern Rocky Mountains

**lava**—molten material erupted on the earth's surface

**limestone**—sedimentary rock composed mostly of the mineral calcite and often containing marine fossils

**magma**—molten material below the earth's surface and from which igneous rock is derived

**mantle**—zone of the earth's interior below the crust and above the core

**marblecake bedding**—swirled, contorted pattern of sedimentary beds caused by deformation before the material was hardened into rock

**meander**—broad, semicircular curve in a stream that develops from erosion on the outside of a bend and deposition on the inside

**Mesozoic**— the middle era of the Phanerozoic Eon, between 245 and 66 million years ago, that is characterized by fossils with shapes intermediate between those of the Paleozoic and Cenozoic Eras

**metamorphic (rock)**—rock whose original mineralogy, texture, or composition has been changed by the effects of pressure and/or temperature

**mineral**—naturally occurring, inorganic crystalline solid with a specific chemical composition

**monocline**—one-armed fold in which steeply dipping beds are sandwiched between horizontal layers like a stair riser between treads

**mudcrack**—sedimentary feature formed when wet mud dries out, shrinks, and cracks

**mudstone**—fine-grained sedimentary rock formed from hardened clay and silt

**muscovite**—silver mica mineral that breaks off in paper-thin sheets

**nonconformity**—unconformity in which older metamorphic or intrusive igneous rocks are overlain by younger sedimentary strata

**normal fault**—extensional fault in which the block above the fault plane slides down relative to the block below

**oceanic crust**—dense crust composed of basalt; forms the ocean basins

**orogeny**—tectonic episode of mountain building

**outcrop**—segment of bedrock on the earth's surface

**Paleozoic**—the earliest geologic era of the Phanerozoic Eon, between 545 and 245 million years ago, that is characterized by relatively archaic fossils

**pegmatite**—very coarse-grained intrusive igneous rock of granitic composition that typically fills fractures to form veins

**period**—the most commonly used unit of geologic time, representing one subdivision of an era

**permeable**—rock formation or soil that is able to transmit groundwater relatively easily and rapidly

**physical weathering**—degradation of rocks by physical processes such as abrasion

**plate tectonics**—theory stating that the earth's crust is broken into separate plates that move and interact with each other

**pluton**—balloon-shaped igneous intrusion of plutonic rocks

**plutonic (rock)**—igneous rock that cooled beneath the earth's surface; characterized by large crystals

**porous**—rock or soil with a high proportion of pore spaces relative to solid mineral grains

**potassium feldspar**—a feldspar containing potassium

**Precambrian**—all geologic time before the beginning of the Paleozoic Era, from 4600 to 545 million years ago

**quartz**—very hard, clear or translucent mineral composed of silica ($SiO_2$)

**quartzite**—metamorphic rock composed of sand-sized quartz grains fused together by heat and pressure

**reverse fault**—compressional fault in which the block above the fault plane moves up relative to the block below

**rift**—long, narrow continental trough formed where a continent is breaking apart

**ripplemarks**—small ridges preserved on sedimentary rock surfaces; formed by moving wind or water while the sediment was deposited

**sandstone**—sedimentary rock composed of sand-sized grains cemented together

**scarp retreat**—gradual retreat of a cliff away from a river caused by undercutting

**schist**—metamorphic rock composed of platy mica minerals aligned in the same direction

**sedimentary (rock)**—rock formed on the earth's surface from the weathered products of preexisting rocks or as the product of biological and/or chemical processes

**shale**—fine-grained sedimentary rock formed from hardened clay and silt that typically splits into thin layers

**silica**—silicon dioxide ($SiO_2$). Igneous rocks with higher silica contents tend to be lighter in color and more resistant to chemical weathering

**sill**—sheetlike igneous rock intruded parallel to sedimentary rock layers

**slickensides**—polished and striated surface resulting from movement and friction along a fault plane

**spheroidal weathering**—form of chemical weathering in which water penetrates cracks around a block, attacking it from all sides to round the block's edges

**spicules**—tiny, silica-rich supports that stiffen the tissues of some invertebrates, especially sponges

**sponges**—ancient marine invertebrates commonly found as brainlike fossils in Paleozoic limestones

**spring sapping**—formation of an overhang caused by the plucking of individual sediment grains by a spring

**stalactite**—conical calcite deposit hanging from the ceiling of a cave and crystallized from dripping water

**stalagmite**—conical calcite deposit crystallized from dripping water on a cave floor

**strata**—layers of sedimentary rock

**stream piracy**—process by which the headwaters of a steeper stream erode headward and capture a lower-gradient stream

**stromatolite**—fossil characterized by thin, wavy laminations in limestone; the only macrofossils present in the majority of Precambrian rocks

**subduction**—tectonic process in which a dense oceanic plate dives beneath another due to plate convergence

**syncline**—bowl-shaped fold

**tectonic**—pertaining to the large-scale processes that deform the earth's crust

**tidal channel**—major channel followed by tidal currents, extending from offshore into a tidal marsh or flat

**topographic inversion**—process by which originally low-lying areas become higher than their surroundings due to differing erosion rates

**trace fossil**—sedimentary structure consisting of a fossilized track, trail, burrow, or tube resulting from the activities of an animal

**travertine**—form of limestone deposited by springs or as a cave deposit

**trilobite**—fossil from a class of Paleozoic marine organisms that are divided into three segments and are related to modern crustaceans

**ultramafic**—very dark, igneous rock with exceptionally low silica content; the major constituent of the mantle

**unconformity**—surface representing a gap in the geologic record where rock layers were eroded or never deposited

**vein**—a mineral filling a fracture or fault

**volcanic (rock)**— igneous rock that cooled on the earth's surface; characterized by crystals too small to be seen with the naked eye

**volcanic arc**—chain of volcanic islands associated with a subduction zone

**weathering**—disintegration and decomposition of rock at or near the earth's surface due to physical or chemical processes

# Index

301

# About the Authors

Lon Abbott received a bachelor's degree in geology and geophysics from the University of Utah and a Ph.D. in earth science from the University of California, Santa Cruz, where he specialized in the study of mountain building. Lon's field work has taken him from the remote mountain peaks of Papua New Guinea to the bottom of a 15,000-foot-deep ocean trench near Costa Rica. Lon's twin passions for teaching geology and outdoor activities led to his current faculty position at Prescott College, where he teaches a variety of field-oriented geology courses that examine the wonders of the American Southwest, including the Grand Canyon. Lon's research has been published in several scientific journals, and he has written an article about the geology of rock climbing for *Rock and Ice.*

Terri Cook earned a master's degree in geology at the University of California, Santa Cruz, where she studied rocks from deep-sea hot springs. Her research results have been published in several scientific journals. Terri's undergraduate degree in archaeology is from Tufts University, and her combined interests in geology, archaeology, and experiencing new cultures have led her across six continents. Having grown up in Connecticut, Terri first saw the Grand Canyon ten years ago, and she returns to experience its wonders over and over again. Terri is an instructor at Prescott College.

*Photo by W. J. Ervin*

THE MOUNTAINEERS, founded in 1906, is a nonprofit outdoor activity and conservation club, whose mission is "to explore, study, preserve, and enjoy the natural beauty of the outdoors. . . . " Based in Seattle, Washington, the club is now the third-largest such organization in the United States, with seven branches throughout Washington State.

The Mountaineers sponsors both classes and year-round outdoor activities in the Pacific Northwest, which include hiking, mountain climbing, ski-touring, snowshoeing, bicycling, camping, kayaking and canoeing, nature study, sailing, and adventure travel. The club's conservation division supports environmental causes through educational activities, sponsoring legislation, and presenting informational programs. All club activities are led by skilled, experienced volunteers, who are dedicated to promoting safe and responsible enjoyment and preservation of the outdoors.

If you would like to participate in these organized outdoor activities or the club's programs, consider a membership in The Mountaineers. For information and an application, write or call The Mountaineers, Club Headquarters, 300 Third Avenue West, Seattle, WA 98119; (206) 284-6310.

The Mountaineers Books, an active, nonprofit publishing program of the club, produces guidebooks, instructional texts, historical works, natural history guides, and works on environmental conservation. All books produced by The Mountaineers Books fulfill the club's mission.

*Send or call for our catalog of more than 500 outdoor titles:*

The Mountaineers Books
1001 SW Klickitat Way, Suite 201
Seattle, WA 98134
800-553-4453
*mbooks@mountaineersbooks.org*

*www.mountaineersbooks.org*

The Mountaineers Books is proud to be a corporate sponsor of Leave No Trace, whose mission is to promote and inspire responsible outdoor recreation through education, research, and partnerships. The Leave No Trace program is focused specifically on human-powered (nonmotorized) recreation.

Leave No Trace strives to educate visitors about the nature of their recreational impacts, as well as offer techniques to prevent and minimize such impacts. Leave No Trace is best understood as an educational and ethical program, not as a set of rules and regulations.

For more information, visit *www.LNT.org,* or call 800-332-4100.

# MORE TITLES IN THE HIKING GEOLOGY SERIES
## FROM THE MOUNTAINEERS BOOKS

**Hiking the Southwest's Geology: Four Corners Region,** *Ralph Lee Hopkins*
A full-color guide to 50 diverse hikes in Arizona, Colorado, New Mexico, & Utah

**Hiking Arizona's Geology,** *Ivo Lucchitta*
Over 40 day hikes organized in Arizona's three major provinces

**Hiking Colorado's Geology,** *Ralph Lee Hopkins & Lindy Birkel Hopkins*
Fifty hikes reveal Colorado's dramatic geologic story

**Hiking Washington's Geology,** *Scott Babcock & Bob Carson*
Over 55 hikes cover 8 regions of the state

**Hiking Oregon's Geology,** *Ellen Morris Bishop & John Eliot Allen*
Over 50 hikes throughout 10 regions of the state

# OTHER TITLES YOU MIGHT ENJOY FROM
# THE MOUNTAINEERS BOOKS

**A Field Guide to the Grand Canyon,** *Stephen R. Whitney*
Comprehensive guide to Grand Canyon's natural history, including geology and species illustrations on over 480 plants and animals

**Pages of Stone: Geology of Western National Parks and Monuments, Grand Canyon and Plateau Country,** *Halka Chronic*
A thorough guide to the area's geological features with photos

**Little-Known Southwest,** *Barbara & Don Laine*
Find great lesser-known destinations such as national wildlife refuges, monuments, historic sites and fun outdoor activity areas without the crowds

**Exploring Arizona's Wild Areas: A Guide for Hikers, Backpackers, Climbers, Cross-Country Skiers, & Paddlers,** *Scott S. Warren*
The best guide to Arizona's 5.8 million acres of wilderness lands, among the largest of any state in the nation

**Mac's Field Guide to Southwest Cacti, Shrubs, & Trees,** *Craig MacGowan*
Handy and fun identification guide on a waterproof laminated card

Available at fine bookstores and outdoor stores, by phone at 800-553-4453
or on the Web at *www.mountaineersbooks.org*

THE MOUNTAINEERS BOOKS